Edge

Ben Lyttleton is a football writer, broadcaster, and director of Soccernomics, the football consultancy that helps teams improve their performance. He is also the author of *Twelve Yards: The Art and Psychology of the Perfect Penalty* and *Football School: Where Football Explains the World*, a series written to encourage children's literacy. He lives in London.

Edge

Leadership Secrets from Football's Top Thinkers

Ben Lyttleton

HarperCollins*Publishers*

HarperCollins*Publishers*
1 London Bridge Street
London SE1 9GF

www.harpercollins.co.uk

First published by HarperCollins*Publishers* 2017
This edition published 2018

A catalogue record of this book is
available from the British Library

ISBN 978-0-00-822639-8

Printed and bound in Great Britain by
CPI Group (UK) Ltd, Croydon

MIX
Paper from
responsible sources
FSC www.fsc.org FSC C007454

To ABC, with love

CONTENTS

PROLOGUE

As soon as I took the call, I knew it was a great idea. It was summer 2014 and I had just spoken to Marcus Christenson, Football Editor at the *Guardian* newspaper. His plan was to tap into the football expertise of his global network and publish a piece called 'Next Generation'. It would identify the top 60 players around the world aged 17 or below.

The feature would run every year, and readers would be able to track previously listed players and check on their progress. It was also quite brave, because if, in three years, say, 55 of the 60 players named had dropped out of football, no one would look too clever.

He asked me to come up with two players who were based in France. I have always been enchanted by French football and have written extensively about the game there. But I did not know all that much about the next generation, and when it came to that age group, it was more like the generation after next.

I called up some of my contacts in the French game and they helped me draw up a shortlist of five names. I had to narrow it down. I looked at video footage of the players but that didn't help; they all played in different positions anyway. So I went back to Marcus and asked what he wanted. Was it the most talented players? Or the ones most likely to make it? He wanted both: basically, a feature that would become an annual celebration of the *Guardian*'s football knowledge pool. 'We just want to get it right,' he said.

This made me think. Would the most talented players be the ones most likely to make it? I asked a friend, a Premier League scout whose speciality was spotting youth-team players in northern France. 'Not at all,' he replied. He was looking for players who influence games, whatever their position. This is not just a matter of technique or skill; it's about working off the ball, and how they react to losing the ball.

So what is he looking for? 'Resilience,' he said. Most scouts focus on the six seconds after a player loses the ball to check for reaction, but my friend keeps an eye on them for ten minutes. One youngster missed a chance to score and spent the rest of the half shaking his head and hitting his thigh in disgust with himself. He was crossed off the list. 'He was nervous when he next got the ball and he won't grow out of that.'

He also talked about adaptability: how a player fits in socially with those around him, and extrapolated that to the potential new contexts that might await him. It was also important that he had a general respect for team-mates and the coach, and a simple enjoyment of the game. 'You can spot the ones who don't want to be there a mile off.' There is a lot more to his job than interpreting body language and the odd behavioural trait. But he made it clear just how many aspects there are to assessing talent.

This was my chance to have a go at it. I had five players whose talent was not in question. Four had been capped by France at Under-17 level, and they were all playing in academies with a good record of bringing players through: Toulouse, Lens, Valenciennes, Rennes and Paris Saint-Germain. I had to narrow it down to two names.

I made more calls and this time was specific about my questions. 'What's his attitude like? How does he react to difficult situations? How motivated is he? Does he get on well with people? Is he adaptable?' There was a lot more fluctuation in the answers to these questions.

The difference in the talent that I could see between these five players was minimal. But there was a big gap in the talent I could not see. Some of it was talent you cannot even measure. How can you tell how motivated someone is, or what their decision-making is like under pressure? What about their adaptability to a new social group, or how they react, not just to defeat, but also to success? These elements all factored in attributes above the shoulder. They could be the difference between making it and not making it.

As I went through the questions about each player – asking about attitude, teamwork, motivation, adaptability, resilience and creativity – I realised these skills were not just relevant in the football world. They make the difference in any professional environment. Talent is the starting-point, but these are the elements that give you an edge. That's what I was looking for. They all had talent. Which ones had the edge?

I was finally ready to send my names to Marcus. One was Jean-Kévin Augustin, a 17-year-old striker waiting for a first-team opportunity at Paris Saint-Germain. The other was also 17 and had not yet made a first-team appearance for his club. He was in the youth academy at Rennes. He was a winger. His name was Ousmane Dembélé. I will come back to his story.

We can all agree that football and business are not the same. Your company will not release its results every three days. The local, national, and sometimes international, media won't pore over every decision you or your colleagues make. The weather is unlikely to affect your performance. The visual acuity of one man who could be 30 yards away won't become a defining moment in your life. Or at least, for your sake, I hope not.

In football, only one team can win the league. In football, managers spend a lot of time thinking and talking about the competition. They change strategies according to the opponent. Most businesses focus on the customer instead.

Then there is the performance itself. In what business do you spend only 5 per cent of your time performing, and the rest of the time developing your skills? If you're lucky, it might be the other way around. Most of us spend 99 per cent of our time on performance, and maybe 1 per cent on self-improvement.

To see how different business is from football you only need to look at the people who straddle both. The game is littered with highly successful businessmen who buy a football club and somehow take leave of their senses. They make crazy decisions. The heart takes over the head. Emotion trumps logic.

In my role working for Soccernomics, a consultancy named after the book of the same name, I have had conversations with the sporting side (coaches, scouts) and with the management side (chief executives, heads of finance) about players. Soccernomics works with club owners, helping them avoid expensive mistakes in the transfer market. I have listened to these people dissect running styles, crossing ability and ball control. Football has traditionally quantified talent through a rear-view mirror: looking at goals, tackles and passes. New data measures distance run, sprints made, speeds clocked, time on the ball, position on the pitch and even expected goals scored. In sport's era of big data, they are just the tip of the iceberg.

Clubs measure the precise contribution of an individual to his team's chances of scoring in a given game. One club wants versatile players and uses analytics to track exactly what percentage of games over a season a certain target might play in different positions. A centre-back who can fill in at full-back, or a defensive midfielder who can push forward, or a wide player who can move into the hole: these are all highly coveted players whose value to a team in being able to cover for more than one position is helpful. Another likes to know the difference between the market valuation of its targets (what clubs will pay) and the intrinsic valuation, a calculation based solely on his output on the pitch. Every club looks for different Key Performance Indicators to develop their winning team.

But how do you measure what the eye cannot see? The biggest talents in football share characteristics that are harder to quantify. The skills of those who provide the real edge are intangible: adaptability, resilience, leadership, decision-making, composure under pressure, motivation, creativity, teamwork. These are the qualities I was looking for when I was scouting for the talented French youngsters.

In this book, I have spent time with clubs who actively identify and develop these traits in their players. They understand that the best results come from thinking about what the eye cannot see. They revealed to me how they get an edge. And you can do the same.

An edge is not a sporting term. It's a competitive advantage, and just as relevant in any professional environment. You are no longer competing with people in your city anymore, but globally. New businesses are disrupting the landscape and changing outlooks. This book will give you tools to respond to these challenges.

Football offers solutions. Jorge Valdano, a former Real Madrid player and coach, who won the 1986 World Cup with Argentina, gave me a unique insight into how to unlock creativity and work with mavericks. He put it best, saying: 'Ultimately, football is just a metaphor for life.'

It's about time that other industries took this metaphor seriously. Over 250 million people play football. It's the most popular sport in the world. Every professional footballer has got past millions of competitors to reach that point. One sports psychologist has calculated that the performance level of players in the Champions League is in the top 0.0001 per cent. That is a narrow elite of specialists that any professional would want to learn from. This book will give you the framework to do just that.

The need to identify and develop talent is crucial to success. This becomes a fascinating challenge when, as I discovered, every coach, sports director or club owner has a different definition of the word 'talent'. How clubs go about optimising their talent is the perfect lens through which we can discover our attitude towards talent and what this means for us.

I know one successful chief executive who puts this into practice. He set up a media business from scratch in 2014. It started with two people and no office. Less than three years later, he manages over 50 staff and has a turnover of over £10 million. How did he do it? 'In all seriousness,' he tells me, 'I base my management style on the coach of my favourite Premier League team. He keeps his messages simple but leaves no one in any doubt about what they need to do; he communicates regularly and with a lot of one-on-ones; he focuses on retaining talent by improving his employees rather than hiring in new people.'

He sees his company's workforce as no different to a sports team, and mentions only a few of the factors that can give you an edge. This book will help you get the best out of your talent, and that of those around you.

I visited the football clubs that have identified new ways to quantify these intangible skill-sets. I'm grateful to all the experts in top-level football that gave me their time and expertise in my quest for an edge. I spoke to club and national team coaches, sporting directors and club psychologists; players, heads of talent identification and performance coaches; heads of academy, club owners and professors. I spoke to World Cup winners, European championships winners and league title winners. I even spoke to one club's 'cultural coach'.

Football is the most hot-housed, intense and financially profitable talent factory on the planet. It's time we woke up to the lessons it can provide. We all want to have an edge. This is your chance to find one.

Ben Lyttleton
August 2017
London

COHESION

ATHLETIC CLUB DE BILBAO
Retain your talent

A unique talent pool / Pride in el sentimiento Athletic */ Social purpose and talent retention / Belonging improves commitment / Different measures of success*

The route started at Basilica de Begoña, the church dedicated to the patron saint of Biscay, the Virgin Begoña. The bus made slow progress onto the south side of the river that runs through the city. It was carrying the players and staff of Athletic Club de Bilbao, one of the oldest football teams in Spain. Their destination was the City Hall, only a 15-minute walk away, but this particular journey took three hours. The starting-point was significant: before every season, the club's directors and players visit the church to pay their respects. And they ask for a good season ahead.

No one was in a rush. The noise came from all sides, people cheering, waving and singing as the bus edged through the crowds. There were thousands of them, waving flags and dancing on either side of the Ayuntamiento Bridge. You could hear them from the Palacio Ibaigane, the old-fashioned central office which Athletic still uses, where the boardrooms are oak and the woodwork a dark, dark mahogany. The vibe there is stuffy English bank rather than community club. But the people here were young and old, grandchildren with their grandparents, making memories that will last forever.

There were even some who hired boats along the river, the Ria de Bilbao, to catch a glimpse of their heroes. There were at least a hundred of them on a catamaran and another five on a dinghy.

The boats cruised in from the north-west, past the Guggenheim Museum, which stands just yards from the place where this story began. That is the *Campa de los Ingleses* – the English pitch – where, next to the river, British émigrés, mainly ship builders from the south coast, but also miners from the north-east, arrived in Bilbao in 1898 and were the first to play football in the city. A plaque marks the spot, inscribed with a poem written by Basque poet Kirmen Uribe:

This is where the English played.
Here on a field by the river.
When there was only grass and a small graveyard.
Sometimes the ball went in the water,
and they had to go and get it.
If it went far they threw little stones
to bring it closer to the shore.
The stones made waves, little waves
which grew bigger all the time.
In the same way Athletic played in Lamiako,
then in Jolaseta, then, finally in San Mames.
One wave, then another, then another.

The English influence is still retained: the name of the team, Athletic Club de Bilbao, is an Anglicised one, while the red-and-white striped kit came from a club member, Juan Elorduy, who sailed to Southampton with the plan of bringing back 50 blue-and-white Blackburn Rovers kits, to match the original Athletic colours. He could not find any, so instead he brought back the first kits he saw, which were the red-and-white stripes of Southampton. He brought back 50 kits in all: 25 were for Athletic Club and 25 for another club that had recently been founded by Bilbao students in Madrid: Atlético Madrid.

The culmination of the celebration came when captain Carlos Gurpegi stood on the balcony of the City Hall and raised the Spanish Super Cup to over 50,000 fans watching below. The date was 18 August 2015 and this was the first trophy Athletic had won in 31 years. They had just beaten the dominant Barcelona 5–1 over two legs, crushing the League and Cup holders 4–0 at its home stadium San Mames (where the VIP bar is called *Campa de los Ingleses*). Aritz Aduriz, a player that Athletic had released twice before, scored a hat-trick in the biggest club game of his career. This victory was sweeter because Athletic achieved it with a team made up only of players from the local region.

As I retrace the journey of this procession, I see Athletic imagery everywhere: cafés with Athletic flags hanging outside, kids wearing Athletic shirts on their way to school; cars with Athletic bumper-stickers. This is a club that unites the community. It makes people proud.

This local-only policy is best explained by former Athletic president José Maria Arrate, who wrote in the club's 1998 centenary book: 'Athletic Bilbao is more than a football club, it is a feeling – and as such its ways of operating often escape rational analysis. We see ourselves as unique in world football and that defines our identity. We do not say that we are better or worse, merely different. We only wish for the sons of our soil to represent our club, and in so wishing we stand out as a sporting entity, not a business concept. We wish to mould our players into men, not just footballers, and each time that a player from the *cantera* makes his debut we feel we have realised an objective which is in harmony with the ideologies of our founders and forefathers.'

The policy was established in 1919, when the club backed the city's movement for Basque autonomy. The relationship between the two was strong; the football club was run by *socios* (members), who could attend general meetings and elect a president and directors to run the club. Athletic is still run on this model. The policy only counted towards players, so it was no problem that the club's first four managers were all English. The most successful of them, Fred Pentland, was appointed in 1921.[1] Basque players – from Athletic and neighbouring Real Sociedad, who dropped its Basque-policy in the mid-1980s – had just formed the bulk of Spain's 1920 Olympic Games silver medal-winning side. Its aggressive style of play was dubbed *furia Espanola*, Spanish fury, a nickname the Spanish were happy to adopt – though it originated as a less than admiring term for a ferocious Spanish attack on Antwerp in 1596.

Athletic won its first trophy with Pentland in charge, the 1923 Copa del Rey. He was persuaded to leave to coach Atlético Madrid and then Real Oviedo, but returned in 1929, in time for Spain's first season with a national league. This was the most successful period in Athletic history, as they won two league titles – the team was unbeaten in the top flight in 1930 – and four Spanish Cups between 1930 and 1933.

Pentland saw coaching as a form of education and embraced the chance to develop up to 80 players in the club's *cantera*, or academy. 'The big clubs will have a coach and ... his business will be to teach the young players unity,' he wrote in 1921. 'This will do away once and forever with young players playing for themselves alone.' In 1932, after Athletic's two straight titles, Spanish newspaper *AS* asked Pentland to explain his success. In a series of articles, he wrote about his philosophy. It was not just technique, but 'the psychological and intellectual aspects of a game ... in which the morality and intelligence of a player are a prerequisite'.

You might think that reducing the talent pool to only three million players – while other clubs in this globalised industry can and do recruit from all over the world – would leave Athletic struggling, or playing catch-up. The opposite is true. No club has provided more players to Spain's national team than Athletic. No province has provided more players to Spain's national team than Biscay.

Athletic have won eight league titles and 24 Cups, and are third in the all-time Spanish trophy table (this is a big deal in Spain). Out of all the teams in the top leagues across Europe, Athletic's total of 32 trophies is tenth in the all-time list. There are only three teams never to have been relegated from the Spanish top division: Barcelona and Real Madrid, as you might expect. And Athletic Club de Bilbao.

The morality and intelligence that Pentland wrote about gives them an edge. Their difference gives them an edge. Even their weakness gives them an edge. I went to Bilbao to find out how.

It's the morning after another night before. Another piece of history was made at San Mames, and again Aduriz was at the centre of it. He lit up a run-of-the-mill Europa League game against Belgian team Genk by scoring each of Athletic's goals in a bizarre 5–3 win. I thought he might not last more than ten minutes: he collided with the post after tapping in his first goal, ending a move that he began with a pass to Iker Muniain from the centre-circle. Muniain beat his man, crossed for Raúl García to head back across goal, and Aduriz scored. He played on, his 35-year-old body energised by a fervent home crowd, and scored two more before half-time. Another two goals in the second half and the papers had their headlines. 'Historica' wrote *Mundo Deportivo*. 'Aduriz Aduriz Aduriz Aduriz ADURIZ,' went *AS*. 'We are lucky to have him,' said coach Ernesto Valverde, with a hint of understatement.

The pick of his goals was the fourth one, when he ran onto a pass from centre-back Yeray Alvarez that split the Genk midfield and defence. Aduriz did not even need to control the ball; he just stroked it first-time into the corner of the net. Before the game, a fan told me about Yeray, a 21-year-old defender with only five starts to his name. 'At any other club, Yeray would not get a chance. We were worried about defence after Gurpegi left the club. But instead of buying someone old and expensive and not very good, we give a chance to our youngsters coming through. Before the season began, I thought Yeray would be a five out of ten. Instead he's playing nine out of ten. I tell you, at no other club would Yeray even get a chance.' (It turned out to be quite a season for Yeray, who was diagnosed with testicular cancer a few weeks after my visit. He underwent a successful operation in December and was back playing 46 days later. Five days after his comeback, he extended his contract, which now has a €30 million release clause, until 2022. Sadly, the cancer returned after the 2016–17 season ended.)

On this Friday morning, I see Yeray with the first-team, having a light warm-down session at Lezama, the training-centre nestled under lush green mountains and farmhouses ten miles east of Bilbao. This is where the club's dedication to developing locally born players into first-teamers is demonstrated. There are six full-size pitches, one with a 1,500-seater stand and a symbolic arch that was removed from the original main stand of the San Mames before its recent reconstruction.

'At Lezama, the work done with the different teams is unique and shared by all the coaches at the club,' runs the club's mission statement. 'The player is the key element, the corner-stone of our development plan, and games are the fundamental means of learning while taking on new concepts. Along with the optimisation of the player's sporting performance, it is about the integrated development of all their personal aspects. It is about reaching the end of the process with a human psychological profile for an Athletic player. Someone who meets the demands of today's football, and who also represents the values and idiosyncrasies of the club.'

Watching on from his office is José Maria Amorrortu. A former Athletic striker in the 1970s, he is now the sporting director. His job is to assess all the talent coming through the club. It's his second spell in the job; he returned from Atlético Madrid (where his talent crop included Spain internationals Koke and David de Gea) in 2011, when current president Josu Urrutia, another former player, was first elected.

He too was impressed with the previous night's performance of Yeray. 'We can say that every day, the kid who plays at centre-back who has not been playing long for the first team, he surprises us. We can see his process of development has been a success.'

In the course of our time together, Amorrortu pinpoints three factors central to Athletic's success that are critical to businesses today. This is where we can learn from Athletic: its social purpose to represent the best qualities of the Basque region; the investment in talent as humans first, so they feel valued and in an environment where they can develop; and the importance of talent retention which, in Athletic's unique case, overrides almost everything.

Every year, 20 children enter the *cantera* aged ten. Maybe two in each year, 10 per cent, will stay and make it to the first team. It's an outstanding return. 'Our strength is to help all of the kids reach their potential. They know and they also push themselves, that's why they stick with it. But that number, it's extraordinarily good.'

When he arrived for his second spell, Amorrortu produced a planning document, called *Construyendo nuestro futuro* (Building our Future), that forms the backbone of Athletic strategy. He shows me the document. It demands a Lezama that is open, modern, supported by its tradition, at the forefront of development, with the best professionals and integrated in Basque sport and football. Under subheadings that include Improvement, Quality, Personal Development, Sportsmanship, Talent Identification, and Recruitment, its focus is on the development of people and not just players. Remember what Arrate wrote in the centenary book: 'We wish to mould our players into men, not just footballers.'

This is a theme we will come back to in this chapter. Companies that invest in the human side of talent get better results than those who only focus on outcomes. Google hire people they find 'exceptionally interesting' regardless of academic qualifications. They look for generalists rather than those specialists who may bring their own unconscious biases. When the company was specifically looking for 'smart creatives', it instigated 'the LAX test'. Google execs were to imagine they were stuck at LA airport for six hours with a candidate: did they like that individual, and would they still be creative or interesting to talk to after six hours? Did they have insight? 'If they don't,' said Google's executive chairman Eric Schmidt, 'I just don't think you should be hiring them.'

Perhaps the most significant page in *Construyendo nuestro futuro* is the one at the back, on Social Responsibility. The task: to reinforce and expand *el sentimiento Athletic*, the Athletic feeling; to stay loyal to players and their families; and to carry the Athletic spirit within our daily actions. This intangible element of the club is what has sustained it for so long.

'We have a 100-year-old culture, and that tradition is to always count on kids from our region. This has hardened into our identity,' Amorrortu explains. 'The values we have are fundamental and they form a culture which is the expression of a way of being. That is what Athletic has.'

So begins an elaborate verbal dance in which I try to tease out exactly what these values are and where the edge exists. Amorrortu talks a lot about feeling, belonging, culture and social capital. These are the pillars of the club, and noticeable the night before when the biggest cheers (apart from the Aduriz goals) came when local boys Iñaki Williams, Sabin Merino and Javier Eraso were all substituted on.

One club director told me part of this culture comes from one degree of separation: 'Everyone in this city knows someone who has played for Athletic. So the sense of belonging is passed down through the generations. It's pride. "I knew this kid and look at him now ..."' Most of the shirts on sale in the club shop don't have player names on the back; the club wants supporters to put their own names on the back, to encourage kids to dream that one day it might be them.

Amorrortu agrees. 'Yes, it's about a pride in belonging to this club, belonging here, to feel part of this club. The chance that the kids might play in the first team gives them great excitement. It is these intangible things that encourage the player to make a bigger effort during his development. To feel part of Athletic is to be in communion with the values of the club. To play for this club means you identify with an idea. It's a feeling and that's a way of being, to feel a part of something. Athletic represents a lot. It is not only the team of the city, it also represents a philosophy.'

Amorrortu's staff of 91 coaches try to bring this philosophy to life. The document talks about encouraging autonomy, allowing players to take responsibility, and focusing on the players' educational and psychological improvement. He compares it to a stone that, if rubbed enough, will change shape. 'It comes from something natural, essential, inside.'

The values relate to the region. 'The culture here in the Basque country is a culture based on hard work, collaboration, common feeling, and of participation, of working together in a team, of a way of being,' he says. 'It is something transmitted down the generations in a spontaneous way. And from that, we can say we form part of a legacy that comes from our ancestors.'

Keeping this legacy going, above all, is how Athletic measures success. Players and staff alike are clearly very aware of it. 'It's a lot more than a football club,' says Aduriz. 'It can't be compared to any other club in the world, it's unique,' adds Williams, tipped to be the new star for Athletic and Spain. 'For me, victory is watching 11 Basque players every Sunday, maintaining the philosophy that's been there for 100 years,' says club historian and museum curator Asier Arrate. 'That's our title.'

They are quite right; but it's by redefining how they measure success that makes Athletic different in the world of football. It also makes them attractive to a corporate world looking to find its own version of *el sentimiento Athletic* to improve performance. 'Professional sport has a set of questions, issues and values that can be very useful for the business world,' Amorrortu tells me. He is a regular at business conferences and says, with typical Basque understatement, that there is 'some curiosity' about how Athletic develops its sense of belonging among the players.

HOW TO GET AN EDGE – by JOSE MARIA AMORRORTU

1. Have an objective and make your ideas clear. What is *your* success?
2. Surround yourself with great professionals and behave in accordance with what you want to achieve.
3. Leave a legacy for society and create value in your surroundings. All companies need to make a profit but the benefits of social purpose are for the whole society.

Amorrortu also talks about the importance of showing patience and building for the long term. Businesses want to replicate a *sentimiento Athletic* but are less interested in emotional development, improving behaviours (not just knowledge) and instilling confidence in employees. 'People think so much about short-term performance that sometimes we lack patience and we need to remember that.' We will see later in this chapter that the effects of short-term decisions can have long-term implications. But Athletic shows patience: in the ten years before my visit, the club has had only three different head coaches, the fewest of any team in La Liga. This is not the case elsewhere: across the 92 Premier League and Football League clubs in England, 36 made a total of 51 managerial changes during the 2016–17 season (Leyton Orient boosted those numbers by getting through five different coaches).

Stability enhances the sense of belonging. An environment that threatens belonging can produce uncooperative behaviour, information hoarding and, according to a study by psychologists at UCLA,[2] an experience equivalent to physical pain. 'When our social needs are being satisfied, the brain responds in much the same way as it responds to other rewards that are more tangible. Being treated with respect and as a valued member of an organisation may activate reward systems in the brain that promote stronger learning of behaviours that predict more of these social rewards in the future.'

There are 13 men's teams in the Athletic structure: behind the first team are Bilbao Athletic (Segunda Division B), Baskonia (division three) – in Spain, youth teams play in the lower divisions – two Juvenil teams (17 to 19 years old), two Cadetes (15 and 16), two Infantiles (13 and 14) and four Alevines (11 and 12). There are also two women's teams.

At the end of one recent season, the coach of Bilbao Athletic's second team, José Ziganda, addressed the board about his team's progress. Their results had improved. The average age had dropped. Things were going well. But Ziganda was still not happy. 'I want to develop players here and then see them stay,' he said. 'But I've not yet heard a player say to me, "I won't leave this club until you kick me out."' His comments earned a round of applause.

At the end of the 2016–17 season, Athletic did make a coaching change. Valverde was appointed Barcelona coach and Athletic promoted Ziganda to head coach.[3] Historians pointed out that Ziganda had replaced Valverde before, during a La Liga match at Real Valladolid in June 1995, when Ziganda came off the bench to take the place of Valverde. Both men, of course, were playing for Athletic at the time.

'It's logical that we also see players staying as success,' says Amorrortu. 'To maintain our competitive level, to play in Europe, and to have the most players from our own *cantera* in the first team.' According to a CIES study, only two clubs in Europe's top five leagues had more internally produced players in their first-team squad in season 2016–17 than Athletic.[4] The average length of time a first-team debutant has spent at the club is 7.2 years, more than any other team in Spain.

Talent retention is an increasing problem for business today. A study by the US Bureau of Labor Statistics showed that in 2016, the average tenure of a job for 18- to 35-year-olds was 1.6 years. In a few years, millennials will make up half the workforce, and expect to stay in that job for under two years. The term millennials refers to the generation born after 1984 who are often accused of being hard to manage. How to get the best out of millennials will crop up throughout this book, as most footballers still playing these days fall into this generation.

The stigma of changing jobs every few years is a thing of the past: millennials who switch jobs are believed to have a higher learning curve, to be higher performers and even to be more loyal, as they care about making a good impression in their short time at each job.

Building a culture helps you keep your talent. Andrew Chamberlain, chief economist for a recruitment company, looks for the driving forces behind why people choose their jobs and what matters to them at work. Using a data-sample based on performance reviews and salary surveys of over 615,000 candidates between 2014 and 2017, he identified the factors that drive professional happiness. His finding: the top predictor of workplace satisfaction is not pay but the culture and values of the organisation, followed by the quality of senior leadership and the career opportunities available.[5]

LinkedIn's Talent Trends survey backed up these findings. Forty-one per cent of professionals saw themselves staying at their current company for under two years. Those who wanted to stay long term, it reported, were purpose oriented and had bought into their company's culture and long-term mission.

The one-club man, who spends his whole career at the same club, is rare in today's football. Urrutia, the Athletic president, was one. A former midfielder, he spent 26 years at the club, playing 348 times. He even rejected an offer from Real Madrid in order to remain with Athletic. He has said that Athletic's policy is about pride in its values, particularly in a world that he calls 'dehumanised' and lacking in values. His career was the inspiration for Athletic to instigate its One-Club Man award, recognising loyalty in other professionals. The first three recipients were Matt Le Tissier (thus further developing the Southampton connection), Paolo Maldini and Sepp Maier. The club thought that affiliating one-club icons as Athletic ambassadors was also a smart way to teach youngsters the value of sometimes resisting the temptation, whether it's a bigger salary or a bigger club, to move on.

The Spanish phrase I hear repeated to me in Bilbao is: 'What do you want to be in life, the lion's tail or the mouse's face?' In English, the equivalent would be the small fish in a big pond or the big fish in a small pond. The business that keeps the 'mouse's face' is the business that retains its talent. The lesson? The grass is not necessarily always greener on the other side.

In each summer after Athletic reached the 2012 Europa League final (which it lost 3–0 to Atlético Madrid), it lost part of the team's spine. Javi Martinez was first to go, moving to Bayern Munich for €40 million. His spell in Germany was decimated by injuries.

Next to go was Fernando Llorente, the forward, who moved to Juventus on a free transfer. He scored 16 goals in his first season in Serie A, helping his team win the *Scudetto*. His next two seasons (seven goals, zero goals) were less effective, and after three years in Turin he moved to Sevilla (four goals). Ander Herrera moved to Manchester United for €36 million, and survived two seasons of upheaval at Old Trafford before being able to show his best form, and winning United's Player of the Season for 2016–17. Llorente's name is still mentioned often in Bilbao. That season saw him embroiled in a relegation fight with Swansea, which was ultimately successful, but there's a strong sense he might regret having ever left Lezama.

Often players only know what they are losing once it's gone. Santi Urquiaga understands this better than most. He was part of the original intake of players when Lezama first opened its doors in 1971. A right-back, he progressed through the Bilbao Athletic ranks and made his first-team debut at 19. He played in the Athletic team that won back-to-back league titles in 1983 and 1984 (that was the last title the team won until the 2015 Super Cup). We meet at Lezama, where he is Facilities Manager. He points to one pitch and says that back in his day it was the only training pitch there. Where a women's team is now training was one of two sand pitches. A tennis court used to be where the main gym now is.

'It is difficult to explain what it was like to win *La Liga* with Athletic,' Urquiaga says with a smile. 'We always say that you have to have lived it to be able to understand. The whole city came out onto the streets for the celebration party. Schools and factories and offices were all closed for the day. These were my friends, my neighbours, the people I grew up with. I lived among them in Sestao. I still do. I'm still the guy that won the title.'

Urquiaga was a Spanish international when he left Athletic and moved to Espanyol. He was successful there too, reaching a UEFA Cup final in 1986. But he says, with a tinge of sadness in his voice: 'Even that was not the same.' So, what is it about this culture? 'When there are difficulties at Athletic, it is not like at other clubs,' he says. 'Nobody is looking to leave; you are playing with the friends you grew up with. That means you become more united when the going gets tough; you fight together, until the end.'

Urquiaga points to the far corner of the first team's training pitch. That's where work will start soon on a new main building. 'As we don't buy players like other clubs, the money made by the club is invested back into the youth system and the facilities,' he says. 'We want this place to be like the best university here, to have the best facilities and give the kids the best chance to make it.'

His choice of the word university is no coincidence. In February 2016, Athletic formalised a relationship with the Bilbao-based University of Deusto. Young players at Lezama can gain a university degree in physical education and sport science. The four-year course contains modules on anatomy, physiology, teaching PE, and theory and practice in sports including handball, volleyball and Basque *pelota*.

Iker Saez teaches the course. He is a regular at San Mames and is working on a PhD that shows education between the ages of 14 and 18 improves sporting performance. 'I believe the best players are often the best students,' he says. 'If I'm smart with my brain, I can analyse the game better. But don't forget the Athletic way is also to develop good people. They want to develop role models for society, and education is at the forefront of that.'

Amorrortu takes a similar view. 'In the end, the kids need to perform in all that they do,' he says. 'Their grades are an expression of their personality. That is something to do with them as a person – it's good to be able to play football well, but you must also be a person who knows how to value effort, who overcomes difficulties, and that is a question of personality. Education forms part of a rounded person, someone who knows about the world around them: politics, business, how things happen. Does it make them a better professional? I'm convinced it does. In the end, someone who knows how to express themselves, who knows how to reason, who has the ability to have relationships with people, that is very important. That is fundamental. That opens you up for everything, and it helps you deal with the pressure.'

The players know that if they fall behind in their grades, there is a chance they may not get picked. What happens in school tells Athletic what is in the players' heads; and the club believes what is in their heads between 14 and 18 can be a marker for future performance. There are four players in the first team with BA or BSc-level degrees, and another six with the high school Baccalaureate qualification. Compare this with England, where Duncan Watmore is the only top-flight player to earn a degree since John Wetherall in 1992. More often, the students come from Bilbao Athletic and Baskonia. Amorrortu says around 60 per cent of the players complete their university courses.

There is one line in Amorrortu's document that is in capital letters. It reads: 'EL NOS ANTES QUE EL YO' (The 'us' before 'me'). Developing this sense of community, through education and belonging, can be powerful. The Athletic model reminds me of Next Jump, an American business that runs employee rewards programmes, allowing discounts from over 30,000 merchants. There are around 200 Next Jump employees based in four cities, and they benefit from a unique company structure. This includes subsidised holidays, free food (a healthy lunch if you attend a lunchtime fitness class), mentors for everyone and Code for a Cause, which offers out employees' IT skills to charities that need it.

The other reason staff turnover at Next Jump is almost zero, and 90 per cent of employees say they love working there, is not the company dance-off at the annual party, but the No Firing policy. Once Next Jump hires you, the contract is for life. 'Hiring managers started treating hiring like adoption: once we take someone into our family, they're here for life, [and] when things don't work, they're responsible for training them, helping them,' explained CEO Charlie Kim. He noticed that training became much more comprehensive, focusing more on character and integrity. The biggest impact he saw was in the effectiveness of performance evaluations. Instead of scepticism from employees concerned about a future firing, there was an honesty and openness in these discussions. Employees spoke frankly about their problems and concerns and, as a result, never took those stresses home with them. With a focus on developing the individuals, employee turnover is down and overall happiness up.

In the ongoing quest for improvement, Athletic can rely on one of their biggest fans: Ignacio Palacios-Huerta, famous in Spain for his outstanding work on the game theory of penalty-kicks. Palacios-Huerta is also on the board at Athletic, where his official title is Head of Talent Identification.

'The wider lesson is that everyone at the club should understand the values of the club and their own importance to their club and community,' Palacios-Huerta says. 'I think that if players feel that the club they play for is *their* club, they'll play with more commitment. They'll be more committed to be better at what they do. They won't feel like ordinary workers, they'll feel and act as if they are owners. If the "workers" feel that they are the ones who give the club its identity and the club feels that they give the club its identity, then you create a family business which can be very efficient in a very tough market.'

Palacios-Huerta describes talent as 'the product of abilities × commitment'. The coaches develop the players' abilities. He is interested in the commitment. He does not want to share too many of the secrets that give Athletic an edge, but a clue into the work he does can be found in his book *Beautiful Game Theory: How Soccer Can Help Economics*. In Chapter 4, he describes a computerised penalty-kick game between 20 pairs of healthy subjects, half of whom were playing while hooked up to a functional magnetic resonance imaging (fMRI) device. Each pair played between 100 and 120 matches; one of them as the striker choosing where to place the ball, the other the goalkeeper trying to stop it.

Palacios-Huerta wanted to know what happens inside the brain during a penalty-kick game and whether neurological data can predict which individuals might be better at strategic decision-making. This is a subject we will look at more closely in Chapter 3. Palacios-Huerta found activity increases in various areas of the brain during the decision-making period, and that brain activity in another area related to better randomisation of choices.[6] Using similar neuroeconomic techniques, he believes he can determine which players would react best in pressure environments.

I remembered these findings during the match I watched. Of the five goals Aduriz scored, three were penalties. He used two different strategies: for the first kick, he picked his spot and smashed the ball into the net, which is known as the Goalkeeper-Independent method. For the other two, he was Goalkeeper-Dependent, waiting for the goalkeeper to move first and rolling the ball into the other corner. I am sure that One-Club Man winner Le Tissier, himself a penalty specialist, would have approved.

Athletic has a triple strategy that businesses can learn from today. It has developed this culture of togetherness and collaboration, helped by its history and geography, that provides an edge. The club invests in its talent as humans first, not machines whose only purpose is to produce results. Their emphasis on education, behaviour and development is testament to that. (So is the players' car park, where I spotted just one sports car and only one convertible; the rest were extremely ordinary. It turned out the convertible belonged to Ernesto Valverde, the coach.) And the club believes that retaining talent is more important than recruiting it. When companies don't develop talent internally or promote from within, it sends a message to employees: we will find external solutions. That can then become self-fulfilling: without opportunities, talent will leave. Athletic retains talent and, in so doing, retains its community.

I catch up with Palacios-Huerta after the game. I ask him how Athletic continues to find its edge. 'We survive on tiny margins. In the player development aspect, in some sense we are like the *Moneyball* of football. We are using data to find as much as we can to gain an edge,' he tells me. 'The reason is because our model is like no other club; it is not about buying or selling. We don't need to sell players and we rarely look to buy them either. It's about developing. And our culture, this social model, it's the biggest part of that.'

HOW TO GET AN EDGE – by IGNACIO PALACIOS-HUERTA

1. Understand better, and from a purely scientific perspective, the production function of talent during the period from 10 to 20 years old.
2. Understand better players' decision-making processes, and how these are formed.
3. I like the definition of talent as the product of abilities × commitment. An edge is obtained by having greater commitment. Understanding and investing in the formation of commitment is key.

GAIN LINE

Measure team chemistry

Defining a team / The TeamWork Index / Turnover and cohesion / Talent portability of stars / Leicester and the super-chickens

Not everyone buys into Athletic's brand of success, or at least the reasons behind it. 'They think cultural input is the reason, but I would argue that it's cohesion,' says Ben Darwin, a former Australia rugby international whose career was ended abruptly after a horrific spinal injury suffered during the 2003 World Cup semi-final against New Zealand.

Darwin's injury came about when a scrum he was in collapsed. He was pushed up vertically and his head caught the inside shoulder of his direct opponent. He heard a crack in his neck and immediately lost all feeling in his body below his chin.

As he collapsed onto the grass unable to move, he knew how serious the situation was. But his mind was in calm, problem-solving mode, as it was programmed to be while on the pitch. 'Mate, I think I've broken my neck, I can't feel anything,' he told the team physio as soon as he ran over.

In the next few seconds, three more thoughts came into his head. One: my coach will be annoyed that I stuffed up that scrum. Two: if I'm a quadriplegic, what will I do with myself? Three: maybe I'll get into computers, I really like computers – okay, that's what I'm going to do with myself.

Darwin did not break his neck – he had suffered spinal shock, and had a prolapsed disc – and miraculously was able to walk out of hospital one week later. For that he owes a great deal to his direct opponent, New Zealand prop Kees Meuws, who heard Darwin whisper, 'Neck, neck, neck.' Meuws crouched over his body to protect Darwin, which saved him from paralysis. 'I think someone just flipped a coin and it went my way.'

Darwin was 26 at the time. He had played 28 Test matches, and was a few years from his peak. He never played again. His biggest loss was the friendships he forged on the pitch. As he put it: 'When you finish a game of football and you've played together and you walk off with your team-mates ... and you've overcome an opposition, you don't have to say anything to each other, you can simply look your fellow player in the eye, and he knows you helped him, and you know how he helped you. And that's enormously satisfying.'

That memory stayed with him. Throughout his coaching career – at Norths in Sydney, Western Force in Perth, Melbourne Rebels in Melbourne, and Shining Arcs and Suntory Sungoliath in Tokyo – he felt that a coach's impact was often negligible. Some seasons, he was part of an ineffective coaching group and the team was undefeated. At Western Force, he did what he felt was his best work and the team came last.

He moved to Japan, coached there – working under England's successful rugby coach Eddie Jones – and won everything, despite doing nothing different. 'I did my worst coaching when I was in Japan, because I couldn't even speak the language.' The team went unbeaten because, Darwin thought, they had been together for so long and knew each other so well.

Darwin returned to the thought that he'd had while lying stricken on the pitch. He 'got into computers'. He set up an analytics company called Gain Line Analytics, based on his belief that there is a fundamental misunderstanding about how teams work. His view is that a team is a system of relationships, and those within it are either aligned or not. The better aligned the relationships, the more successful the team.

The numbers backed him up. Sports teams made up of players who had existing and long-term relationships, those had played with each other for a long time, were a better indicator of performance than salary. In some cases, he saw that the levels of understanding between team-mates impacted on performance by between 30 and 40 per cent.

This is known as the Juggler Effect. It confirms that skill develops in a cohesive environment. If two jugglers work together for five years, they will know each other well and improve as individuals, not just as a pair. If a juggler constantly changes his partner, he will spend more time working on developing new combinations than his own skill. In this respect, high cohesion also allows for greater skill development.

We have seen that Athletic finds its edge by building a community, developing players through education and retaining its talent. Darwin takes this one step further and explains why cohesion offers significant added value for a business. Later in the chapter we will look at a club that did not have the geographical, historical or cultural advantages of Bilbao and still managed to develop its own identity in a cohesive environment.

Darwin set himself the task to measure the intangible of team chemistry. He initially developed an algorithm to calculate team cohesion that had three measures:

- Internal experience (within current team, maybe the youth academy)
- External experience (outside of current team)
- Externally shared experience (for example, club-mates playing for a national team)[7]

He called it the TeamWork Index (TWI). Based on research from nine different team sports, including football, across 30 seasons, it showed a clear correlation between the quantity and intensity of linkages within a team – to put it simply, cohesion – and team performance. He added more measures, among them playing system, combinations and skill-sets, and now has a more robust TWI that, he says, predicts outcomes with greater accuracy than bookmakers. The higher a side's TWI, the more unified the team, the more likely the club is to enjoy sustained on-field success, off-field stability and heightened brand engagement.

His first clients were rugby league teams in Australia. Gain Line Analytics now works in rugby union, Australian Rules football, cricket and football. Darwin offers a Performance Audit to help owners and stakeholders benchmark expectations; a Performance Capacity to calculate squad skill output multiplied by cohesion; a Cohesion Score to assess weak points in clients' teams and opposition teams; and a Cohesion Predictor to assess possible outcomes with different line-ups in the short and long terms. One Premier League manager who uses Gain Line's Cohesion Analytics said: 'I've always felt this about sport, but no one has put it into data.'

At the root of Darwin's philosophy is the belief that high turnover of players reduces cohesion. He looked at data involving 10,000 players and came up with some key findings:

1. A player's output on the field at their previous club is not just solely because of that individual. Their output is a product of the knowledge and understanding that player has with the other players around them. This is something unique for each player at each club, and is not transferrable. So it should be expected that a player who has recently changed clubs would under-perform at the new club.

2. On average, it takes three years for a player to hit their peak after moving clubs, and that is if they manage to hit their peak. Some players are never the same after moving clubs, through no fault of their own. Add in an overseas move, or a foreign language, and it's even tougher.

3. A player's new club is expecting them to perform at the same standard as they did during the last game (or perhaps the best game) at their previous club. Players

who have changed teams will struggle to deliver on this. The number of times we have heard players being described as 'not the player he was at his old club' is remarkable.

4. Moving more than three times rings alarm bells. The more times a player changes clubs, the harder it becomes to settle in to the new club.

This final point is in contrast with some attitudes in football that associate players moving clubs with shows of ambition. Fans love a new signing because it sends a message that the club has the ambition to improve (a director once admitted to me that one player was signed for precisely that reason). I spoke to a coach about one player, a France international who had played for three huge clubs before he was 21, and the coach was worried that the youngster's entourage were more interested in signing-on fees than the player's development.

Darwin warns that highest-risk transfers involve a young player moving from a high-cohesion team to a low-cohesion team. The fact that a player might leave a high-cohesion team also tells its own story. 'If I was a young athlete, I would find a cohesive organisation and take a 50 per cent pay cut, as the rewards would come later,' says Darwin.

His findings are backed up by studies in individual sports, including basketball[8] and football,[9] which neatly summarises the challenge of recruitment. 'Signing players of higher quality will increase team quality but will reduce team cohesion,' wrote Dr Bill Gerrard, Professor of Business and Sports Analytics at Leeds University. 'And the same goes for changing the head coach, which immediately wipes out all of the player–coach Team Shared Experience (TSE). The new head coach will start with zero shared experience with the existing squad.'

Gerrard concluded that the most significant impact on team performance was the interaction of player TSE combined with the length of time that the head coach has spent with the team. And the biggest cohesion impact can come when a new coach takes over a team with a low TWI.

I thought of Darwin when Arsenal coach Arsène Wenger bore the brunt of fan-base anger on the eve of the 2016–17 Premier League season. Arsenal's title rivals had made many expensive new signings but Wenger, whose degree was in economics, had, at that stage, bought only Granit Xhaka.

'There is always demand for new, but new is just new,' Wenger told a baffled press corps at the training ground. 'Football players have to meet their needs. When they meet their needs they express their quality. What a football club is to be built on is to make sure the players meet their needs and can develop afterwards. The fact that it's new, after six months it's not new any more. You come every day, you drive in here, the first day it's new, after six months it's not new any more. What is new makes news. But apart from that it makes noise. The noise is not necessarily always quality.' Spoken like a true Darwin disciple – until, in the last week of the transfer window, Arsenal signed two more players, Shkodran Mustafi and Lucas Perez.

I ask Darwin about the England team and its performance at Euro 2016, where it lost in the Round of 16 to a far less talented, but more cohesive, Iceland team. Darwin was in no doubt where the problem lay. 'It's not about skill level but too much choice,' he says. 'If an English player has one bad game, he is dropped. But look at Iceland: if you have a bad game for them, you keep your place because there is no one around to come in.' There may still be a clear skill deficit, but cohesion helps reduce that gap.

According to Darwin's TeamWork Index, England was the *worst* team at Euro 2016. 'Their numbers were diabolical,' he says. 'The skill is there and, from that point of view, the individuals are getting better, but the cohesion is not, and so the collective is getting worse.'

Darwin cited a 260 per cent difference in cohesion between Iceland and England. 'It looked like the England players had an AVO [Apprehended Violence Order, like an ASBO] put out on them. They were not allowed to go near each other.'

So what's the answer? 'Patience with players. Not changing systems and line-ups all the time. How players handle pressure is related to cohesion and relationships within the team. England has done everything it could possibly do except for keeping the same people in the team. Patience!

'The psychologist is on board, the beds are super-comfy, they even re-created the Wembley grass at St George's Park. But what does the type of grass matter if it's a different guy receiving the pass every time? This is also why low-cohesion teams struggle away from home; we call it complexity under duress but basically they fall apart under pressure. It's not about developing skill. The thing to remember is that the talent you see is not the talent you get. They are different things.'

The TeamWork Index has a universal principle applicable to all businesses. 'Not everyone can afford to bring in the best people, and if you do, you will have problems,' Darwin continues. 'You might be judging talent on the wrong standards if they are coming in from a different system to yours. New people may be indoctrinated into other systems. It's more important to think about if your new hire is a good person – can they adapt to your system? – and remember that the younger they are, the more adaptable they are.' We will look at the importance of adaptability in Chapter 2, where we will find out just what happened to Ousmane Dembélé after he appeared in the 'Next Generation' feature.

The question does not always have to be a 'build versus buy' one: some positions are more suited for buying in talent, and others for developing your own. One study looked at the portability of talent, by position, in the more measurable environment of American football.[10] It took performance data from 75 star wide receivers – whose results are often linked to the relationship and understanding of set plays with their quarter-back – and 38 punters, whose job of kicking the ball is based more on individual skill. The data took into account the best season the player had and the two seasons that followed, dividing the groups into switchers (those who moved teams) and stayers.

The result: star wide receivers who switched teams suffered a decline in performance compared to those who stayed put. All wide receivers decline over time, but these declines were steeper than normal. Punters who switched teams did not experience a greater drop in performance than those who stayed. This suggests that punters have more portable skills than wide receivers – and in business terms, that wide receivers have what is known as company-specific human capital. David Moyes developed his company-specific human capital over ten years at Everton, so a short-term performance decline was inevitable after he moved jobs. Although, when he was appointed manager of Sunderland in summer 2016, Moyes had his own approach to talent portability. He went back to his former clubs to sign eight players: Steven Pienaar, Victor Anichebe, Joleon Lescott, Bryan Oviedo and Darron Gibson, whom he worked with at Everton; and Donald Love, Paddy McNair and Adnan Januzaj from his period at Manchester United. Sunderland finished bottom of the Premier League, and none of those signings improved on their previous performances. You could say that these players did not have the portability skills Moyes had hoped for.

'Managers should consider minimising the portability of certain star positions in order to retain those individuals as a source of competitive advantage,' the study concludes. In other words, if your star player wants a huge pay hike in his new contract, you pay it.

Darwin knows one cricket coach who has a tactic right out of the Athletic playbook: he makes training sessions voluntary attendance. 'They all turn up of course, but that's because he is empowering them and relying on their character to be professional. That leads to stronger relationships within the group.'

I ask Darwin if he could identify underlying reasons for Leicester City's surprising Premier League title-winning campaign in 2015–16. The team began with a relatively low TWI that had them down as a mid-table side. What helped is that they were playing in the Premier League, where cohesion has dropped by over 30 per cent since it was launched in 1992. The cohesion dynamic of the competition itself affects teams as much as their own cohesion does. The Premier League had four different winners in the years between 2012 and 2016 and the last team to successfully defend its title was Manchester United in 2008–09.

Leicester were able to jump up the table because so many other teams lacked cohesion: the Manchester clubs were struggling under coaches approaching the end of their reigns, Chelsea was in freefall under José Mourinho and Jürgen Klopp joined Liverpool after the season had started. As the season went on, Leicester's cohesion rating topped their rivals'. They had no injuries and coach Claudio Ranieri picked his best XI every week. He would also regularly play down the team's ambition to win the title, saying it was not possible until the point at which it was almost impossible not to win it.

There was also the super-chicken factor. An evolutionary biologist called William Muir was interested in productivity, and he devised a study of chickens, assuming theirs would be easy to measure as you could just count their eggs. Chickens live in groups, and so he left one group of chickens for six generations and monitored their productivity. He then created a second group, taking only the most productive chickens from the first group. He called the second group a 'super-flock'. He waited another six generations, and then compared the results.

The first group was getting along just fine. The chickens were plump and feathered and their egg production was up. The second group, the one with the 'super-chickens', was not so good: only three were alive. They had suppressed the productivity of the others and pecked them to death. 'Most organisations and some societies are run along the super-chicken model,' says Margaret Heffernan, an expert in corporate cohesion.[11] 'We've thought success is achieved by picking the superstars, the brightest ... in the room and giving them all the power. The result has been exactly the same as in Muir's experiment: aggression, dysfunction, and waste.'

Leicester's win was a triumph of the collective over the individual, of the group chicken rather than the super-chicken model. Even the three best players – Jamie Vardy, Riyad Mahrez, and N'Golo Kante – always put the group first. Mahrez gave up his penalty-kicking duties against Watford in November to allow Vardy to score in a ninth successive game (he would go on to break Ruud van Nistelrooy's record and score in 11 straight games).

And what about the slump that happened the following season? Because of their original low TWI, Leicester dropped back to their long-term Performance Capacity (remember, that's skill multiplied by cohesion), while their runs in the FA Cup and Champions League diluted in-season cohesion because of the squad players being rotated in (having sole focus on the league in 2015–16 was a huge advantage).

So a team with a low TWI *can* have a good season, but Darwin's data suggests that they cannot sustain it. The last team with a low TWI to win the Premier League was Blackburn Rovers in 1995. That side was relegated in 1999.

What makes one group more successful than another? A team from MIT tried to answer that question, bringing in 697 volunteers, putting them into groups and giving them hard problems to solve. Each team worked together to complete a series of short tasks, one involving logical analysis, another brainstorming; others emphasised co-ordination, planning and moral reasoning. Overall, the groups that did well on one task did well on the others. Anita Woolley, one of the academics who conducted the study, identified the three characteristics that marked out the best teams.

'First, their members contributed more equally to the team's discussions, rather than letting one or two people dominate the group,' Woolley explained. They also showed high degrees of social sensitivity to each other.[12] And thirdly, the teams with more women outperformed teams with more men.[13] (Athletic Club de Bilbao understands that its policy is open to the charge of lacking in diversity, but the club has six women on the executive board, which is more than any other club in Spain.[14] In Chapter 5 I will look at how one French club found an edge by appointing a female head coach.)

Woolley's MIT experiment showed that social connectedness is key to performance. Heffernan visits companies that have banned coffee cups from desks because they want people to talk to each other around the coffee machine. Idexx, an American company specialising in diagnostics and IT solutions for animal health, built allotments on site so people from different areas of the business could meet each other. 'What people need is social support, and they need to know who to ask for help,' she says. 'Companies don't have ideas; only people do. And what motivates people are the bonds and loyalty and trust they develop between each other. What matters is the mortar, not just the bricks.'

When you put all of this together, you get just what Athletic have achieved in Bilbao: social capital. 'Social capital is the reliance and interdependency that builds trust,' says Heffernan. 'The term comes from sociologists who were studying communities that proved particularly resilient in times of stress. Social capital is what gives companies momentum, and social capital is what makes companies robust. What does this mean in practical terms? It means that time is everything, because social capital compounds with time. So teams that work together longer get better, because it takes time to develop the trust you need for real candour and openness. And time is what builds value.'

The Athletic directors Amorrortu and Palacios-Huerta agree with Heffernan's hypothesis. Social capital builds trust: that's the Athletic way. Then there is that term 'culture'. If something is happening in a group and we can't see the explanation, it's often put down to the culture. 'Culture is an ambiguous word that can refer to many intangibles in sport,' Darwin adds. But don't confuse it with cohesion. For Darwin, culture cannot be measured; cohesion can.

HOW TO GET AN EDGE – by BEN DARWIN

1. Understand the state of an organisation so that decisions can be made (and expectations understood) in context.
2. The knowledge of success or failure must be held in the organisation, not in an individual.
3. Decisions with the short term in mind will impact long after in ways not envisaged.

ÖSTERSUNDS FK
Find your USP

The Solidarity Gala rap / Dangers of blame culture / Swap stress for bravery / Create your own distinction / Swan Lake and reindeer lasso / The Privilege Walk / What is art?

As one of the oldest clubs in Spain, it makes sense for Athletic Club de Bilbao to make tradition, history and community such a critical part of its USP. But what about the clubs who don't have that kind of history, or a start-up looking to create an edge in the market: they cannot rely on a past, or even a point of distinction, that doesn't yet exist. That was the conundrum that faced a genial young Englishman who found himself in a freezing part of northern Sweden with his wife and new-born son and a team that was under-achieving at all levels. As we will see, he worked on an identity. He developed cohesion. He found an edge. And the results followed.

'Ladies and gentlemen, you have just seen the football-playing, music-making, love-making, heart-breaking, booty-shaking, fist-pumping, legendary UHHH-EFFF-KOE!'

In September 2016, in Frösö Convention Centre, a former aircraft hangar in a small city in northern Sweden was packed to the rafters. Graham Potter, dressed all in black, was on the stage addressing a crowd of over 1,600 people. The audience was going wild. They had just seen players from their local football club, Östersunds FK, known as ÖFK, put on a show like no other. Potter was ÖFK coach.

This was the Solidarity Gala, and it was raising money for people driven from their homes by war. It began with Iraqi striker Brwa Nouri addressing the venue with a plea for community. 'Solidarity is a collective that takes responsibility for something, without having any self-interest in it to look after the well-being of a group.'

Former ÖFK player and now marketing executive Jimi Eiremo then played a haunting tune on the näverhorn, a traditional Swedish instrument similar to a didgeridoo, made out of birch-bark. Around him, the team sang the melancholy regional anthem 'Jämtlandssången'. Potter even sang a solo verse, as did Christine, one of the club cooks. Christine is a refugee from Congo who settled in Östersunds and is one of the most popular figures at the club. Her performance, given the context, was poignant.

Nouri, Sotte Papagianipolous (Greek/Swedish) and Saman Ghoddos (Swedish) then stepped forward to perform a brilliant rap based on Ison & Fille's hit 'Jag skrattar idag' (I laugh now). The song is about living for the moment and not having regrets. Next up was youth coach Andreas Paulsson, who shouted into the mic, 'Let's speed this up!' and after an impressive beat-box session, sang Justin Bieber's 'Love Yourself' in perfect tune. Curtis Edwards, a former Middlesbrough academy player, then belted out the George Michael song 'Freedom'.

The first-team squad joined together in singing 'Ain't No Mountain High Enough', 'Human' and 'We Are the World'. This one was an emotional one, as drawings from children saying 'Tack ÖFK' – thanks ÖFK – were shown on a giant screen behind the stage. The kids weren't the only ones giving thanks. 'Football was my saviour, and by that I don't mean the actual kicking of a ball, but more about what this club stands for and the values it has,' said Nouri.

Every member of the squad, including the coach and his assistants, performed during the show. It ended with a burst of red-and-black confetti and the first-team players and youth play-ers wildly dancing to 'Can't Stop the Feeling'. The mood was joyous. Relief was mixed with pride. The show was sensational.

'It was a wonderful night,' Potter tells me a few months later, as he prepares for a pre-season training camp in warmer climes than northern Sweden. Potter has guided ÖFK from Sweden's fourth division to the first division, and survival in the top flight, in the space of six years. In 2017, ÖFK also won the Swedish Cup, the first major trophy in their history. Potter is a hero in the 'Winter City', which until recently was more famous for its Nordic sports.

Östersunds has a cross-country ski stadium and a snow piste. It has hosted several Nordic Games and ski orienteering world championships. But now it has another source of pride. One journalist who visited Potter's house saw a bouquet of flowers on the kitchen table and a note from AnnSofie Andersson, the mayor, saying, 'Congratulations, you are amazing. We are so glad you live in Östersunds.'

Potter was an average player (his words), who considers himself fortunate to have been a professional for 13 years. He played in the top flight, for Southampton and Stoke, but most of his career was in the lower leagues. He always had a thirst for knowledge. One afternoon he was idly skimming a newspaper when he realised how much time he had on his hands. He signed up to an Open University degree in social sciences and studied American and European Union politics. When he retired from playing, he wanted to combine his continuing education with some coaching. So he became a football development coach at the University of Hull and continued his early coaching career at Leeds Metropolitan University, where he enrolled in a Masters course in leadership and emotional intelligence.

He explored leadership theory and how success is related to overall environments. He wrote a thesis on the importance of reflection and self-determination in individual development. Potter learned that self-awareness was the foundation of emotional intelligence; it's a lesson that remains with him today. He was the only sports coach on the course. His course leader was a former military man, and everyone else was either in the army or a surgeon. 'They were all highly technically gifted but needed support around emotional management and particularly when mistakes happen and their responses to that.' It was fascinating for Potter, whose own environment had been based heavily on a blame culture, where coaches would tell him to cut out silly mistakes, and players were castigated for individual errors. Potter decided he wanted to be different.

That's when he met ÖFK chairman Daniel Kindberg, who was then the club's sports director.[15] Potter was offered the job of academy head. He turned it down. Over a year later, Kindberg had become chairman. One of his first moves was to return to Potter and recruit him as head coach.

The duo spoke the same language. Kindberg is a former lieutenant-colonel in the Swedish army. He saw active service in Congo, Liberia and the Balkans. It was there that he learned how stress and fear limit decision-making. 'It's simple: if you're in a combat situation, and you make a mistake, your friends die,' he tells me. 'So if you're stressed, it's harder to make the right decision.' When he returned home from tours of duty overseas, he spent time thinking what it was like to be afraid and how it affected him. It made him confront future problems in a different way. 'We need to take away the stress, to encourage bravery, and to be convinced by your inner self.' Even if it doesn't work? 'You don't know unless you try!'

Potter said that there was 'a philosophical connection' between him and Kindberg. Sir Alex Ferguson always said that new managers weighing up job offers should not choose the club, but the chairman they work for. Potter liked Kindberg's vision. The chairman wanted to do something different, to create an identity, to make a difference and to have a football club to be proud of. Even though the club had just dropped into the fourth tier; even though the fans were deeply unhappy and leaving in their droves; even though Potter did not know Swedish football; even though he had a wife and new-born son, he moved to northern Sweden and took the job. This was practising the boldness and risk-taking mentality that he preached.

It was much harder than he thought. The club was in a negative spiral. There was a strong blame culture. Recruitment decisions were not working. And his wife, Rachel, found it hard to adapt. The climate was fierce, as arctic Kallvastan winds whipped off the giant lake, Storsjön, at temperatures as low as minus 25°C. Potter was working 12 hours a day and Rachel was a new mother who didn't speak the language. She has now learned Swedish and, along with her three children, is the one who has to encourage Potter to speak it more often. They are now both fluent, as are their children.

Kindberg's vision had included ÖFK getting into the top division and eventually playing in Europe. 'From where we were, you could argue that was an insane target,' Potter says. It's not so insane now.

His first step was to bring some element of joy back to the club. The focus had been outcome-based, valuing results only, rather than performance. Potter tried to create a new environment, one that recognised potential and was built on trust and mutual support. No more blame culture. It related to the values Kindberg wanted the club to espouse, which were published on the club website shortly after Potter's arrival. It is to the great pride of both men that these values remain in place today, and that their power has had a social impact on the Östersunds and wider Jämtland community. They were: Openness, Long-term, Sincerity and Honesty, Reliability, Professionalism.

Your organisation may or may not have a mission or values statement. The likelihood is that it does, but you just don't know it. Such a statement can be a useful tool to generate feedback about whether the business is fulfilling those values, or implementing that vision. It may seem unnecessary but in the case of ÖFK, whose values are a clear source of pride, it has proven extremely beneficial.

It's also easy to forget about the importance of relationship-building in today's workplace, where deadlines are usually yesterday and stress is never far from the surface. We are given short-term growth targets to meet that are inhibiting and stressful. A culture of short-termism and need for profit restricts employees' risk-taking; they are too scared to deviate from the normal for fear of blame if targets are not reached. How can this be an efficient environment for success?

It's much harder, and braver, to look long term and develop deeper respect and connections between colleagues by devoting time to ÖFK's intangible values. This is particularly true when working with millennials. Simon Sinek, an author on modern management whose work is admired by a coach we will meet in Chapter 3, claims that millennials have it tough: brought up by parents who told them they were special and could do and have anything they want, they often find that not to be the case in the real world of professional business. So they often suffer from low self-esteem, have little resilience and a reliance on technology, rather than real-life connections, as a coping mechanism. ÖFK have found smart solutions.

'We have built a working environment based on hard-core values that we all have to follow,' says Kindberg. 'It's a standard of how we look at each other, at people, at society and at football. In this environment, creativity, initiative and courage blend with competing every day to be the best. The same is true if you are the striker or a clerk in the office. Everyone here is the same.'

The pair embraced the need to create an identity, practically from scratch. But where to start? Potter carried out due diligence. He looked at the competition; studied what other teams in Sweden were doing, the culture of Swedish football, the recruitment patterns; and looked at ways to compete, and possible advantages that Östersunds could find. If ÖFK competed on the same terms, they would fail, because they had less money than their rivals. So how could they develop an edge?

'We had to find different players, and give them a reason to come here,' says Potter. 'We wanted to improve careers here, and work on players as people too. We used our location in northern Sweden as an advantage; it helped us create a tight-knit group. Swedish football was compact and physical; we looked for players who had different qualities, and came from different areas. This diversity also helped us. We looked at personality attributes and those who played football in a different way to other teams in Sweden. Our style was possession-based. We wanted players who could control the ball, who were flexible [position-wise] and, most of all, who wanted to improve.'

The universal principle of this is clear. Every business would like to create a USP but it can only do so by understanding the market and the competition; only then can it harness advantages for the greater good. This can be as true for the individual as the business. Potter simply asked: 'What is my distinction?' By choosing diversity as his USP, he has gone for the polar opposite of Athletic Club de Bilbao, for whom proximity is the USP.

Kindberg reduced the concept of hierarchy by empowering five individual departments to run themselves. He estimates that the board takes 1 per cent of decisions, he takes 4 per cent and 95 per cent are generated by empowered employees.[16] 'Everything we do has the aim of helping us win football matches,' he said. 'We use different methods to widen our eyes, improve our social conscience and take responsibility for ourselves. We cannot compete with other clubs financially. So we find other ways.'

One of those ideas came about after a meeting with Karin Wahlén, whose father Lasse Lindin is ÖFK general manager. Wahlén was a bookish child who grew up wanting to be a librarian. She ended up working for a publisher, then setting up her own cultural agency to promote museums and literacy for groups who don't normally engage with culture.

Kindberg missed his initial meeting with Wahlén, who was convinced that meant he was not interested. When they did meet, she went in heavy with her pitch. 'Getting the players into culture will improve their performances. It will take them out of their comfort zone and make them braver on and off the pitch,' she said. 'When we are brave we can explore our creativity without being afraid of the unknown.'

This chimed with Kindberg's view, so he set up a two-day workshop where the players met authors, dancers and artists, and shared views on the creative process. It was a success, but nothing changed. So Kindberg asked Wahlén for more. He appointed her ÖFK's 'cultural coach' and, later that year, the whole club put on a play. The coaching staff performed monologues, the players acted a meta-comedy about not knowing how to put on a play, and the youth academy did a dancing and singing extravaganza that required over 20 costume changes. 'Everyone loved it, and the results improved soon after,' said Wahlén, a passionate ÖFK fan whose daughters are careful not to stress her out on match-days.

Other cultural projects followed. In 2013, the club put on an art exhibition. In 2014, they published a book, *My Journey*, featuring every club employee's story. In 2015, there was an art/dance piece, called 'Strength through Diversity'. One year later, the club performed a modern dance interpretation of *Swan Lake* at the city's local theatre on the main square, Storsjö. Maria Nilsson Waller, the choreographer, described dance to them as 'movement of the soul'.

In rehearsals, the players began with nervous giggles as they divided into pairs and lifted each other up. But their inhibitions quickly left them as Waller's drills had them moving in harmony. The rehearsals were like training sessions, a safe area for learning (and making mistakes), and peppered with positive feedback and support structure. Everyone was out of their comfort zone and helping each other. In football parlance, it was a real leveller. The power of touch in the dance also brought an intimacy to the group.

Psychologists have shown that sporting teams win more if they touch each other as a way of establishing bonds of trust. One study of NBA teams found that those who touched more (defined by a fist-bump, high-five or a hug) won more games.[17] The smallest touch is a bonding tool of support. You are not alone on the field. Someone has your back (literally, in this dance). We will discuss the importance of tactility in the methodology of one of football's most intriguing managers in Chapter 2.

And so, to show-time. There were 450 people in the venue, mostly theatre-going types. Midfielder Monday Samuel opened up with a graceful solo, before his team-mates joined him. The movements were elegant, the dances polished and, most of all, the focus was intense. This was not a joke for the players. Potter also performed a solo: lying on his stomach, legs bent at 90 degrees, on the gold confetti-covered stage. He slowly lifted his head and neck, but not his shoulders, and looked around him. There was a refined dignity, a stillness, to his movement. It was excellent. Afterwards assistant coach Billy Reid sang The Drifters' 'Saturday Night' and the mood turned joyous as the whole team danced around him. They were back in their comfort zone.

Once mocked for its cultural projects, ÖFK was now having its performances reviewed by Stockholm's high-culture media. 'It was beautiful,' Sverige Radio's cultural expert Gunnar Bolin tells me. 'The sincerity and power of expression made it extremely moving.' Two theatres in Stockholm asked ÖFK to perform *Swan Lake* at their venues. The team declined. Bolin had noted that it was not just the players who were dancing, but all the club employees. 'Even the ones who were not quite so flexible as the younger players,' he smiles.

'The cultural theme allows us to be more open, to be braver, to improve decision-making,' Kindberg says. 'It helps the group come together. When we look at players, people look at qualities like physics, technology and understanding of the game. But we believe the mental part is the most important. By allowing players to venture into situations they do not know, and challenge their own fears, they grow as individuals. By extension, that gives them greater courage on the pitch.'

Potter agrees. 'The environment we have established means everyone is prepared to trust the process, but it's definitely a challenge and by no means comfortable for any of us out there. You have to overcome some inner demons and insecurities to get out there and do it.' Potter found his *Swan Lake* solo particularly tough. 'We had just got promoted to the *Allsvenskan* [Swedish first division] and there was a huge buzz around the performance. It was very difficult to do, and I felt a right wally at times.'

Potter understands the positive effect of the coach showing his nerves and vulnerabilities to the group. 'Culturally, everyone thinks a leader needs to only show strength and be this macho figure, but it doesn't have to be like that.' Potter was not scared of his team seeing his weaknesses. Sometimes giving them that glimpse can be transformative.

The time spent working on the dance also taught a valuable lesson. Time is important. Things don't happen straightaway. The players in the squad are used to instant gratification: being able to watch TV on demand, order things online and even meet partners instantly on smartphones. But it takes patience to write a book, to put on an art show, to learn a dance. It can be arduous and punishing, but ultimately it is worth it. The lesson that ÖFK players took in from *Swan Lake* was not just about cohesion; it was also about self-confidence, job fulfilment and patience.

Management has changed from the days when Potter was a player. Millennials will no longer put up with always being told what to do. 'It just won't work any more,' he says. 'If you rely on your position of power, or control over the group, it's only a short-term solution. You need to be authentic in the relationships you have, show the qualities you want to inspire in the group, and sometimes it's about not having all the answers. As long as you are dedicated to improving yourself and those around you, are able to adapt and make good decisions, then you can manage. It helps to have some self-awareness, as if you understand yourself then you can understand others. That's how you can build relationships that withstand the pressures of losing games.'

This was also apparent in the preparation for ÖFK's 2017 cultural project: an investigation into the Sami culture, to culminate in an exhibition comprising photo, film, crafts, music, song and speech. Known in English as Laplanders, the indigenous Sami live in the Arctic area of Sápmi, which encompasses parts of northern Norway, Sweden, Finland and Russia. The whole club has learned about the Sami's language, faith and narrative tradition, with help from Maxida Märak, a hip-hop artist, activist and Sami expert. One lesson was about reindeer husbandry and, in the absence of a real reindeer, Potter wore fake horns and challenged striker Alhaji Gero to lasso him. So he did.

Potter's studies at the Open University, Hull and Leeds reinforced his interest in self-reflection and forced him to think about what kind of leader he wanted to be. He did not want to repeat the patterns he saw from his own playing career. So, what type of leader is he? 'I value people and I value relationships and I am as authentic as I can be. My job is to understand the person first and foremost, and help them improve. For me, this role is not about winning matches or winning leagues, it's simply about whether you can affect someone's life in a positive way.'

Potter is convinced the cultural projects can work in another environment, though he warned against going from doing nothing to performing Swan Lake. 'It was a gradual process,' he says. 'But the fundamentals are the same across industries: if you have people who are very good at doing something, whatever that is, and you want to explore a new way to challenge them, or develop the team, or find out about themselves, this is a way to do it. Lots of professional life is about coping with the struggles and attitude to that. In football it's a misplaced pass or a lost game – or an angry fan. In another environment it might be a grumpy client or a difficult moment. But being comfortable in uncomfortable situations is a way of teaching people in a new way.'

The cultural work is not just crystallised into the performances. Kindberg sees the whole process as one of self-improvement. 'We want to show that our football is more than football. We are happy, we are open, we are braver than the normal standards, and we use this to challenge people by taking them out of their comfort zone.'

This is where Wahlén comes in again. As well as collaborating with Kindberg on the cultural projects, she organises regular workshops for the team. The players are encouraged to make emotional connections with each other. She remembers the conversations that followed the Privilege Walk, when the whole squad stood in a line in the middle of the room and were asked a series of questions:

If you are a white male take one step forward.
If there have been times in your life when you skipped a meal because there was no food in the house take one step backward.
If you have visible or invisible disabilities take one step backward.
If you attended school with people you felt were like yourself take one step forward.
If you grew up in an urban setting take one step backward.
If your family had health insurance take one step forward.
If you feel good about how your identified culture is portrayed by the media take one step forward.
If you have been the victim of physical violence based on your gender, ethnicity, age or sexual orientation take one step backward.

> *If you have ever felt passed over for an employment position*
> *based on your gender, ethnicity, age or sexual orientation*
> *take one step backward.*
> *If English is your first language take one step forward.*
> *If you have been divorced or impacted by divorce take one*
> *step backward.*
> *If you came from a supportive family environment take one*
> *step forward.*
> *If you have completed high school take one step forward.*
> *If you were able to complete college take one step forward.*
> *If you took out loans for your education take one step*
> *backward.*
> *If you attended private school take one step forward.*
> *If you have ever felt unsafe walking alone at night take one*
> *step backward.*

Some players ended up at the back of the room, while others were now right at the front. One player had taken so many steps forward, he was up against the wall. He had never realised how much privilege he had, compared to his team-mates. 'It was such an interesting way of making us all aware of who we are,' says Wahlén. 'It was an intense session, but we were able to openly discuss why and how these issues had affected our lives.'

Wahlén admitted that she had preconceptions that footballers can only play football; she realised the players had the same assumptions of themselves. 'They only see themselves as foot-ballers, but they are not; they are sons, fathers, husbands; they are emotionally aware, socially responsible and confronting their own biases.' They are also regularly having conversations that Wahlén never imagined. How does music move you? What makes dance, dance? What is the meaning of art? How does this photo-graph make you feel?

The players have started their own voluntary book group, and not a single sporting title has been chosen. Instead, more heavyweight subjects are being tackled, such as identity, race and love (*Americanah* by Chimamanda Ngozi Adache[18]); the Vietnam War (*The Things They Carried* by Tim O'Brien); friendship across generations (*The One-in-a-Million Boy* by Monica Wood); and our role in the world (*Ishmael* by Daniel Quinn).

The players tell Wahlén that they like to read a lot now because everyone else is. She hears them talking about books and finds their conversations more fascinating than those of the cultural elite she often works with in Stockholm. 'The players don't have any literary truths, so they interpret what they read with authentic openness,' she says. 'It's much more interesting for me.'

The fans have picked up on the players' behaviour. At a time when fan violence is not uncommon in Sweden, ÖFK supporters have responded to their club's efforts and become socially responsible. At the last home game of the 2016 season, there was a Gay Pride flag in the stands to mark ÖFK's certification as an LGBT supporter, the first of its kind in Swedish football.[19] There is a closeness with the fans, who have taken a lead from the club and embraced their differences.

At the start of the 2016 season, Kindberg wrote an open letter to the fans. I have not seen a mission statement quite like it. 'Together with you, we want to be role models!' he wrote. 'Östersunds Fotballklub, ÖFK, is a club with clear values. We go our own way. Our belief is that our players perform better both individually and as a team if they are offered an environment that is challenging and stimulating across many human levels ... ÖFK stands for openness, diversity, and tolerance. We stand for sincerity and honesty. We will always be trustworthy and professional. We want to create a new kind of football culture. We want to be good role models. We propose that all ÖFK supporters endorse these five simple rules of conduct:

1. The stadium is a place for everyone. We behave in a way so every visitor, from a small child to a 100-year-old, feels safe and welcome.
2. We may have opinions about a player but we never use derogatory or offensive words.
3. The players and supporters of our opponents are our friends. We do not boo them when they come onto the pitch. We do not boo when they do something good. In general, we boo as little as possible.
4. We may have views about the referee, but we never use derogatory or offensive words.
5. We always stay away from violence.

We are ÖFK. We go our own way!'

In return, the fans are inventive with their banners, even making a special one for Potter's wife Rachel. Behind the goal, in the pre-season friendly against Everton, the fans unfurled a giant red *tifo*, a banner with 'RACHEL' written on either side of giant white hearts. The head of the supporters' group, the Falcons, also wrote a thank-you letter to Rachel. It included the lines: 'I don't know you and you don't know me, but I just want to say thank you. I'm not sure if you realise how much you, indirectly, affect me (and many others) every single day. You need to know how much joy you've given us. And still do. Everyone in Östersunds is talking football nowadays. Everyone is proud of ÖFK ... That wasn't the case in 2011 but much has changed since you and your husband first arrived five years ago.'

'I wanted the people of Östersunds to be proud of its football club,' says Kindberg. 'This city is warm, welcoming, safe and secure.[20] The fans are also part of our team and they recognise these values that we have. We want to take a stand against society and use our role for good. That's another product of the environment we have built. If it connects with the core values in the club, then fine. I believe that can give us an edge and help us win games.'

The project is not over yet. Kindberg told Potter when they first met that Europe was the target, and he was not just talking about going to Tenerife on a pre-season training camp. 'We still see this as the start of our journey.'

Key to the journey is Potter, who was voted Swedish Manager of the Year after the team finished eighth in its debut top-flight campaign in 2016. 'Graham is extra-extra-extra-extraordinary,' says Kindberg. 'He is one of most promising managers in Europe. I can stand up every day and argue that. He is open-minded, has values and fantastic leadership skills.' And emotional intelligence? 'Of course!'

Is Kindberg prepared for the day when Potter moves to another club? What will happen to ÖFK's edge then? 'I will be the proudest chairman on earth when a top-five club in the Premier League comes in for him, but they would have to pay a very big compensation. I will only talk to another club [about him] if it's Barcelona who want him!' Kindberg is smart and has already considered a succession plan – which sets him apart from most club chairmen I have encountered. He is convinced that ÖFK will one day win the Swedish title and compete in the Champions League. 'We will be winners in a totally different way. We refuse to compete in any other way. That's our belief.'

He enjoys taking advantage of football's conservatism, and derives great pleasure from signing unpolished diamonds like David Accam (now playing for Chicago Fire in the MLS) and Modou Barrow (now at Swansea). 'We look to recruit players that don't follow the others. They might seem strange, or different, but they have a brain that others don't recognise. The conventional football environment kills geniuses. That's where we can find players.' He is particularly excited about an English midfielder, Curtis Edwards, rejected from Middlesbrough's academy, but with a huge potential for development.

HOW TO GET AN EDGE – by DANIEL KINDBERG
1. Create the environment where everybody promotes creativity, initiative and courage.
2. Delegate decision-making.
3. End the blame culture.

Potter is preparing for the new season ahead. I wonder if it might be his last in Sweden, before an offer comes in that Kindberg cannot refuse. He has already rejected approaches from other teams in Sweden. In six years, Potter has turned around a club in a negative spiral to an upwardly mobile, community-bonding, booty-shaking success story.

The ÖFK identity has come a long way in a short time. 'We embrace diversity as part of our identity and are open-minded around how we explore different parts of ourselves as a team to develop the individual,' Potter says. 'We play an exciting, interesting and attacking brand of football with players from all over the world. We are a team that people are proud of, that's grown a lot and that has made a difference to a small part of the world.'

I can't let him leave without one final question. What *is* the meaning of art? 'It's about expression,' he smiles, with no hesitation. 'It's a way of expressing yourself. In some ways, football is similar. In its simplest form, kids and everyone else who plays the game express their emotions through it. It's just like art.'

Potter has not followed the traditional path for English coaches, and that sets him apart from most of his peers (other exceptions are Paul Clement, former assistant coach to Carlo Ancelotti at Paris Saint-Germain and Bayern Munich, and Michael Beale, who left Liverpool's youth academy to join Brazilian club São Paulo for a seven-month spell as assistant coach).

If there is a bias towards appointing foreign coaches in the Premier League, might it be because the English coaches lack experience outside of England? Potter has shown remarkable adaptability to cope with the serious challenges that ÖFK presented. We will look at the importance of adaptability, and how to develop it, in more detail in Chapter 2. It starts with a moment of stunning skill in Dortmund, in the presence of another culturally engaged coach who sees football as a true art form.

HOW TO GET AN EDGE – by GRAHAM POTTER

1. Make sure people feel they can improve in a learning environment.
2. Find out the unique advantage that separates you from the competition in the market-place.
3. Hire managers who understand people and relationships, even if others may have more seniority and experience.

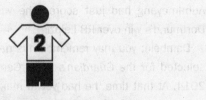

ADAPTABILITY

THOMAS TUCHEL
Be a rule-breaker

Dembélé and adaptability / The Rulebreaker Society / Forget success / Power of small rituals / Talent, aesthetics, and Nietzsche / Segmenting motivation / Mistakes don't exist / The Lemon Tart and curiosity

Ousmane Dembélé's first touch was outstanding. He trapped the ball brilliantly, lifting his left leg above waist height and killing it dead. He was on the halfway line, and his next move was to knock it down the touchline and run past his marker to pick it up again. He was approaching the corner of the penalty area, at speed, when he did it again. He played the ball to the defender's left, and ran around the other side – known in France as a *grand pont*, a big bridge – to leave his poor marker flustered and floundering. But would there be an end product? Dembélé had just run 50 yards at speed and beaten two men. He looked up and fizzed in the most enticing cross imaginable: at perfect velocity and height, eight yards from goal, a little too far for the goalkeeper to reach.

His team-mate Pierre-Emerick Aubameyang only needed a small jump to power his header into the goal. The move had taken only eight seconds. In that time, you could see just how devastating Dembélé could be. This was February 2017, and Aubameyang had just scored the winning goal in Borussia Dortmund's win over RB Leipzig.

Dembélé: you may remember his name. He was the player I selected for the *Guardian*'s 'Next Generation' feature back in 2014. At that time, he had yet to make an appearance for his club, Rennes. I was told that this 17-year-old boy, as he was then, had a natural gift for dribbling; that he did so with grace, agility, lightness, fluidity and ease. In some ways, that run-and-cross against RB Leipzig could not have been more appropriate. His unpredictable way of playing is the antithesis of modern football.

I wanted to speak to Dembélé, but Borussia Dortmund was keen to protect its talent. Instead, my colleagues at French TV station BeIN Sports sat down with him for an interview in February 2017 and, on my behalf, asked how he felt when he was named in the *Guardian*'s 'Next Generation'. 'I don't pay too much attention to it,' he told them. 'It's not an extra pressure for me, it's just what I do. I'm on the road I have to follow and I don't think about anything else. I train to get into the team and I'm enjoying my football here in Dortmund.'

As well he might: in the Dortmund club shop, the name of Dembélé is the only one on the back of the shirts of the mannequins; not the top scorer Aubameyang, or the local Germany player Marco Reus, or the cult hero Shinji Kagawa.

In this chapter, I speak with the two managers who hold Dembélé's future in their hands. I went to Germany to meet his club coach at Borussia Dortmund, Thomas Tuchel, and to France to see national team coach Didier Deschamps. They were excited about Dembélé and his potential. It's their job to confirm that into talent.

As the season went on, it was clear that whatever they were doing was working. Dembélé provided some of the outstanding moments in European football: a dribble, burst of pace and outside-of-the-boot cross for Aubameyang to score in a Champions

League knock-out tie at Monaco; a cutback, which left his marker David Alaba dizzy and grounded, and a curling left-foot shot, which went in off the crossbar, to win the German Cup semi-final at rivals Bayern Munich (and a nice celebration to follow, running straight to Tuchel for a hug). He repeated the move in the German Cup final, scoring a similar goal in a Man of the Match performance to seal Borussia Dortmund its first trophy for five years.

On the final day of the Bundesliga season, he pulled off an outrageous assist, scooping the ball over five Werder Bremen defenders for Aubameyang to volley home another goal. He was outstanding in an end-of-season friendly against England, scoring the winning goal in a 3–2 victory. In late August, just a few weeks before this book was first published, Barcelona signed Dembélé for a reported £135 million, a fee that made him the second-most expensive player in the world. (His new coach would be Ernesto Valverde, formerly of Athletic Club de Bilbao.)

Dembélé was not our only topic of conversation. Both coaches gave me a unique insight into the challenges of modern leadership. Their stories can teach us a lot about the importance of communication, self-development, motivation, disruptive thinking and, above all, adaptability, in today's professional environment.

Deschamps does not like to talk about individual players but he made an exception for Dembélé. 'There are times when maybe during a game there's not much going on and then he will do something special,' he told me. 'It's about getting that quality to express itself over the long term. But as far as he's concerned, psychologically he considers himself ready. He's also exposed to daily demands at a club that's structured to deal with a player of enormous potential. He has got something.'

Tuchel agrees. In training sessions, the coach will tell the players to only play one-touch passes, or two-touch give-and-goes, or do a spatial awareness exercise. 'It's no problem for Ousmane. Within minutes, he gets it and I say, "Hey please, what was that?" He adapts so quickly to everything.'

This is crucial to success. In his short career so far, Dembélé has adapted to all the contexts he has had to face. These have involved new teams, relationships, venues, levels of performance, cultures, countries, languages, and levels of media attention. Tuchel and Deschamps understand this better than most: they have also learned to adapt to get their edge.

Thomas Tuchel walks into the Italian restaurant around the corner from the Borussia Dortmund club offices, a five-minute stroll from the Signal-Iduna Park stadium, looking nothing like a football coach. He is wearing high-top trainers, skinny jeans, a grey jumper, leather jacket and a flat cap. He looks more like an artisanal coffee-shop owner than the most exciting coach of his generation.

But that's what he is. He has been known to change his team's formation up to six times in one game, and his original tactical ideas have led to comparisons with Pep Guardiola. In his first job as head coach, at Mainz, he took a tiny club to its highest-ever league finish and a place in Europe; at Borussia Dortmund, one of the best-supported clubs in Germany, he improved what the *New York Times* called 'the most gifted collection of young players anywhere in Europe, crafted into a team of rich spirit and endless adventure' – until, after we met, he left his position as coach, ending his second season at the club with victory in the German Cup Final.

Tuchel talks about adaptability as a necessity of leadership, though in his case it requires bravery and humility: bravery to stick to his philosophy, even if results don't support it (which doesn't happen too often); and humility to know he doesn't have all the answers, while remaining open-minded enough to constantly search for them.

'Tuchel's team of the future may have no systems of defence, midfield or attack,' wrote Cathrin Gilbert in German broadsheet *Die Zeit*, 'but simply "action principles" based on how his players behave in certain situations, the respect they have for the space, and how their character shows itself in the way they play football.'[1]

He does not know what his next tactical change will be, or where his next idea will come from, but he is open to anything – even, as he said, playing with only two defenders (most teams play with four, though some, Dortmund included, play with three).[2]

'Two at the back, really?' I say.

'Why not?' he responds, his clear-blue eyes glinting with mischief.

I ask Tuchel if he is trying to reinvent football. 'No! A clear no. It's not reinvention. That would mean I am changing for the sake of change. I'm not looking for change. I'm looking for an edge!'

He remembers Mercedes chief executive Dieter Zetsche comparing business to walking up the down escalator. If you do nothing, you go down. If you walk at a certain speed, you stay where you are. So you'd better run. 'You have to adapt,' says Tuchel. 'It's not about reinvention. It's to adapt and to adapt and to adapt and to find the solutions quicker than others.'

And if that means doing things differently, then he will. Just before we meet, a year-old video of American basketball coach Geno Auriemma has gone viral. He coached the USA women's basketball team to Olympic gold in 2012 and 2016 and has led the Connecticut Huskies to five straight national titles. 'On our team, we put a huge premium on body language,' Auriemma told a press conference in 2016. 'And, if your body language is bad, you will never get in the game. Ever. I don't care how good you are … When I watch game film, I'm checking on the bench. If somebody is asleep over there, if somebody doesn't care, if somebody's not engaged, they will never get in the game.'

'I know what he's talking about,' Tuchel agrees. 'We call it "the eyes". Does he have good eyes or not? Can I trust this guy? It's about binding relationships and respect and belief and faith.

Even if you just sense it's not there in a player, it's already complicated.' Tuchel sometimes looks over at his bench during a match and might see a player disengaged from the game. He will decide then not to bring them on. 'You have to adapt.'

I've never heard a coach say this before. Instead, when Mario Balotelli needs two minutes to get someone else to tie his shoelaces during a game for Nice, or when Paris Saint-Germain substitute Serge Aurier takes seven minutes to get ready to come on, they are indulged as 'characters'. Tuchel would not be so forgiving.

Tuchel tells me that shaping the personality of his players is just as important as improving their football ability.[3] This is part of his own methodology that he has developed to improve performance.

This is why Tuchel was the first sporting leader asked to address a fascinating group of disruptive innovators called the Rulebreaker Society. It was founded in Switzerland in 2013. Its members include Walter Gunz, who set up Media Markt, Europe's largest retailer of consumer electronics; Gabor Forgacs, a medical entrepreneur who has pioneered 3D bio-printing technologies to produce human tissues for medical and pharmaceutical use; and Tan Lee, whose company Emotiv uses electroencephalography (EEG) to track mental performance, monitor emotions, and control virtual and physical objects with thoughts.

The Rulebreaker Society claims to bring together people who seek to innovate and inspire through their visions. They see progress in business and society through the creative destruction of conventional rules. Its inner circle has put together a manifesto, not of rules (of course!), but as a platform for inspiration:

1. No company will be market leader for a long period of time.
2. If I don't cannibalise myself someone else will do it.

3. If someone else attacks my business model it will be a more radical and damaging approach than if I did it on my own.

4. The development of a business model happens through creative destruction and a so far unknown re-combination of business elements.

5. Most rules made to be broken are mental rules. They exist only by your own cognition.

6. The unspoken rules are the most solid rules. They need to be broken first.

7. Digitisation and Internet technology will change every business.

8. Asymmetry of information will vanish by the digitisation of society. As a result of that, you need to model your business without those asymmetries.

9. I always look at the market from the user's perspective.

10. If rule-makers get nervous I am on the right track. If rule-makers start to fight me, I am almost there.

During his final season at Mainz, Tuchel addressed the Rulebreaker Society at a get-together in Rorschacherberg, St Gallen. Wearing a plain black T-shirt and jeans, he explained that it had been a tough summer before his third season at the club, probably his toughest ever. Mainz had sold three influential players – Zdenek Pospech, Nicolai Muller and Eric Choupo-Moting – and lost two more with long-term injuries. They signed ten new players who were still bedding in. They had a Europa League qualifier second leg away to Romanian side Gaz Metan Medias. Mainz dominated the game, with 46 shots to the opposition's four, but lost on penalties.

That night the team had an 11 p.m. flight back to Frankfurt, and would be starting a new Bundesliga season on the Saturday in a brand-new stadium against the previous season's runner-up,

Bayer Leverkusen. As they sat in the departure lounge, Tuchel looked around. 'I've never seen a team more empty and more disappointed than my team in that moment,' he told the society. 'I'll never forget the players' faces. Everyone was just empty. We were awake for the entire flight, and the journey home, thinking, "What can we do here? The way everyone is feeling now, there's no point in us turning up to play Leverkusen. It's impossible for us to play."'

Tuchel broke one of his rules. He did not show video analysis of the Gaz Metan game, as he normally does after a match-day. Instead he gathered his players into the video-analysis room and put this quote on the big screen:

'I've missed more than 9,000 shots in my career. I've lost almost 300 games. Twenty-six times, I've been trusted to take the game winning shot and missed. I've failed over and over and over again in my life. And that is why I succeed.'

Michael Jordan

For the next five minutes, he showed footage of Jordan in action, featuring all his achievements and successes. The message was clear: 'We will fail, we will be labelled failures and we'll lose games and we'll have the most disappointing moments in order to develop ourselves.' The players understood and changed their frame of mind. They ended up beating Leverkusen 2–0. The lesson Tuchel wanted to give is one that we should all remember.

His Mainz side was measured by what they achieved in his second season when they finished fifth. They beat every team they faced at least once. With Tuchel in charge, Mainz famously beat Bayern more often than they lost. That was what they were always judged against. The best moments. The over-achievement. That was a burden. Tuchel called it 'a heavy load we have to bear'.

Ending his talk, he proposed what he called a controversial theory. I don't believe it is. Rather, it is something we should all carry with us in our everyday lives. He said: 'It's more important to forget and move on from the greatest, most unexpected success you might have than to forget and move on from the failures.'

This attitude is right out of the Netflix playbook. Company founder Reed Hastings had the original idea to set up a video subscription after he was fined $40 for the late return of *Apollo 13*. He broke the rules of late fees, turning his company into a subscription-only service (subscribers could keep DVDs for as long as they wanted). That was a success in itself. But rather than stopping there, Hastings adapted; he recognised that broadband services would speed up and so launched Netflix as we know it, a company that breaks the rules in other ways: episodes can vary in length as they don't need to fit into a schedule; dramas don't need contrived cliff-hangers; and the company doesn't release viewing figures, apparently to build 'mystery and intrigue'. This is the equivalent of content trumping results, which is exactly how Tuchel wants it.[4]

I ask Tuchel if he is still a rule-breaker, and he refers me to one of the valuable lessons we learned from Athletic sporting director José Maria Amorrortu in Chapter 1. How *do* you measure success?

'Points are not the only way to judge my work, so how else can we judge it?' asks Tuchel. I come up with some suggestions. For some people, it might be chances created and conceded; or the development of individual players; the joy felt by 80,000 fans every other week; the emotion conjured up when you think of the team; the spirit you feel when you come into the stadium. After all, the Dortmund team slogan is '*Echte Liebe*' (True Love). 'I never wanted to become a rule-breaker but we just did it this way,' he adds.

The genuine warmth of the greeting Tuchel gave to the restaurant owner when he walked in came as no surprise. The pair shook hands and hugged like old friends. Tuchel believes in the power of small rituals like this. In his first few days as a senior coach, it was one of his most important messages.

It was back in 2009 and the circumstances were unique. Tuchel had been Under-19 coach at Mainz 05 for one year (beating Borussia Dortmund in the youth cup final), the first team had been promoted into the Bundesliga but coach Jorn Andersen had been sacked after falling out with the sporting director, Christian Heidel. Tuchel had never played in the Bundesliga before. His career was limited to eight appearances for second division side Stuttgart Kickers. He had never coached a senior team before. He was 35, younger than some of the players in his squad. And four days before the Bundesliga season was due to start, Heidel put him in charge.

On his first day Tuchel outlined his most important rules, hand-written on a flipchart. Among them was that everyone greets each other with a handshake. It was to start with the coach, by looking each player in the eye and greeting them – not a cursory greeting but one that said, 'I'm happy you're here and I'm looking forward to training with you in a few minutes.'

He soon realised that mealtimes were a problem. He noticed some players leave the table just as he sat down for his lunch. The next day, he asked them all to wait for him to say, 'Enjoy your meal,' before tucking in. The buffet on offer was plentiful: soup, meat, fish, fruit, three different desserts. As Tuchel put it: 'Grilled this, poached that.' But before he'd finished his soup, half the squad had left again. It really bothered him. So he addressed the squad at the end of training the following day. 'Sorry guys, I'm embarrassed to speak about eating as a team again, but I have one more thing to ask. I'd like for us all to spend at least 20 minutes eating together.' The players agreed. Very quickly, the mealtimes became a period to reflect and bond with each other. Eighteen players would sit for 45 minutes on two tables of nine, and no one would leave until the last person had finished eating.

Tuchel did not ask them to spend that long together, but he was happy to establish what he saw as a basic principle of respect. The players got to know one another.[5]

Tuchel wanted to create a ritual that reinforced the culture of the team; a ritual that says, 'This is who we are and this is how we behave.' The stronger those relationship ties are, the better the team will operate. Teams that perform small acts of kindness for and with each other shore up bonds and develop trust. There is egalitarianism in eating together. Tuchel is part of the same group, no one is better than anyone else: we are all in this together.

I have been in offices where similar rules exist. A friend who works in a high-pressure TV news studio in Paris laughs that everyone in his office spends the first ten minutes of their day double-kissing their colleagues every morning. Even when he is on the phone to someone, a colleague waits to greet him in a formal way. But he accepts there is an atmosphere of respect, goodwill and collaboration.

Mauricio Pochettino instigated a similar ritual when he took over at Tottenham Hotspur. The players shake hands with one another every day before they start work. 'It is a small thing but it means a lot to create a real team. It shows you are interested in the people with whom you shake hands.' That rule has now become a habit. When chairman Daniel Levy turned up at the training-ground canteen and every player greeted him with a handshake, he may have suspected it was a wind-up.

In an office I visited in Zurich, everyone eats together and no one is allowed to eat alone at their desk. The team is multinational and once you get past the punch-line potential – there was an Australian, a Spaniard and an Irishman all eating goulash overlooking Lake Zurich – the mealtimes are a small but positive part of team-building. They reinforce collaboration between the company across all levels. Managers will speak with juniors, and vice versa, and often this will act as an ice-breaker for future work together. You don't build trust sitting at a conference or in a meeting-room – or in Tuchel's case, just on the training ground. You do it slowly and with consistency. By creating mechanisms for real interactions to take place. These connections trump technology.

This respect for people helps shape personality. Tuchel sees that as a key part of his role: not just to improve talent but to develop personality, which is essentially formed by what happens off the pitch. When a Dortmund player snapped, 'Where's my shirt?' at the kit-manager during half-time, and it turned out he was sitting on it, Tuchel took him aside the next day and told him that was unacceptable. The player apologised to the kit-manager straightaway.

'I will tell the player that type of behaviour is not what we do here and, by the way, it's not cool either. Because if I go to training and I'm not looking forward to saying hello to every player there, then it's the first problem. So you don't let them off the hook. If he doesn't say hello to someone, it's not good enough. These are my values. For some players, it's tougher to adapt to thanking the physio, or saying hello in the morning, than to playing football. But life is not only about the green grass. If you want to become the best, you have to shape your personality.'

Sometimes it can be a slow process. He remains embarrassed that he and his team fly to so many cities (in 2016–17, Dortmund played in Madrid, Warsaw, Lisbon and Monaco) but never see anything beyond airport, hotel, training pitch and stadium. 'I want to develop personality for the players and I am sure that if we knew something more about Lisbon, for example, it would help us in our game preparation. I want to see more of the cities.' It's another form of respect he strongly believes in: respect for the opponent. In future, he might ask certain players to give a talk about what their home country means to them. On the day we meet, in discussions about Dortmund's planned summer tour to Japan, he had requested an extra day in Tokyo so players could visit the city and learn more about the culture.

This respect extends to the training ground, where slide tackles or fouls out of frustration are forbidden. The rules need to be respected. Things can fall apart very quickly, with one small disagreement potentially leading to a rift. That didn't happen at Mainz. The team did well. So well, in fact, that Mainz never worried about relegation. They finished ninth in his first season, their highest ever position. The following year, when everyone tipped them for relegation citing 'Second Season Syndrome', they won their first seven games and finished fifth, qualifying for the Europa League. The next season was harder and Mainz ended up thirteenth. Not once did they drop to sixteenth (the relegation play-off spot, which plays the team that finished third in the second division) in the table. In Tuchel's five years in charge, only the big four German teams of Bayern Munich, Borussia Dortmund, Schalke and Bayer Leverkusen accumulated more points than his side.[6]

How did Mainz develop an edge under its new coach? In part, it came from *Querdenken*, the German word for thinking outside the box. Based on Tuchel's analysis, Mainz would copy how other teams would play in training, learn different formations to cope with that, and the players, constantly adapting to new systems, would intuitively understand their jobs. 'We wanted to establish flow. This willingness of my players to play in different positions and systems, combined with the opponents' continued use of that old-style, outdated thinking, allowed us to establish a competitive advantage over those teams.'

A turning-point in his own education came at Mainz, after the club had approached the local university looking for analysis on players' endurance and sprint abilities. 'I presented the sprint results directly to Mr Tuchel [then Mainz head coach] and his coaching team, and later we spoke for several hours about the benefits of Differential Training on technical and tactical training,' said Wolfgang Schöllhorn, Professor of Training and Movement Science at the Johannes Gutenberg University. 'I still remember that straight after our meeting, his team used some of my suggestions in their practice sessions.'

So when he wanted to teach his players to make diagonal runs towards goal, he changed the training pitch into a diamond shape. When he wanted his players to stop grabbing shirts while marking at corners, he gave them tennis balls to hold while playing. He is a problem-solver. A *Querdenker*.

We will look at more working examples of Differential Training later in the chapter. 'That influenced me a lot because it changed my role as a coach completely,' Tuchel says. 'With this, there is no right and wrong. You cannot make mistakes. I'm not there to tell them right and wrong, I'm just responsible for the ideas and principles of how we play. Within those they are free to find their own solutions.' Tuchel is an expert in analysing opposition, and explaining to players how to use space to make chances. 'I can find the spaces but *you* have to find the solutions.'

This is why Borussia Dortmund hired Tuchel to replace Jürgen Klopp as coach in summer 2015. Borussia Dortmund: German league and Cup double-winners in 2012, Champions League finalists in 2013, the only club that has pushed Bayern Munich in the last decade and famous for its 80,000-capacity stadium with its iconic Yellow Wall at one end, the standing-only south stand with room for 25,000 passionate, cheering fans behind the goal. *Echte Liebe*. True Love.[7]

In his first season at Dortmund, Tuchel refreshed a side that had become stale under Klopp. He got the best out of the team's spine of Mats Hummels, Ilkay Gündogan and Henrikh Mkhitaryan, who all had outstanding seasons. They were so good, in fact, that Dortmund, now much more tactically versatile, ended up selling all three for a combined total of over £80 million.

In their place, the club signed young players, who were convinced to sign because Tuchel was there. That's why Dembélé said he joined, after turning down interest from Manchester City and Klopp's Liverpool. Nineteen-year-old Emre Mor signed for the same reason. Christian Pulisic, who had a break-out 2016–17 season aged 18, extended his contract at Dortmund after Liverpool tried to sign him.[8] In the first half of 2017, Dortmund confirmed the signings of two highly rated youngsters, Mohamed Dahoud (midfielder, 21, from Bayer Leverkusen) and Dan-Axel Zagadou (centre-back, 18, from Paris Saint-Germain).

The team finished third in the Bundesliga and won the German Cup final, the club's first trophy for five years. For a second successive season under Tuchel, the team was unbeaten at home in the league. The campaign will never be forgotten, though, because of the events of 11 April, just a few days after I met with Tuchel. Shortly after Dortmund's team bus set off for the Champions League quarter-final against Monaco, three bombs stuffed with metal pins were detonated. The devices ripped through the reinforced glass and, incredibly, only two people – defender Marc Bartra and a policeman – were injured.

The game was postponed but, within an hour, was rescheduled for the following day, less than 24 hours after the attack. Dortmund lost the game 3–2 and Tuchel was not happy. 'We were informed by text message that UEFA was making this decision,' he told reporters after the game. 'We would have liked more time to take stock. A decision made in Switzerland that concerns us directly. We will not forget it. It is a very bad feeling. A few minutes after this attack the only question that was asked was: "Are you ready to play?" As if we had thrown a beer on our coach.'

It later emerged that Dortmund had three options: to play the next day, to forfeit the game 3–0 or to leave the competition voluntarily. None of them ideal. The incident made headlines across the world and Tuchel won backing for the compassionate support of his players and public reminders that they are husbands, fathers, children first, and players second. Dortmund chief executive Hans-Joachim Watzke, annoyed Tuchel had gone public in his complaints against UEFA, admitted there had been a disagreement with the coach about whether to play the Monaco game.[9] 'As always, it is not only just about the sporting side, but also about strategy, communication and trust,' Watzke told local paper *WAZ*. His words suggested the fall-out was a heavy one, and so it proved. Three days after Borussia Dortmund ended the campaign by beating Eintracht Frankfurt 2–1 in the German Cup final, Tuchel and Dortmund parted company. The severance meeting, which lasted just 21 minutes, took place in the same hotel where Dortmund was staying before the bus attack. It somehow seemed appropriate.

Before he left his job, Tuchel spoke about his responsibilities as coach of these talents in a fascinating panel discussion with Stanford University's only German academic, Hans Ulrich Gumbrecht.[10] In a conversation that spanned the definition of aesthetics according to Kant and Hegel, Nietzsche's *Thus Spoke Zarathustra*, and whether Faust or Mephistopheles (the evil spirit to whom Faust sold his soul) most resembles football's complex drama, Tuchel set out his role as a teacher. 'I see myself more as someone who accompanies these talents, personalities and different characters,' he said. 'I'm responsible for the timing and the speed at which they learn. I set the stimuli that they need.'

'To develop a player like Ousmane Dembélé is practically an educational obligation,' Gumbrecht told him. 'So is the key ingredient for him now a sprinkle of humility, or would encouragement work better?'

'It definitely has to be encouragement,' Tuchel responded. 'But modesty also plays a part: to set yourself the daily task of working on your imperfections, to go about your own regeneration professionally so that you don't have to be substituted with cramp, as is the case now. It's important to show modesty with respect to your own huge, huge talent. To show everything in the stadium and to have no fear, regardless of how old or young you are; to take the first penalty; to still have an ice bath afterwards, even when it hurts.'

Tuchel describes talent as an extraordinary gift that comes with a responsibility and an obligation to improve. One of his talents is that he knows how to bring out the enthusiastic 12-year-old that exists inside a footballer to perform at their best; to find the individual motivational drivers for every player. He believes all players have one dominant motivating force. He has segmented them into three types:

- *Aggressive motivation:* These are the ones who want to be the best: the goal may be to become captain, be on the front page of a magazine or win an individual award. It does not make that person aggressive, and it may only be a fleeting moment of understanding that motivation. But you are doing it for yourself.
- *Binding motivation:* These are the ones who are happy to have close relationships, they are a strong part of the team and happy to deliver and stay in the background.
- *Curious motivation:* You want to see what level your skills can work out at and how far your talent can take you. Can you do this move against Bayern Munich? What about something spectacular in an away game? They are curious and want to be tested all the time. They have to solve problems all the time and they cannot be trained with simple A-B-C exercises. This is the group for whom Differential Training can, well, make a difference.

Tuchel believes we all have elements of each motivation but one is usually dominant. Understanding his players in this way can also help identify their best position. He does not want his full-backs to be too curious. That's one of the reasons why Raphael Guerreiro, good enough to play left-back for Portugal in their triumphant Euro 2016 campaign, switched roles to central midfield. 'He is very brave, always smiling, so skilful and very curious,' says Tuchel, who seems to me a prime candidate for curious motivation (he says he also has a strong binding motivation).

Tuchel looks back at some of his team selections and thinks they were particularly brave. At the time, they seemed totally logical. Even now, when he is interviewed before kick-off on Sky Germany and he's asked: 'You have made six changes today and have a different formation ...,' it surprises him. 'I think, what? Really? Six changes, that many? But that's still a good team that I've picked!' We never picked a team as the means to an end; we stuck to the systems that we played.'

The systems are fluid, can change during games, and require an open mind to see what works and what doesn't. Midway through his first season in Dortmund, he trialled a 3–2–4–1 system, in a 1–0 Europa League win at FC Porto. He stuck with it in matches against Bayern Munich (0–0) and Tottenham Hotspur (3–0), and at times in 2016–17 it was devastating: Dortmund beat Hamburg away (5–2), Bayern Munich (1–0), Borussia Mönchengladbach (4–1), Bayer Leverkusen (6–2) and Benfica (4–0) using the formation.

'I knew nothing about this system until we tried it – and now I love it! It changes everything depending on what players you use: it could be four midfielders, or three strikers, and often we play with two full-backs in the back three!'

This is Tuchel's curious motivation brought to life. When he saw Pep Guardiola, as Bayern Munich coach, pick 5 foot 9 inch Joshua Kimmich to play at centre-back, he thought, 'Why now? What's changed? Things change all the time and you have to adapt to the speed of the change. Even better, to be ahead.'

This approach, process-based and built around curious motivation, has similarities to those we saw at Athletic Club de Bilbao and Östersunds FK. The process is more important than the result. Tuchel once said, 'I couldn't envisage being at a club where the result – winning a game 1–0 – came before everything else.' He wants to reframe that now.

'I know more about clubs now and every club has a spirit,' he says. 'There are certain clubs like Ajax, Arsenal, Barcelona, AC Milan who like an aesthetic game: it's not only about winning but how you win and how you play. Others, like Chelsea now, or Atlético Madrid, are more win-at-all-costs. Each club has a charisma and an aura: Tottenham Hotspur, for example, is like Borussia Dortmund; they take risks, they like excitement. My philosophy is an aesthetic one: aesthetic means to control the ball, the rhythm, to attack in every minute, and to try to score as many goals as possible.' In short, to provide entertainment, as well as winning results.

So what happens, then, if a win-at-all-costs team wants to give him a job? Tuchel makes it clear that, above all, he too wants to win every game, but the aesthetic is also important. 'I have to be honest with myself and ask if I'm the right person with the right character and the right approach for this club to make the people happy. Or is it so much against me that I'd better say, "Guys, we will have a misunderstanding here?" But the clubs themselves should be aware of what they stand for.'

Tuchel knows what he stands for, and accepts it's hard not to be only result-focused. In one recent game, he was annoyed with himself for settling for a 1–0 win, which he felt was fortunate, and not daring to change things. 'I told myself not to trust the result and if you have an idea, then to do it, change it and take responsibility. Do what leaders do!'

He strikes me as an empathetic leader, but he couldn't describe his own leadership style. 'I don't know!' he sighs. 'I don't even feel like one [a leader]. I do my thing. I try to bond, but can still get on players' nerves, though I have a good sense when it's too much and when to back down and give everyone their space.'

The description of his thought process before games would make a brilliant response in every post-match press conference. The starting-point comes from Schöllhorn: that there are no mistakes. 'I prepare myself for this game and I feel my team, and somebody might be injured or having a bad time or on fire, and I see spaces that I predict we can find to beat the opponent and then I take a decision, and I cannot wait until after the result to decide if it was right or not!' Sadly this does not suit the narrative cycle of winning = right decisions and losing = wrong decisions, but the sentiment is admirable, and one I'm sure other coaches would agree with. We all make the best decisions we can at any given time.

Tuchel loves music and is friends with Clueso, a top-selling German singer-songwriter. They have the same personal manager, a charming entertainment impresario who sees more similarities between football and showbiz than he ever imagined. The three men often swap ideas about talent, optimising performance and how to find an edge.

'For sure, those conversations help,' says Tuchel. 'But at the end of the day, I am not the musician, I am the conductor. People don't come to the concert to see the conductor. They come for the music. So you have to be clear that you're there for players. I am there for them. To develop their talent. Bring out their best. Develop their personality. Influence them. Help them overcome obstacles. Push them. Not make it easy for them. Give them the rhythm and the confidence and the freedom to perform. That's my job.'

Tuchel seems to me more like a chef, always looking for the perfect dish: someone like Massimo Bottura, head chef at Italian restaurant Osteria Francescana, rated by Michelin as the best restaurant in Europe. Like most chefs, Bottura gives all employees several different jobs in the kitchen before finding the right role for them (a form of Differential Training). He also keeps them thinking creatively by constantly exposing them to music and art:

famous prints by Picasso, Magritte and Duchamp cover the staff bathroom's walls. I think Tuchel would appreciate Bottura's most famous dish, 'Oops, I Dropped the Lemon Tart!' It has its own special plate, which looks as if it has been dropped and stuck back together again, and contains broken biscuit, splashes of yellow, lemon and sugar all deconstructed. It's a playful and beautiful (and bright yellow) vision of creativity, just like Borussia Dortmund at their best. How does it feel when this perfect image of space and movement comes together in a game? 'It feels like a part of me. Wow, wow, wow!' Tuchel smiles. 'It might only last for ten seconds, but that was it. We found it!'

I wonder where this curiosity comes from. He had a comfortable upbringing in Krumbach, a small town near Augsburg, in Bavaria, where he would swim and play football with his friends. He grew up supporting Borussia Mönchengladbach and wept when his mum told him, while he was on a skiing holiday in 1987, that coach Jupp Heynckes had left to join Bayern Munich. 'It's true!' he laughs. 'I really cried about it.'[11]

His father was demanding as he grew up, pushing him to his limits. Perhaps that's how he has developed a knack of knowing when to stop challenging the players. 'I have a sense for that. I know when to trigger them, when to leave them, and when to push them out of their zone.'

One of the biggest influences in Tuchel's coaching career was Ralf Rangnick, who we will meet in Chapter 4. The pair met at third division SSV Ulm, where Tuchel was a young defender. Tuchel was always a keen learner: he combined his playing career with studies in English (his is perfect, including colloquialisms) and sports science. He also took a physiotherapy course. When a knee injury ended his career at the age of 24, he did a Business Administration degree at the Berufsakademie in Stuttgart. He gained his Pro Licence coaching qualification with a 1.4 (1 was the highest mark, 6 the lowest); and while studying he worked at a bar in Stuttgart twice a week. He liked the anonymity it gave him. 'People recognised me for who I was, not someone who used to be half-decent at football,' he said. This is a reminder of how highly Tuchel values personality.[12]

Tuchel abandoned a playing comeback after two months. He had contacted Rangnick, then coaching Stuttgart, who invited him to shadow the youth coaches. He eventually asked Tuchel to coach the Under-15 side. 'Not being able to play hurt so much, but he [Rangnick] helped me discover a new passion. I was very curious to learn more.' He also worked alongside Hermann Badstuber, father of Germany defender Holger, who encouraged his *Querdenken*.

Rangnick could tell that Tuchel was a coach in the making. 'You could see from the questions he was asking, and his critical approach to our games, that it was clear he was a gifted young man with a future as a coach. It was obvious very early on.'

Tuchel spent five years in the Stuttgart academy, coaching the Under-19 side that won the championship in 2005. He then moved to Augsburg, as head of the youth academy, and in 2008 to Mainz, where he won the Under-19 championship in his first season in charge. A few weeks after that, he was leading the first team. His Mainz side beat Bayern Munich in his third game in charge. He may be a rule-breaker but he is successful. His methods work.

Rangnick, who has become one of the most influential figures in German football, can testify to this: he tried to hire him as RB Leipzig coach in summer 2014. 'He was a bit hesitant [to join Leipzig],' says Rangnick now. 'But he did everything right, and he has been very successful with Borussia Dortmund. I am sure he can be the head coach of any team in the world in the future.' The pair have been rivals, though Rangnick still takes pleasure from Tuchel's success; at least, he says he does.

I wonder if the intensity ever gets too much for him. Tuchel constantly questions his own decisions and reflects on his approach to certain games or situations. 'I'm always asking myself, "Why did you do this, what did we do here, was my approach wrong here?"' This process has always been part of his character. If a teacher or a friend ever said to him, 'This is the way it is,' he would always look for reasons to prove them wrong. He has not stopped doing that. As item number five of the Rulebreaker Society's manifesto goes: '*Most rules made to be broken are mental rules. They exist only by your own cognition.*' That is helping me imagine a Tuchel side playing with two defenders in the future; or his picking a team of eight midfielders all of whom use and interpret space in harmonising ways.

'There's something I want to make clear, this is really important,' he says before he orders a tomato soup for lunch. 'I don't know the solution. I can do it my way but I never want to say, "I know how it's done." I know nothing, I just try my things, and every day is new. There are lots of people out there in business who say they know how it's done. But there's not just one way to do things. You have to adapt.'

And so he continues to adapt. He keeps on looking for an edge.

As for Dembélé, Tuchel is impressed with his rate of progression. 'He can play at the highest level,' he says. 'There are still many traps out there, but they are not in football terms.'

Differential Training has helped Dembélé develop his game: the constant changes in each training session provide challenges that Dembélé responds to every time. 'The idea,' says Tuchel, 'is that training is more complicated than the game.' When the game comes around, everything is a doddle by comparison.

It seems to work for Tuchel, and for Dembélé. When they were together, it worked for Dortmund too. So planning my next appointment seemed obvious. I had to see Professor Wolfgang Schöllhorn of Mainz University.

HOW TO GET AN EDGE – by THOMAS TUCHEL

1. Have the passion to never get stuck: do it a new way, and do it better. Always keep trying for that new way.
2. Be honest with each other, smile and help each other. It matters if you say good morning and thank you.
3. Be available. No one hesitates to come to my office. I'm always around.

WOLFGANG SCHÖLLHORN
Train differentially

Differential Training / Correction slows learning / Qi-gong and the sadness of comparing / Barcelona and Van Gogh / No answers, just questions / Flautists, mechanics and ADHD

The first thing you notice about the office of Professor Schöllhorn is the seating arrangement. There are chairs placed around a low table near his door, and each is different. There's a bright green stool on a spring-loaded base; a black leather wobbly backless (also known as ergonomic) seat on top of a beautifully crafted wooden stool; a low Indian 'Yogi' chair; and a red office chair. The key is in their difference. Schöllhorn calls his interiors choice Differential Furniture. He would.

Schöllhorn is the former athlete and physicist who played a major role in Thomas Tuchel's coaching philosophy. He calls it Differential Training, and it's based on his belief that repetition and correction hold back learning.

He gives me an example. Two groups of 12- to 14-year-old students in Mainz are given a skipping rope before every maths class for one month. The first group is told to skip in a consistent way, only looking straight ahead, for three minutes before every lesson. This happened four times per week for three weeks; 12 lessons, 36 minutes of skipping.

The other group can do whatever they want with the skipping rope. They can skip with crossovers, double jumps, high knees, alternating legs, running skips, front-to-back or back-to-front. They can adjust or change any joint in their body. Again, only for three minutes before each lesson. If anyone in the group makes a mistake or drops the rope, it's no problem. There is no one to correct them.

The result? According to Schöllhorn, one month later, there was 'significant improvement' in the maths results of the second group. He puts this down to the effect that the training had on the brain state. The rope-skipping exercise, which is equivalent to a 45-minute run at around 80 per cent intensity (not ideal just before a maths lesson), puts the brain in an Alpha-Theta state, which is the ideal frequency for learning, creativity and problem-solving (Alpha) and relaxation and intuition (Theta).

Schöllhorn peppers his conversation with Chinese proverbs, maybe because his current research work is based around Qi-gong, the Chinese equivalent to Indian yoga that also achieves Alpha-Theta state. One of his favourites is: 'If you want to be unhappy, just compare more.'

He says that ten minutes of yoga every day for four weeks will produce anatomical changes in the amygdala, the neuro-function in the brain that copes with emotions. It allows athletes to cope better with strong emotions, to keep anger in check and become more reflective. 'I would say it's a good thing to be less driven by emotion on the pitch,' he says. 'That would certainly make you less likely to get a red card.'

As a result of not being corrected or criticised, athletes in Differential Training naturally start to be less critical of themselves and take more risks. No two players are the same, so if they are doing a training exercise, there will naturally be different results. Schöllhorn's premise is that if you are training to a manual, and it has to be a certain way, then you are always comparing, and you will always lose.

He started his career as a gymnast, but on growing too tall became a high-level handball player. After a knee injury ruled him out of contact sport, he switched to decathlon, and then bobsleigh. Whenever he had a problem, he would source the solution to help him and move on. As a student of biomechanics in Frankfurt, one of the first challenges he set himself was to find the commonalities in great athletes.

His biggest findings were that all athletes have an individual 'fingerprint' in their movement; and that it is impossible to have an identical repetition of a movement. 'If there was a bank robbery in England, and you had CCTV footage of how the robbers walked, assuming you had their details on a database, you would be able to recognise them 99 per cent of the time,' says Schöllhorn, who identified every top athlete on the basis of 200 metres of their movements.[13] These findings made him question the traditional approaches of learning based on repetition. If there is no such thing as an identical repetition, why should an athlete repeat in training? As a coach, Schöllhorn noted that top athletes understood their bodies and were able to find their individual technique, which is adaptable in new situations.

Any two members of a team, therefore, will have their own style of movement. Each one is different, and they would fail if they tried to copy someone else. They should also be treated and trained differently, as what might work for Dele Alli, say, might not work for Marcus Rashford.

Schöllhorn sees athletes' potential to learn through their 'fluctuations': these are the instability measures that naturally occur in Differential Training. It's rare to complete any task at 100 per cent, but if the struggle is encouraged as part of the process, it will organically lead to improved performance. Schöllhorn realised this very early on, when he worked to improve the sprinting technique of Eintracht Frankfurt strikers Andy Möller and Tony Yeboah in 1992. The team was second in the German Bundesliga at the time.

Schöllhorn had sessions with them twice a week over one month, which was all it took to improve their sprinting. He asked them to vary their angles in practice, to raise one knee higher, to push more from the hip, to change the rhythm of their arm movements. They learned to relax their muscles, to achieve the Alpha-Theta state and to run faster.

One coach who quickly understood the benefits of Differential Training was Marcus Nölke. He was coaching the Austrian ski-jumping team, and he adapted Differential Training to ski-jumping. Austria won two gold medals and a silver medal for ski-jumping in the 2006 Turin Winter Olympics.

Another was Paco Seirul·lo. A legendary figure at Barcelona, he was head of their physical department in 1995, when Johan Cruyff was coach. He worked with Pep Guardiola, who was a 15-year-old youth-team player. When Guardiola was Barcelona coach 23 years later, Seirul·lo was still there. Seirul·lo has worked with Spanish athletes across all disciplines, including climbing, boxing, martial arts, basketball, handball and bullfighting. He says all of them improved their performance.

Seirul·lo, now working under the grand title of Head of Methodology at Barcelona, understood the benefits of Differential Training and introduced it to *La Masia* (The Farmhouse), the Barcelona youth academy that developed Andres Iniesta, Xavi and Lionel Messi. Coaches used no more than three repetitions of every exercise. They brought in more variation in training. Seirul·lo says the best physical coaches make their players fall in love with training: 'I want them to say, this is the nicest thing I am doing in my life. It's not having fun, it's falling in love. That's different.'

Seirul·lo's latest protégé is Rafael Pol, a key figure under Barcelona's former coach Luis Enrique, who was employed after the coach liked his thesis, 'Preparation: Physics in Football'. Pol says he has no answers, only questions. 'Why do you train technique when you are not tired? Why train tactics and try and eliminate tiredness? Why do we value endurance without reference to the state of the game? Are we training them technically for [only] the first minute? Training must be like matches, so that the games can become part of the training.' It is not always easy for his players, though. 'Football is about spirit and Pol always has you switched on even if you are not at 100 per cent physically,' said Nolito, the striker who trained under him at Celta Vigo before moving to Guardiola's Manchester City.

For Seirul·lo, Differential Training in football is like learning a language or how to paint. 'Do you paint like Van Gogh or Rubens? The context in each case is different, the methodology is different and the path is different too. That's why we will not see Van Gogh painting women in the forest … And if we do not evolve, we end up doing the same thing as everyone else. So we have to take a step forward.'[14]

Schöllhorn says something very similar. He combined his sporting ability and knowledge of physics to seek improvement solutions. 'If I wanted to develop extraordinary athletes, I had to apply extraordinary methods.' The athletic team he coached in the late 1980s won German Junior championship titles in sprinting, hurdles and decathlon.

There is no end to the ways in which Differential Training can be used. The professor developed a DVD showing 200 different exercises just for a goalkeeper's kicking and ball-receiving movements. He invites coaches to discover creative solutions at his Institute, and now teaches the next generation of German coaches on courses put on by the German FA. 'I show them the method or philosophy and it's up to them what they do with that knowledge,' he says.

Schöllhorn has taken the universal principle of Differential Training and applied it to different environments. In car factories, Audi mechanics were told to vary the order in which they fixed parts, and there was an immediate reduction in employees' sick days; at Mercedes, employees used Differential Training to introduce the mounting of a new car series, and there was a spike in productivity; in music learning, varying movements and breathing patterns can quickly improve performance. He recommends that flautists vary breathing (strong, soft, interrupted or continuous), finger movements (fast, slow, wide or narrow) and finger posture (straight, flexed, different flexions in wrist or elbow).

Differential Training has already had successful applications in psychotherapy,and the rehabilitation of stroke patients. Schöllhorn's next challenge is to improve medical research around Parkinson's and ADHD. Differential Training produces more dopamine in the brain – of which, studies have shown, sufferers of Parkinson's and ADHD have a deficit. Schöllhorn is investigating what effect his methods have on the heart and brain in parallel, and whether more intensive Differential Training can benefit Parkinson's and ADHD sufferers.

Schöllhorn claims that he is currently too busy to support a team, even his local side Mainz, but he could not ignore the progress that Borussia Dortmund made under Tuchel. Winning a first trophy for five years, and the way they did so, is a fantastic advertisement for Differential Training in another environment. Not that Schöllhorn will celebrate too much. 'As the Chinese say,' he smiles, 'in the beginning it's good or bad. But when you reach a certain level, that's just the way it is.'

HOW TO GET AN EDGE – by WOLFGANG SCHÖLLHORN

1. See the big picture: we all play a role in a team, and in society, and because this role changes many times during our career, we need to adapt to different fields all the time.
2. Have the desire to improve: if we stop moving forward, we will drift backwards in the river of life.
3. Be hungry to learn: learning is an evolutionary necessity that comes with a child's curiosity and enthusiasm, but is often lost in traditional education.

TYNKE TOERING

Control your learning process

Taking charge of your learning / Impulse control / Mkhitaryan and the ice-bath / Restraint is contagious

I was struck by how aware Thomas Tuchel was about his learning process. He was comfortable that he did not have the answers; it kept him looking for an edge. Even in the cut-and-thrust of league football, where games come every three days and there is barely time to draw breath, he makes the time to reflect on his own performance, to think about the decisions he has made and to look for better solutions.

Some leaders who expend energy making tough decisions all day are at risk of *ego depletion*. This is when they are in a hyper-controlled state at work, and when they get home, their will-power is gone. They have nothing left. This is not the case with Tuchel. He may sometimes worry, but he is not an obsessive. He is devoted to his young family, he likes playing Padel tennis and enjoys trips to foreign cities where he can walk around *incognito* (that might not be possible for much longer).

He clearly benefits from taking charge of his own learning. This is known as self-regulation and is seen as a factor that correlates to success.

Tynke Toering knows all about self-regulation. She is a Dutch psychologist working at the Norwegian School of Sport Sciences. She studies what differentiates the players who make it from those who don't, and believes the way each individual approaches the processes around learning and development can predict future performance.

She found that youth players who self-regulate their learning well seem to benefit from practice more than others by being more engaged in reflection. As she puts it: 'The self-regulated learning process appears to help players become aware of what is required at several performance levels, which then sets the standard for their practice efforts.'

She produced an academic study evaluating the responses of 639 professional footballers in the top two leagues in Norway.[15] They were each asked to rate their level of agreement with 13 statements on a 1–5 scale (where 1 is not at all and 5 is very much) about their levels of restraint and impulse control. Restraint refers to whether athletes 'give it their all' while impulse control refers to keeping themselves under control.

The statements included (in brackets is the aspect each question refers to, where R = restraint and IC = impulse control):

- I wish I had more self-discipline (R)
- I have a hard time breaking bad habits (R)
- I do certain things that are bad for me, if they are fun (IC)
- Sometimes I can't stop myself from doing something, even if I know it's wrong (IC)

There was a slight, but not statistically significant, difference in the responses depending on the league in which the respondents played. On restraint, the mean score of the Norwegian Premier League players was higher than the second division players (3.52 compared to 3.38). The same was true on impulse control (3.94 compared to 3.86). Toering's opinion is that restraint and impulse control seem related to professional footballers' lifestyle and performance: 'Because the population studied included players who had already reached professional status and they had relatively high scores, it is possible that a minimum level of self-control is a necessary requirement to become a professional player.'

More significant was the difference between the 79 players who had represented their countries at senior-level international football and the 525 who had not. The mean score on restraint was 3.62 for internationals and 3.42 for non-internationals; on impulse control, 4.15 for internationals and 3.86 for non-internationals. This is a relatively big difference. 'For each point scored on impulse control, players were 83 per cent more likely to have national team experience,' says Toering. That's a big number, but she urges perspective and reminds me that there are a lot of additional factors that have an impact on football performance.

There was also a strong correlation between the team's average rating on restraint in pre-season and their final league positions. The higher their restraint score, the higher up the table they finished. Restraint scores were related to team performance, while impulse control scores were associated with individual performance (in terms of international recognition). Toering said that while we need to remember that these results were based on self-assessment, they still show some interesting tendencies given the tests cover two complete leagues and a total of almost 650 players.

Talk of restraint and impulse control made me think one of the players that Borussia Dortmund sold in summer 2016. Thomas Tuchel had told me that his role model player was Henrikh Mkhitaryan. He was the playmaker, the creative star of the side, but he was also the most humble. When Borussia Dortmund returned from European away matches, it was Mkhitaryan who would carry the biggest boxes out of the team bus; and no one would work harder to recover from games – after away matches in Europe, he was the player sitting in an ice-bath at 4 a.m. 'So when you lose him, you lose more than a great player, you lose a role model: someone who arrives early and leaves late, can take criticism in the heat of the half-time talk, who adapts to everything.' Mkhitaryan had high levels of restraint and impulse control, and his coach believed that those benefits were contagious to the rest of his squad. Could Tuchel be right?

'I believe that restraint may be "contagious" in the sense that, if a high-performing culture is created, these standards will impose on all the people involved,' Toering responds. 'We, as human beings, are affected by the people we interact with. So, "the way we do things here on a daily basis" will probably have an effect on how I do my job as a player. In professional football, one could expect that if players higher up in the hierarchy show values related to restraint, the rest will probably follow.' She believes that impulse control is a more individual characteristic.

One Premier League club carried out a study in 2011. They wanted to measure the personality attributes of youth players. The sample size was too small to learn much of significance, but the ultimate finding was most peculiar.

The survey measured nine personality traits with a series of statements about each one. These included:

- *Mental toughness:* I criticise myself when things go wrong during a game
- *Teamwork:* It's not that important to think of and play for the team
- *Leadership:* I don't like having a special responsibility in the team
- *Discipline:* Even when I'm tired during training, I never find it difficult to get going
- *Competitiveness:* When I play football I need to be the best player
- *Openness to feedback:* I know better than the coaches what I should be practising

Each player was asked to give himself an Ability Rating score, based on what percentage of players they are better than amongst those they play with and against. So if a player thought he was the best in his group, and never came up against anyone better, he would rate himself 100 per cent. The mean rating was

74 per cent. That score was then placed alongside the Ability Rating from the four youth coaches at the club. The end result was a scatter plot that looked like this:

The first thing to note here is that there was no correlation between how the players rated themselves and how the coaches rated them.

By combining the data from the players' personality statements and their Ability Rating score, the two aspects most significant to a high rating were Mental Toughness and a lack of Openness to Feedback. Remember, this was the players' self-assessment. It was a small trend, and not statistically significant. The coaches' Ability Rating scores combined with the players' personality statements provided a different trend: that Discipline was the overriding attribute.

Now most of the players are in their early twenties, we can get a sense of how they have progressed. Player A, for example, only rated himself at around 55 per cent. Yet he spent the 2016–17 season at a top-six side in the Premier League. Player B, on the other hand, rated himself at 100 per cent. He was at a Championship bottom-half side in 2016–17. Player C plays in non-league football.

Six years later, the people behind the study were able to draw some more conclusions. Of the 53 people in the youth group at the time, only 30 completed the self-assessment. Eleven have now dropped out of the game. The players that the coaches rated the highest have had the best careers. Five out of the top seven players, as rated by the coaches, went on to represent their country. The coaches knew the talent better than the players did.

There was one clear correlation from this very small sample. It was that if the player did not complete the survey, he was more likely to be successful. We don't know the explanation for this: maybe the group of 53 was split into two, and only the bottom group completed it; maybe the better players had more power even then and just didn't bother doing it; or there was a systemic bias within the club, which only asked those players they were unsure about. Looking at the 'downstream effects' five years later shows us that the players are not always right about their own ability; that the coaches know their stuff; and that even at 17, the best of the bunch are already treated differently.

As the manager responsible for the development of Ousmane Dembélé, Tuchel knows he has someone with talent on his hands. Or as he put it: someone with 'an extraordinary gift that comes with a responsibility and an obligation to improve'. Dembélé has undoubtedly improved at Dortmund. And one of the beneficiaries of that is the France national team whose coach, Didier Deschamps, happens to share Tuchel's desire for self-improvement.

HOW TO GET AN EDGE – by TYNKE TOERING

1. Follow your heart. Go for what you're passionate about and do it your way, at the same time realising that you're part of a world that's bigger than just you.
2. Act upon the standards required for the level you pursue, and make sure that this is reflected in your daily activities.
3. Keep innovating. There's always a different way. There's always a better way.

DIDIER DESCHAMPS
Listen like a true leader

Are leaders born? / Injustice of millennials / Body language matters / Three domains of leadership / How to listen well / Promises cause problems / That crucible moment

It cannot be a coincidence. There was a time when France playing at major tournaments used to be a byword for trouble: players refusing to train (2010 World Cup) or insulting coaches (Euro 2012), falling out with each other (Euro 2008), or swearing at journalists (Euro 2012). 'Gross incompetence and cartoonish dysfunction' is how the *Wall Street Journal* summed up the 2010 campaign, which ended with one player sent home early, the captain rowing with the coach, the team going on strike and the head of France's football federation resigning.

That kind of thing doesn't happen so much now. Occasionally, the odd scandal does appear, like the bizarre plot in which Karim Benzema was accused of blackmailing his team-mate Mathieu Valbuena over a sex tape, but these days it gets shut down, and shut down fast. Benzema and Valbuena never played again for France after that story broke. These days, France is respected by its opponents and loved by its fans. The reason? He is sitting opposite me in a hotel bar in Monaco. It is a cloudy afternoon in February and, as the Mediterranean waves lap the shore outside, France coach Didier Deschamps is explaining the art of leadership.

This is where he took his first job in management, coaching a Monaco side that was almost relegated in his first season and two years later reached the 2004 Champions League final, beating Real Madrid and Chelsea on the way. The walk from the Monte Carlo casino to our beachside rendezvous is full of reminders of football's elite; walking along the seafront, I pass the Fairmont Hotel, where football club presidents and secretaries stay for the UEFA competition draws. Opposite the Rolls-Royce and Bentley showrooms is the Grimaldi Forum, the venue where those draws take place; just across the road is Café Sass, beloved by former UEFA president Michel Platini (not to mention George Clooney and Bono) when in town; and nearby, where the real high-rollers stay, Le Méridien, the only hotel with its own beach.

There are few men in football better qualified to talk about leadership. Deschamps was captain of every team where he was a regular starter, at Nantes, Marseille, Juventus and of course France, whom he skippered to success at the 1998 World Cup and 2000 European Championship. He also won the Champions League with Marseille and Juventus and the FA Cup with Chelsea.

What makes Deschamps's success all the more significant was his own ability. He played as a defensive midfielder, as solid as they come. You would never see him dribble round one or two before laying the ball off to a team-mate. His appearances in the opposition box were rare. His best goalscoring season ended in four goals and he was infamously described by Eric Cantona as 'a water-carrier', a term that annoyed him greatly. He was not a spectacular player, but compensated for that by other means: he made sure that his role on the pitch would be important.

Plus ça change. At his first club, Aviron Bayonnais, he was made captain six weeks after joining. 'He took charge without being authoritative – he would only use nice words – and the others listened,' remembered his first coach, Norbert Navarro. 'In two weeks he went from the junior beginners to the Under-16s. And on the day of his birthday, 15 October, I gave him the captain's armband. A little boy of 11 with 13–15-year-olds!' The leader was born – although Deschamps believes his moment came long before then.

'I don't think you just become a leader,' he says, leaning forward in a low armchair and sipping an espresso. 'You can't wake up one morning and say, "Right, now I'm going to be a leader." I think it is something that's in you, that you're born with, and which develops. Some people have that character, that personality and it comes naturally. You can't force it. It has to be authentic and natural. Innate. It comes from you, your early years, your attitude as an adolescent, how you are with a group and as the one who influences things.'[16]

Over the next few hours, as we sit across an asymmetrical table, Deschamps will explain how his style of leadership provides an edge. There are learnings that can be applied to almost any other professional context. He tells me how to get the best out of millennials, how to build trust in relationships and how to be a good listener. He talks about the importance of adaptability and why he wants to learn more. He relives his darkest moments as a coach and admits his managerial mistakes. He is confident but not afraid to talk about his failings. He is open-minded but knows his own voice. He is a leader for the modern age, and one from whom we can learn a lot.

Deschamps received his football education at the Nantes academy, famous in that era for producing Marcel Desailly, Claude Makelele and Christian Karembeu. He left home to join it when he was 14, among kids older than him; they were all fighting for a contract. 'It was a jungle,' he says. 'I wasn't yet 15 and here I was being confronted by life. It makes you grow up fast.'

When he came home for the summer holidays, Deschamps would ask his father for permission to visit Georges Etcheverry, an osteopath who lived two doors down on the same road as the Deschamps family in Anglet. Even at that age, Deschamps knew that his body was his work-tool. He would ask Etcheverry how to prepare, how to stretch, how to eat. 'And he never had any serious injuries,' Etcheverry said.

Nantes coach Miroslav Blazevic saw something in the young Frenchman, who then wore patched flared jeans and turtleneck sweaters knitted by his mother. He is much more stylish today, in black jeans and trainers and tight white T-shirt and dark sunglasses. Blazevic appointed Deschamps as Nantes captain when he was only 19. 'I was one of youngest in the group, but already if I had something to say, I would say it, because it was always for the good of the team. The older guys at Nantes never made things difficult for me, never doubted my capacity to fulfil that role. There were guys who were 30 but they accepted my leadership.'

The same happened in the France team, when he was called up at 21. 'I was 29 when he joined the team and he was just a kid,' remembered Bernard Pardo. 'I wanted to make him feel at ease by telling him: "We're going to play side by side, so do what you need to do and I'll be there to cover." But it was the opposite, it was him covering me!'

He was already a coach in spirit, said his former team-mate at Marseille, Marc Libbra. 'I remember [he was] a bloody nuisance on the pitch, giving orders, barking, ushering people about. He'd unleash hell. I was young and thought he was angry with me about something, but clearly not. He has a go at you to bring the best out of you. He's someone who is always on your back, whether you're his team-mate or his opponent.'

It was only ever team dynamics and optimising the talent of the group that interested Deschamps. In that respect, his position on the pitch probably helped. 'Being a leader is about having time for others. And for you to be able to spend time with others, you must be in a situation where you don't have a problem with yourself.' The more you have to work on your game, the less time you have for others. Is this why other holding midfielders, the likes of Pep Guardiola or Carlo Ancelotti, have made such impressive managers?

This selflessness comes up throughout Deschamps's career. 'Lots of players may have the technical qualities of Didier Deschamps, but very few have the same energy and heart and ability to work for the team and help them win,' said Mathieu Bideau, the Nantes academy head of recruitment. Landry Chauvin, Rennes academy head, put it another way: 'Zidane does not need anyone else to win the *Ballon d'Or*, or to pull off exceptional moves, but he needs Deschamps to win titles.'

In the past, Deschamps has credited Aimé Jacquet (France's World Cup-winning coach) and Marcello Lippi as great influences. He spoke of Jacquet's man-management skills and Lippi's tactical smarts. But when I ask what he has taken from different coaches, he snaps. 'I didn't *take* anything!' His fist slaps into his palm to make his point. 'Everything you go through has to fit in with the way you are and your own ideas. You wouldn't be able to do today what coaches did when I was a player. I say something to my son and he tells me I'm prehistoric. You have to live in your time, be of today.'

This is one of the key lessons that Deschamps is keen to impart. Leaders may be born but adaptability can be developed. And for managers today, it could be the most important of all. Just because one plan worked at a certain time with a certain group, it's no guarantee that the same plan will work again elsewhere. 'The key thing is knowing how to adapt,' he says.

'Adapting to the group that you have at your disposal; adapting to the place where you're working; adapting to the local environment. This is crucial: adaptability. It means being aware of the strengths and weaknesses inside the group; being aware of all the outside factors that can influence your sphere; and adapting to all of that, then modifying what you've done, and not being afraid to change.'

Deschamps is talking on a personal level, but the same is true of today's modern behemoth companies. PayPal began as a cryptography company, Google used to sell its own search technology to other search engines and Facebook started out as a campus-only social network. Apple was not the first to create a smartphone, a tablet computer or a digital music player: they just did it better than others. They all adapted to capture new value in the market. Deschamps's job is to do the same.

During his 15 years as a coach – at Monaco, Marseille, Juventus and France – Deschamps has had to adapt. Some players in the France squad were not even born when he lifted the Jules Rimet Trophy at the Stade de France in 1998. He openly admits that managing millennials today is a challenge, and not just in the sporting context.

'The role of the leader is much more complex today,' he says. 'In society at large, mentalities have changed. In any professional sphere, an 18-year-old wants everything and they want it straightaway, because they feel strong. They have mastered new technology, which gives them a certain power over generations above them. And these days an 18-year-old has no qualms about wanting to take the place of someone who's 30 or 40, who has experience. These days there are no borders; kids feel strong and confident. They have a desire to explore and to conquer. These can be good things but there can be a bad side as well.'

This often involves an entourage whose motivations may not always tally with the player's best interests, or a social network that provides the player with a link to fans and additional commercial revenue. These are outside influences that never concerned Deschamps as a player. 'They see players as a cash cow and that cow has to keep giving milk.' Deschamps gives an example of the player who has been dropped, and whose agent tells him, 'The coach is an idiot,' and demands a move straightaway. He has seen it happen.

'One of the words I hear a lot is injustice,' he continues. 'But what is considered injustice for them may not be something you agree with. So it all becomes a question of how you interpret words and where you put your cursor on the importance of words. For a lot of young guys these days, very quickly they will say that's totally unfair!'

This may be familiar to those who work with millennials in a non-sporting environment. They are accused of being entitled, narcissistic and unfocused, attitudes that confound their managers.[17] Social networks have created a generation who crave instant recognition. Technology empowers them to challenge authority. We will see in Chapter 5 how one top club mitigates against this instant gratification by introducing a salary cap. Simon Sinek urges leaders today to understand how social media also affects behaviours.[18] Engagement with social media releases dopamine, the same chemical triggered by smoking, drinking or gambling. Dopamine is addictive and social media gives people access to that hit. As this generation switch their craving for approval from parents to their peers, so they rely on social networks: for likes, retweets and shares.

'As they grow older, we're seeing that many kids can't form deep-meaning relationships,' Sinek told *Inside Quest*. 'Many friendships are superficial; they can't rely on them; their friends may cancel on them. They don't have the right coping mechanisms for stress, so when it comes in their lives, they turn to a device and not to a person.'

That means a different type of management is now required. It's one that involves an exchange of views, an understanding of opinions and a mutual trust. As Deschamps tells me how he builds that trust, I am surprised by the rigour with which he approaches his role.

He thinks about every word he utters; is acutely aware of his body language and how he delivers his message. 'It's not just about the words you use, but the way you use them, and the message that puts over. Also your face too, and the way you project your message. If you're telling the group to stay calm, be good, and you have beads of sweat dripping down your forehead, you're in trouble ...'

Deschamps takes in as much as he can. He has created a circle of trust that both empowers the group and provides him with more information to make better decisions. This is how he gains an edge.

Every new player called up to the France squad has a one-on-one chat with Deschamps. He tells them what he thinks of them, what he wants from them, and warns them what to expect in the future. Once that player is an international, the way people look at him will change forever; as will expectations, from his support structure, team-mates, opponents and the media.

Deschamps ensures that all players have a copy of his Code of Conduct in their rooms at Clairefontaine, the French training-centre. In it, he asks them to respect the jersey and the national anthem, to display an open and friendly attitude, to be genuine and humble, and in a section on how to handle the press, to remember that 'your behaviour, attitude and words shape your image as it is replayed to the public by the media, which are an unavoidable and indispensable part of your journey. They mould the image that you show to the entire country, so be professional with them, too.'

You can get a gist of his message from how Deschamps defines talent. He thinks all young players have potential, not talent. 'Talent doesn't exist in young players. Talent is something that you are able to show at a high level over a period of time. We're talking about consistency, that's talent. Talent has to be confirmed. It's the confirmation of potential. It's getting to the top and maintaining that level over a period of time.'

The player needs to understand his message. 'What I don't want them to think is that if they have to come to Clairefontaine, they have made it. This is the first step only.'

Deschamps then keeps an eye on how they settle in with the squad; not just on the pitch but off it. 'It's very interesting for me to watch that.' Deschamps will give a youngster a wider margin for error, but he will not accept a lack of effort, a lack of determination or a lack of desire.

'If it happens, they get a warning, and I see how they will

react. It comes down to a relationship based on trust,' he says. 'The role I have as national team coach is about having a moral contract. I don't pay these guys, their club does, which is why I'm talking about a moral engagement. It's about creating a link based on trust. The human relationships these days have become almost as important as what's on the pitch. Being a manager is about recognising talent and knowing how to use it in the right context. You need to spot that thing which tells you, "He's the guy who can bring me what I need here." Your choices are human investments: you have to put time in, to get to know them better. They have different lives, personalities, cultures, backgrounds, even views on life. So you have to be able to tune in to their station. Man-management has become extremely important.'

This is where the dialogue comes in; not always face-to-face in his office, but sometimes the odd word on the training ground or during a meal. It's all considered and thoughtful. The information on his players is out there, available to us all. 'What interests me is knowing the man behind all that.'

So how does he do that? When he was a club manager, Deschamps established a leadership group of three 'captains'. Each one represented a domain of leadership: physical leadership, technical leadership and psychological leadership. He felt the whole squad was covered by at least one of those three. It was important to have an odd number in case a vote was tied. In the national team, he increases the three to five; one of the extras is a young player who sits in on the leadership group's 'Cabinet meetings' and passes on messages to the younger players in the group, and vice versa, so their message is relayed to the coaches. A vice-captain also joins, so the number remains odd. This 'inner circle' is crucial to Deschamps's work. His back-up staff is in constant communication with other members of the group, and the coach rarely needs to intervene in an issue. If he does, it's already out of hand.

Deschamps emphasises that this is not a one-way conversation. It's important for the Cabinet to tell him what the group feels or requires as well. Their job is to bring back information to him. Speaking and passing on the right messages is part of modern leadership. 'For me being a good manager is very much about listening. And we must remember that listening and hearing are two different things. The players have to feel like they can express themselves. Your role is not just to give orders: it is also to console, to encourage and to listen.'

Deschamps has learned how to listen. Listening is not about being quiet when others are speaking, using facial expressions to encourage conversation or repeating back what you have heard. Academics Jack Zenger and Joseph Folkman collaborated on a study of listening, taking 3,492 managers and identifying the listening characteristics of the top 5 per cent according to their colleagues.[19] They discovered that good listeners ask questions that promote discovery and insight; include interactions which build the other party's self-esteem, by supporting and conveying confidence; use feedback in both directions as part of a co-operative conversation; and make suggestions.

There are also different levels of listening. These include responding to body language, or non-verbal cues, which is estimated to make up to 80 per cent of communication; also asking questions, offering ideas without hijacking the conversation; and understanding what the other person wants from the conversation.

I can see that Deschamps has an awareness of these. One of the key levels is about attention. I had noticed him clearing away his phone from the table, so his focus was only on the conversation in hand. In turn, this influenced *my* attitude and made *me* a better listener. Behavioural scientists from Virginia Tech University noted the importance of this in any form of conversation. Their study divided 200 participants into 100 pairs of two. Each pair sat in a coffee-shop and was given ten minutes to discuss either a meaningful or trivial topic. A lab assistant noted the non-verbal behaviour and whether any of the pairs took out a mobile device during their chats. Every participant was then asked to measure how they felt during the chat, on a scale related to empathetic concern and feelings of connectedness to their interlocutor.

The key finding was that if either participant put a smartphone on the table (even face down) or held it in their hand, the quality of the conversation was less fulfilling. There was a lowering of empathetic concern, which was more pronounced among those who already knew each other. 'The mere presence [of phones] as environmental cues can distribute individuals' attention and guide the behaviour of those who are nearby without their awareness,' wrote the study's author Shalani Misra.[20] Phones kill conversation. Their presence leads to absence. If you want to have a proper conversation, keep your phone out of sight.

Deschamps is the first to admit he does not have all the answers. At one club he coached, he made the wrong choices for his leadership group. 'Once you make that mistake it becomes very complicated,' he says. One player from that period, who went on to play in the 2004 Champions League final for Monaco under Deschamps, confirmed that the leadership group initially chosen was the wrong one. Monaco had finished fifteenth in Deschamps's first season. 'It takes balls to recognise your mistake and change it,' the player said.

That's not the only mistake Deschamps has made. 'Never make promises,' he tells me when I ask for more examples. 'What may be true today may not be the case tomorrow. And if you make promises then you're in trouble. Then you have to go back and justify, and you don't want to be in that situation. Sometimes, to be nice to someone, you might be tempted to make a promise. And then as the days go on, you can't do what you said. So don't commit to things before you're absolutely certain. Leave yourself free to make decisions when you're ready.

Be careful of what you announce and what you promise. Obviously people have the right to ask things and I have the right to say no. But one thing I feel is important: if I say I will do something, then you bet I will do it. You must be true to your word as a leader. If you say yes, you do it.'

Deschamps defines a good leader as someone who is recognised by his peers as exemplary and who guarantees the respect of the rules put in place. He repeats the need for authenticity and adaptability. It's also important to give praise, positive recognition.[21] 'When to give a pat on the back is something that I haven't always known how to do. It's easy to point the finger when something's going badly, but never forget words of encouragement when things are going well. But even when things are going very well, my way of thinking is, "We can still do better."'

That was not the case on the evening of Friday, 15 November 2013 in Kiev. France had played a catastrophic first leg of a World Cup qualifying play-off against Ukraine and lost 2–0. Deschamps had been a coach for over ten years and calls that period the defining moment of his leadership career. This was a new situation for Deschamps and he had to adapt fast.

'I had to dig deep into my resources and find the answers,' he remembered. All sorts of people contacted him telling him what he needed to do: change this, try that. He stayed in what he called 'my bubble' with his staff. 'I return to a phrase from my youth: *c'est dans le succès que tu fais la plus grande connerie.* You make the biggest cock-ups in times of success. I find that's true: success makes you euphoric and can lead you to make bad decisions.[22] But in difficulty, at times of failure, that's when you learn the most. I've always found I've learned more from times of difficulty. This period, that's where I found the true meaning of my role as national team manager. That's where I really felt that I was there for a reason.'

Deschamps lifts up his glass of water and declares himself 'a glass half-full type of guy'. Even at 2–0 down against Ukraine, after a shocking French performance, he kept that attitude. He reframed the stats: instead of telling his players that no team had ever overcome a 2–0 first-leg deficit to reach a World Cup before, he said, 'It's about time that stat changed.'

The message was never about what *Les Bleus* would try to do. He banned the word *essayer*, or try. 'We don't try. We do everything we can to get where we need to be. Don't TRY! You do your best. When you're at the top, you don't try. You do. Not "I will try to win" but "I want to win, I'm going to win."' Deschamps was decisive. Within 12 hours of the first game finishing, he knew what changes to make. 'I got inside the players' heads and made my decisions.'[23]

For the second leg he switched the centre-backs from Eric Abidal and Laurent Koscielny (sent off and suspended) to Raphaël Varane and Mamadou Sakho. He dropped Samir Nasri and selected Yohan Cabaye. Out went Loic Rémy and Olivier Giroud, and in (ironically) came Valbuena and Benzema. These were sweeping changes. Deschamps knew that defeat would cost him his job. He needed a team not just to win the match, but to win it by three goals.

Let's not forget the context to the game. The France team's popularity had been at an all-time low when Deschamps took over. One poll even asked if fans wanted the team to qualify for the World Cup. There was no love for this group of players.

The home leg changed everything. Sakho converted a Franck Ribéry cross after 22 minutes and Benzema doubled the lead shortly after the half-hour mark. Ukraine went down to ten men in the second half and Sakho, a centre-back playing only his sixteenth game for *Les Bleus*, scored again to make it 3–0. France had done it. They had qualified for the World Cup. Deschamps had found the right formula for his players, who had finally delivered. Just as significant, that one performance thrilled and united the fans at a raucous Stade de France. Deschamps had turned the mood around. After the final whistle, the French players did a lap of honour and gave their coach the bumps.

The team went on to reach the 2014 World Cup quarter-final, losing 1–0 to eventual winner Germany. France played Euro 2016 on home soil, and despite the pressure that brought, they reached the final. France did beat Germany this time, winning a dramatic semi-final 2–0 in Marseille. Deschamps' team only lost the final to Portugal after extra time. He is getting closer to a title, and winning one will make him the most successful figure in French football history (if he is not already). That win over Ukraine gave him the platform to build on.

This was Deschamps's crucible moment. A crucible moment is a transformative experience through which an individual comes to a new or an altered sense of identity. Academics Warren Bennis and Robert J. Thomas interviewed over 40 top business leaders and found that the one thing they all had in common was that such an experience became the source of their future leadership abilities; a tough moment needing deep self-reflection. 'It required them to examine their values, question their assumptions, hone their judgment,' they wrote.[24] 'And, invariably, they emerged from the crucible stronger and more sure of themselves and their purpose – changed in some fundamental way.' Like Deschamps, they all became better leaders as a result.

There is no simple answer to the question of what makes a great leader. Sadly this is one even Deschamps cannot answer. But Bennis and Thomas discovered that the most critical skill for a leader – aside from engaging others in shared meaning, a distinctive and compelling voice, and a sense of integrity – was an 'adaptive capacity'. This implies the need to weigh up the right factors in their context (in Deschamps's case, making the decision to change certain players) and to persevere without losing hope ('You don't try. You do').

Do we all need a Deschamps in our office lives? Imagine what we could achieve with an inspirational leader in charge, one who has a proven record of success and a desire to improve those around him; who understands the art of listening, and will put away his phone when he talks to you; who makes a moral contract to help you develop, as long as you show the requisite desire and effort to do so; who may adapt to changing situations, but has the confidence to remain his authentic self.

And Deschamps is not done yet. He is passionate about his role in the French game (unlike some international coaches, he is heavily involved in pathway development for future French players). He does not see himself as the finished article, as a great leader who can learn nothing more. In fact, the opposite is true: 'When I get up every day, I never say I know. What I say is, I know that I don't know, and that I can still learn. And that's why you need to be able to listen. You can have situations when you don't have the best solution: in that case, knowing the *least bad* decision is already an important quality. It's up to you to find the most suitable response.'

Experience has taught Deschamps to step back from his decisions and not take everything to heart. He used to steam into the dressing-room at half-time. Now he waits three minutes, 'for my temperature to come down'. He cuts himself off from external noise, is not affected by any criticism and doesn't waste energy on battles he will not win. He remains open-minded and is willing to adapt anything he reads, hears or watches to his own needs. The night before we met, he watched a TV show about South African explorer Mike Horn. 'Fantastic! The guy defies nature, but it also showed the importance of being able to inspire people, and how they will follow you. The head rules the body. We can all learn from that. The mental state is what's important.'

He might use something from Horn in a future team-talk. Some coaches sit the players down for 20 or 30 minutes and give a deep team briefing. With today's players, Deschamps reckons he has their attention for ten minutes, tops. 'Then someone will see a fly buzzing around and you've lost them.' So he looks for the right formula, the best form of motivation, sometimes returning to familiar themes. 'It's an immense pleasure for me to prepare these talks: you're looking for the right buttons to push, on the human, psychological and tactical side. A huge pleasure!'

He finds it hard to define his own style. 'My method is more about who I am, where I am, my roots, my personality. I wouldn't have the pretension to say this is "my way".' Perhaps that sums up why he is so successful. He is still looking for the answers. The bedrock of his leadership culture is based on trust, authenticity, communication – and, above all, adaptability.

Deschamps is willing to adapt everything – methods, communication style, decisions – depending on each individual situation. As he put it, his players have different personalities, cultures, backgrounds, even views on life, so why wouldn't he 'tune into their station'? In the next chapter, we will look at why this individual model of development works so well – and how it can help us make better decisions. And so, I bid *au revoir* to the lapping waves on the Monégasque coastline, and head for the tranquil canals of Amsterdam.

HOW TO GET AN EDGE – by DIDIER DESCHAMPS

1. Listen to other voices and hear them. Remember you're not on your own. It's an exchange, not a monologue.
2. Establish the bond of trust, work with confidence and serenity, and be demanding.
3. Don't be afraid of mistakes. You have the right to get it wrong. It's much worse *not* to do something than to do it and get it wrong.

DECISION-MAKING

CRUYFF FOOTBALL

Establish the individual paradigm

Total Football and Dutch disruption / Constraints predicting success / Individual development principles / Cruyffism as religion

It's autumn in Amsterdam and the Olympic Stadium is a hub of activity. Flags from across the world are going up ahead of the city's marathon, which finishes at this landmark stadium in the south-east of the city. A huge sign, 'I Am Sterdam', is wheeled into position in front of the rather small entrance to the stadium running-track, which is visible from the roadside. The stadium was built in 1920 for the 1928 Olympics and, every night, the five Olympic rings light up the city skyline.

There used to be a bronze statue in front of this stadium, depicting the moment that Johan Cruyff won a penalty for Holland in the first minute of the 1974 World Cup final. It was created in 1978 by artist Ek van Zenten, and it seemed like the perfect spot for Cruyff. The Olympic Stadium played host to what Cruyff always referred to as one of his favourite games as a professional: Ajax's 5–1 victory over Liverpool in the European Cup second round, in December 1966. It became known as *De Mistwedstrijd*, 'The Fog Game', because the conditions were so poor. TV cameras could barely pick up the ball, but Ajax, wearing all-white kit to better see each other, managed just fine. Cruyff scored one goal. It was a precursor to Ajax's dominance in the competition that would see them win three consecutive European Cups between 1971 and 1973. Cruyff was at the forefront of that success.

Cruyff's apartment in Amsterdam was near the Olympic Stadium. His charity, the Johan Cruyff Foundation, rents workspace within the stadium, in Unit 5, while his educational programme, the Johan Cruyff Institute, is on the other side of the street. The statue has not moved far either: it is now at the back of the stadium.

Cruyff died in March 2016 but his legacy lives on. That's why I am here: to speak to the team behind Cruyff Football, an educational consultancy that calls itself 'the official heir and worldwide guardian of Johan Cruyff's football legacy'. Its job is to spread the Cruyff football philosophy worldwide; in so doing, they offer practical lessons that can provide an edge in developing talent, providing infrastructure for individual improvement, and learning to make better decisions.

You can feel the impact of Cruyff by just walking around Amsterdam. It's impossible to walk more than a few kilometres without stumbling upon a 'Cruyff Court', a 3G urban space which provides a safe area for children and the local community to play sport. Each court has two goals built into them at either end, as well as basketball hoops. There are over two hundred courts in Holland. Some have even popped up in England, with Dennis Bergkamp contributing £75,000 from his testimonial for one in Islington, near Arsenal's ground, which opened in 2008. There is another Cruyff Court in Tottenham, while there are two more in Liverpool: one at Anfield, the other at Everton.

Outside each court the 14 Rules of Johan Cruyff are displayed. There are 14 because that's the number he wore on his shirt.

1. *Team player:* you can't do anything on your own, you have to do it together.
2. *Responsibility:* be frugal for what you get and what you can do with it.
3. *Respect:* respect your opponent.
4. *Integration:* pull others into your activities.
5. *Initiative:* you are there to do something new.
6. *Coach:* in a team, you have to help each other.
7. *Personality:* be who you are.
8. *Social involvement:* important in sport but especially outside.[1]
9. *Technique:* the foundation.
10. *Tactics:* know what you do.
11. *Development:* sports develop your body and your mind.
12. *Learn:* try to learn something new every day.
13. *Play together:* be a concrete part of the game.
14. *Creativity:* the beauty of sport.

You can separate Dutch football history into Before Cruyff and After Cruyff. Before Cruyff, Holland had only ever qualified for one World Cup, in 1934. After Cruyff, this country with a population of 16 million, not even in Europe's top ten, reached three World Cup finals, two semi-finals and won the 1988 European Championship. By comparison, England has reached two semi-finals (at Italia 90 and Euro 96, on home soil) since winning the 1966 World Cup.

It was Holland's good fortune that a few months after Cruyff, aged 17, had made his debut in late 1964 for Ajax – then a semi-professional club in the east of Amsterdam – Rinus Michels, a gym teacher for deaf children, became coach. Ajax were struggling at the bottom of the table at the time, but Michels won his first game in charge 9–3, convinced the players to quit their jobs and turn professional. Ajax avoided relegation, and won the Dutch Championship for the next three seasons.

The partnership between Michels and Cruyff made it happen. 'Like Lennon and McCartney, they often quarrelled, but together they revolutionised Dutch and global football,' wrote Simon Kuper, who grew up in Holland in the 1970s and said listening to Cruyff talk about football was 'as if you could read a conversation with Albert Einstein ... every few days'.[2]

Their philosophy was called Total Football: it involved playing with two wingers, defenders who attack and players who could swap positions. It was innovative and challenging and required smart thinking as much as technique. It was football for the intellectual class, reflecting a spirit of the time, one that questioned authority and challenged the staid order of things.

Hubert Smeets, a Dutch writer, thinks that Cruyff did more than anyone to shape modern Holland. 'He changed the personality of the country,' agrees David Winner, author of *Brilliant Orange: The Neurotic Genius of Dutch Football*. Cruyff was a disruptive thinker and the country buzzed with creativity and originality. Holland may have lost the 1974 World Cup final to West Germany, but Cruyff saw it as a moral victory, because people remembered that Holland had played the better football.[3] For Cruyff, even in a World Cup final, the result did not matter; we will see that this attitude never left him.

Cruyff was the original rule-breaker. The Rulebreaker Society that Thomas Tuchel addressed could have written its ten-point manifesto with Cruyff in mind. The man who set up the society, a German called Sven Gabor Janszky, now runs a consultancy that predicts cultural trends. In 2003, he warned that music labels would need to change their business model; in 2007, he predicted TV would become personalised. Recent projects have included how driverless cars will affect the rail industry, the rise of intelligent assistants to replace smartphone apps and how the digitised cinema of the future will revolutionise viewer experience.[4]

As Ajax coach between 1985 and 1988, Cruyff developed the club's youth system in his own image. Technique was more important than size; thinkers more important than athletes; and developing talent always at the heart of it. As he put it: 'You play football with your head, and your legs are there to help you.'

With a team of mainly home-grown players, among them Edgar Davids, twins Frank and Ronald de Boer, and Clarence Seedorf, Ajax won the 1995 European Cup. The club was at the forefront of player development. They were also open to fresh ideas. One was to assess the psychological factors that predicted career success: without a time-machine that could measure and quantify what was in Dennis Bergkamp's mind aged 10, 14 and 18, it was a tricky question.

So, in 1994, Ajax allowed a reverse-engineering study to take place, in which 65 academy players in four youth teams from Under-15s up to Under-18s were asked a series of questions about their mental approach to becoming professional players.[5] Fifteen years later, their results were assessed based on whether the players met their goals, became professionals and reached certain levels.

The starting-point of the study was earlier work by psychologists who had identified three measurable aspects associated with high-level performance.[6] They were:

- *Motivational constraint:* The commitment of the player to reach a difficult goal, which includes hours of purposeful practice, dedication, and willingness to make sacrifices. Sample statement: 'Quite frankly, I don't care if I achieve my goals or not'
- *Effort constraint:* The ability to recover from training without feeling exhausted or burnt-out, which includes two forms of coping mechanisms: problem-focused, where you can change the outcome, or emotion-focused, where the outcome is hard to change. Sample statement: 'You were fed up with anything having to do with football'

- *Resource constraint:* The tendency to seek social support from friends or loved ones when confronted with problems or drawbacks to form a network of mutual assistance.
  Sample statement: 'You talk to someone to find out more about the situation'

Eighteen of the 65 players went on to have successful professional careers, where success was defined as playing professionally for at least ten of the 15 years following the original study (all 18 played over 100 games for a top-flight team).

Measured across all three constraints, 85 per cent of the players were correctly classified as successful or unsuccessful based on these three predictors.[7] Taken alone, the motivational and resource constraints were more effective predictors of success than the effort constraint, which showed no real difference between those who were successful or not.

The biggest surprise in the study was that, relative to the unsuccessful group, successful participants had more siblings and more often had divorced parents. The study's author, Nico van Yperen, speculated why: 'Siblings may form a kin group bound by strong ties of trust and support, and may increase social skills, which may be helpful to progress in team sports in particular. And having divorced parents may help to develop coping skills and attitudes that are helpful in dealing with all kind of problems or drawbacks.'[8]

Cruyff's parents did not divorce. His niece Estelle, though, did marry one of his former protégés at Ajax, Ruud Gullit (they divorced in 2012). Along with Marco van Basten and Frank Rijkaard, the three Dutchmen were at the heart of the AC Milan side that won back-to-back European Cups under Arrigo Sacchi in 1988 and 1989. By then, Cruyff was coaching at Barcelona, where he won four straight La Liga titles, and beat Sampdoria in two European finals, the Cup Winners' Cup (1989) and the European Cup (1992). More significantly, he established the same system in the Barcelona youth academy, *La Masia*, which went on to produce talents like Xavi Hernandez, Andres Iniesta and Lionel Messi.

The coach who led that trio to its most successful season (in 2009, Barcelona won all six trophies it contested) was Pep Guardiola, an avowed Cruyff disciple. 'He was unique, totally unique,' Guardiola said at the launch of Cruyff's autobiography, *My Turn*, published six months after his death. 'Without him I wouldn't be here. I know for sure this is why I am, right now, the manager of Manchester City and before that Bayern Munich and Barcelona.

'Before he came [to Barcelona] we didn't have a cathedral of football, this beautiful church, at Barcelona. We needed something new. And now it is something that has lasted. It was built by one man, by Johan Cruyff, stone by stone. That's why he was special. I would not be able to do what he did. You hear all these people saying: "Oh Pep, what a good manager he is." Forget about it. Cruyff was the best, by far. Creating something new is the difficult part. To make it and build it and get everyone to follow? Amazing. That's why, when I was Barcelona manager, I went to see Johan many times. I made especially sure I went a lot in my first year when we won everything, absolutely everything. The influence of Johan especially, because he was the one I shared most time with, was very important in my becoming the coach I am.'

Guardiola, who once said he would never have played in a higher league than the third division if he had not met Cruyff, was not the most influential figure behind the recent dominance of Barcelona and Spain's national team. Cruyff was. This is summed up by his response to the 2010 World Cup final, a match that pitted Spain against Holland. Spain played Cruyffian football, using space and movement imaginatively. Holland were pragmatic and violent, a style embodied by an early challenge from Nigel de Jong which caught Xabi Alonso just below the neck.

Cruyff was furious and vociferously supported Spain, the eventual winners.

Cruyff losing his temper was nothing new. He believed in a 'conflict-model', where discussions were commonplace and arguments encouraged. As item number ten on the Rulebreaker Manifesto puts it: *If rule-makers get nervous I am on the right track. If rule-makers start to fight me, I am almost there.* This was not always a positive: he fell out with the Dutch football federation and didn't turn up to play in the 1978 World Cup; then Dutch squads infamously imploded at major tournaments in 1990 and 1996. The relationships with his former clubs were also turbulent; he lasted one month as Ajax technical director in 2008, and four months as Barcelona honorary president in 2010.

After Ajax lost 2–0 at Real Madrid in a Champions League tie in September 2010, Cruyff vented his frustrations in his newspaper column for *De Telegraaf*. 'This isn't Ajax any more,' he wrote. 'Let me get to the point: this Ajax is even worse than the team from before Rinus Michels's arrival in 1965.'

The column had enormous impact. It kick-started what became known as the Velvet Revolution, a period of intra-club warfare as Cruyff, who had an advisory role at the club, demanded wholesale changes to the youth system. His view: Ajax was not able to spend big money on players, so why not go back to his heyday and create them? The former coach put together a group of his former players – Wim Jonk, Dennis Bergkamp, Marc Overmars, and later the manager Frank de Boer – and empowered them to develop the Cruyff Plan, a way of training and developing successful talents.

Among the fans who chanted 'Stand up if you support Johan!' in minute 14 of home games was Elko Born, an Ajax fan who had never seen Cruyff play. 'Like some ethereal presence, or a splinter stuck deep in our collective consciousness, Cruyff was everywhere, always ... amongst Ajax fans, Cruyff had cult status;

he was omnipotent and revered as a deity,' said Born of this period.

And so it turned out: in March 2011, Ajax chairman Uri Coronel and his executive board resigned. Cruyff's technical team took over. With De Boer as coach, Ajax, who had not won the Dutch league since 2004, won the next four league titles. So what was special about this plan?

It had five pillars, which included having a targeted transfer policy; playing attractive, Cruyffian football; co-operation at national and international level; and the academy head being involved in major decisions. It was the final element, individual player development, which gave the club its edge.

Cruyff never forgot the influences of his own career, not least Jany van der Veen, his first youth coach at Ajax. Van der Veen took Cruyff out of the Under-17s youth team when he was 16 as he felt he lacked strength. He sent him to train three times a week at the local athletics club. He dropped him, even though he knew that the team could lose without him. He put the player's development before the team results.

Wim Jonk, the head of the Ajax academy, did the same with Jaïro Riedewald. A talented centre-back, but playing within his comfort zone in the Under-18s, Riedewald was moved by Jonk and played as a defensive midfielder for a whole season. The team may have suffered slightly, but Jonk prioritised Riedewald improving his awareness and speed of action. At 19, Riedewald became a regular in the Ajax senior side at centre-back. In his second season, under a different coach, he played in midfield. That same season he won his first cap for the Holland national team. When Ajax reached the 2017 Europa League final, with a side we will hear more about later in this chapter, Riedewald played at left-back.

Cruyff himself was a product of what he called 'the player paradigm'. Putting the player first is at the heart of the Cruyff Plan. When results are on the line, it can be easier said than done. 'No matter your industry, your employees are your company's real competitive advantage,' says Chris Boyce, chief executive of Virgin Pulse, which provides tech solutions to create a culture of wellbeing and increase employee engagement and loyalty across businesses. 'They're the ones making the magic happen – so long as their needs are being met.' Pulse echoes the thoughts of Virgin owner Richard Branson, who puts employees first, customers second and shareholders third. In the case of Ajax, both Van der Veen and Jonk felt that taking Cruyff and Riedewald out of their comfort zones would produce a short-term deficit that was worth it for a long-term win.

'The player paradigm' was the one pillar that actually happened at Ajax. None of the other four pillars were properly developed and so, after some discussions with the Ajax board and supervisory board, Jonk left the club in December 2015. Cruyff left too, and so did 13 other members of staff whose job it had been to implement the Cruyff Plan.

Ruben Jongkind was one of them. He co-wrote the Cruyff Plan and for four years was Head of Talent Development at Ajax. A former running coach with a Masters in business administration, his speciality in Business Process Re-engineering came in handy when he oversaw the changes following the Velvet Revolution. He has a Spanish mother and a Dutch father, so perfectly understood the two worlds Cruyff inhabited.

Jongkind worked closely with Cruyff in developing their specific player paradigm model. That also was based on five principles:

1. *Individual development is not linear:* Players' development may vary based on biological patterns, and is rarely linear.
2. *The player is key:* Training is centred around the player, and the staff and organisation do all they can to help improve that player's technical, tactical, physical and mental qualities.

3. *The coach as mentor:* The coach observes and adjusts learning environment to stimulate the player to develop. Creates a safe space for mistakes. Make it fun and let the player explore his own solutions.

4. *Prepared learning environment:* Supervise and facilitate self-regulation. Adapt facilities to appropriate age group.

5. *Potentiality versus actuality:* Coaches who focus on results in the future, not right now, find players with high potential more interesting.

Jongkind's work on the player paradigm model directly benefited three players who went on to play in the Premier League. Christian Eriksen's one-on-one work with Jongkind three times per week improved him from a moderate runner to covering the most distance for Ajax in Champions League matches (Jonk also worked on his finishing in intense sessions). Eriksen was the only Premier League player to cover an average of 12 kilometres per game in the 2016–17 season, running more per 90 minutes than even PFA Player of the Year N'Golo Kante (second) and James Milner (third). Jongkind also made technical improvements to the running style of Toby Alderweireld, improving his agility; and with Daley Blind, enhanced his running economy.

In youth football, the team paradigm is a more typical context. This is because many youth coaches are former players who make results the priority. Jongkind relates this issue to Maslow's hierarchy of needs, a five-stage model with each new stage motivating people until it is met. The stages are: physiological (food, water, warmth), safety (security), love and belongingness (friendship, relationships, intimacy), esteem (feeling of accomplishment) and self-actualisation (achieving full potential).

In football terms, youth coaches often aspire to be an assistant or head coach, where they can earn more money, get more visibility and raise their prestige. The best way to do this is to win matches at youth level so their work can no longer be ignored. The more visible they are, the faster they rise up the club – and the more other youth coaches replicate the same path. This puts the team result ahead of individual development. No wonder one of Cruyff's ideas was to regularly rotate coaches across all levels of the organisation, so that the first-team assistant coach would take charge of the Under-8s for one week (it didn't catch on).

When Cruyff, Jonk and Jongkind all left Ajax, they took the Cruyff Plan with them. The result is Cruyff Football, this development solution that spreads the legacy of the Cruyffian football philosophy. Jongkind is second in command at 'Team Jonk', which owns the exclusive licence to Cruyff Football. 'We implement strategy at clubs and national federations around the world to develop more creative players, and those who can play a more dominant game, with the long-term goal of producing a successful team,' says Jongkind. Some of their clients are in Europe, but most are in emerging markets like the United States and Asia.

Cruyff's son Jordi has shown how the philosophy can work abroad. He was appointed sports director of Maccabi Tel Aviv in 2012, at a time when the club had not won the Israeli title for nine years. Cruyff changed the training schedule of the players – it used to be just one session per day – and made them share mealtimes together (taking a leaf out of the Thomas Tuchel management book). He also found up-and-coming coaches who fit the playing style he wanted: Oscar Garcia, Paulo Sousa, Pako Ayesteran, Peter Bosz. All went on to bigger clubs: Bosz coached Ajax in 2016–17, before replacing Tuchel as Dortmund boss.

The club was reborn. Maccabi won three consecutive Israeli league titles, the Israeli Cup and the Toto Cup, and qualified for one Champions League group stage and two Europa League group stage campaigns. There was also a focus on local talent: every Israeli player in the first team had represented Israel at youth level, while the Israel side that competed in the 2018 World Cup qualifying featured up to six Maccabi players. 'Cruyff has become the symbol of Maccabi's resurrection,' said Israeli football writer Raphael Gellar. Just like Johan at the Olympic Stadium, fans have called for a statue in Jordi's honour at Maccabi's stadium. 'Jordi is the man who changed everything here,' said Inbal Manor, editor of Israeli sports website ONE. 'I think you can compare his influence at Maccabi to the influence of his father at Barcelona.'

Taking Cruyff Football to new markets is the natural conclusion of the work of Cruyff's individual disciples like Arsène Wenger, Arrigo Sacchi and Guardiola. It's full-scale evangelism of the philosophy on a global scale. The spread of Cruyffism has been compared to that of Christianity. Religious language appears throughout his career. His first coach at Ajax, Vic Buckingham, called Cruyff 'God's gift to football', while Guardiola spoke of 'the cathedral' at Barcelona. A few pages back I found myself referring to Holland BC, Before Cruyff.

'Cruyff's admirers don't just like the way he and his teams played. They believe the world could be a better place if his vision of football prevailed,' says Dutch football expert Winner, who reminds me that Cruyff even has the same initials as Jesus Christ. 'Cruyffian football, they feel, is more beautiful, more fun and more spiritual than other approaches ... Just as Christianity spread almost everywhere and adapted to fit local cultures, so too entire countries have adopted Dutch methods and added a few characteristics of their own.'

Jongkind and his team see themselves as educators rather than evangelists. Above all, Cruyffism is a form of education, with clear links, as we will see later in this chapter, to the Montessori method of teaching. And that's exactly what employees want from their managers. When Professor Boris Groysberg of Harvard Business School asked search consultants what strong candidates look for in prospective employers, the answers were not about wealth accumulation or career advancement: 'Candidates want to work with people they respect and can learn from.'[9]

Google's people analytics team set up Project Oxygen, a multi-year research initiative that examined data from thousands of employee surveys and performance reviews to find out which behaviours characterised its most effective managers. Number one on the list: be a good coach. Even the Google employees were using football-speak. Perhaps Cruyff Football is missing a trick by only focusing on educating within football.

Their work around mindset, Jongkind continues, requires a vision of what each client needs. At Barcelona, for example, their game is based around keeping the ball, so players need to enjoy possession and the in-game pleasure that brings; they need a group effort to regain the ball as soon as it's lost; and to know that they are working to create one-on-ones for the star strikers, Lionel Messi, Luis Suarez and Neymar, to score. Cruyff's framework was based around players having the skills to create something out of nothing being helped by their team. Cruyff Football develops athletes to have the mindset to fit the appropriate team. Another team may have more of a worker-bee mentality and need more aggression, concentration and equality in the ecosystem.

We are talking less than a year after Cruyff died and Jongkind still finds himself talking in Cruyffisms. 'The starting-point of it all is the idea that you can develop and get better, that's what he always said,' he tells me. This is the key message for managers today. Are you using the individual player paradigm over the team paradigm? In other words, are you allowing your employees to develop and improve?

I ask what other lessons Cruyff preached (I just can't stop this religious terminology). Jongkind continues: 'Know your strengths and make them better. Dare to make mistakes, as only then you can truly learn. Try something new. Don't copy but think ahead all the time. And make good decisions.'

HOW TO GET AN EDGE – by RUBEN JONGKIND

1. Do what you like and what you're good at.
2. Dream big but go forward with baby steps.
3. Focus on accomplishing those steps, be happy about it and don't worry about money or a bad result.

GEIR JORDET
Learn to anticipate

Perception, exploration, anticipation / Lampard's Prospective Control / The 11 model of performance psychology / Xavi, an ideal CEO

This is where Dr Geir Jordet comes in. He is a Norwegian professor of psychology who played football for lower-league side Strømmen IF. He wrote his Masters thesis and PhD on the role of vision, perception and anticipation in elite-level performance: in short, the areas of performance where psychology can directly affect the outcome on the pitch. He has analysed Ajax players, shared his findings with the Ajax staff and works with Jongkind as a consultant to Cruyff Football. He will teach me about the art of decision-making, and show me a revolutionary new tool to improve that and other behaviour types that correlate to success.

He breaks down the key factors of decision-making in football into three segments. These also work away from the pitch. The first is visual perception, which he describes as the ability to take in and interpret information; the second is visual exploratory behaviour, or the ability to actively search and scan to collect information; the third is anticipation, or the ability to see what is about to happen.

Jordet started out his research by taking a camera to matches and filming one player for the full 90 minutes. A bit like the art-house Zinedine Zidane film *Zidane: A 21st Century Portrait*,[10] but starring Jordan Henderson instead. Jordet filmed about 250 players with close-up images, and realised that they all did different things before they received the ball.

He showed me a video of Andres Iniesta in the 2010 World Cup final. In the ten seconds before he scores the winning goal, you can see Iniesta in the middle of the pitch, scanning for information. He is making sure his eyes are exposed to the most relevant information on the pitch. That is his starting-point: before his cognitive processes kick in, before he makes a decision, before he uses signal detection and memory, he makes sure that the relevant information has hit his retina.

Frank Lampard was the same. Better, in fact. Jordet has a 16-second clip of Lampard that has become a YouTube favourite. Filmed in October 2009 during a Chelsea game against Blackburn, Lampard is in the opposition half. He looks over one shoulder, then the other. He jogs into space, and looks over both shoulders again. He is capturing information for when he has the ball. He looks around ten times in seven seconds before he gets the ball, looks up, jinks past one man (whom he saw coming) and plays a team-mate into space.

Lampard had the highest 'Visual Exploratory Frequency' in the Premier League during the period of Jordet's research. He counted exploratory behaviour as: 'A body and/or head movement in which the player's face is actively and temporarily directed away from the ball, with the intention of looking for information that is relevant to perform a subsequent action with the ball.'

The study looked into the search frequency of 64 players over 118 games, covering 1,279 game situations. Lampard averaged 0.62 searches per second before receiving the ball. Steven Gerrard was very close on 0.61. Jordet believed that players who actively scanned their surroundings before they received the ball would produce a higher percentage of successful passes once they received possession. Was he right?

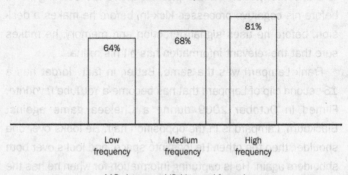

Exploratory Behaviour Frequency
Passes Completed

Low frequency: 64%
Medium frequency: 68%
High frequency: 81%

118 players – midfielders and forwards
Jordet, G., Bloomfield, J. & Heijmerikx, J. (2015)

Jordet divided the data into three sections: those who looked the least, those who looked the most, and those in between. The pass completion for those who looked the least was 64 per cent; for the middle group 68 per cent; and for those who looked the most, 81 per cent. This was an important finding but not yet proof that looking around more leads to enhanced performance. After all, maybe the 81 per cent of passes were all safe passes to the side or back to where the ball came from. He changed the variable so the data only looked at forward passes completed.

The sample set was smaller, down to 55 players, but the result was more powerful. The highest-exploring third hit nearly twice as many forward passes, 75 per cent success rate, as those players who did not explore as much, 41 per cent.

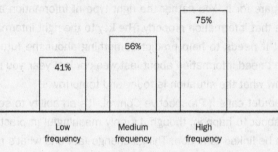

Exploratory Behaviour Frequency
Forward Passes Completed

41% 56% 75%

Low frequency | Medium frequency | High frequency

55 players – midfielders only
Jordet, G., Bloomfield, J. & Heijmerikx, J. (2015)

He tweaked the variable one more time and looked at forward passes completed in the opposition half. Again, the same results.

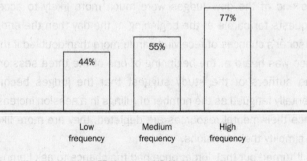

Exploratory Behaviour Frequency
Forward Passes Completed in Opposition Half

44% 55% 77%

Low frequency | Medium frequency | High frequency

55 players – midfielders only
Jordet, G., Bloomfield, J. & Heijmerikx, J. (2015)

The finding that there is a close relationship between exploratory behaviour and performance did not surprise Jordet. Increased Visual Efficiency Behaviour (VEB) leads to more information, which allows athletes to improve the ability to effectively process this information.

The same is true in our daily work. You have a meeting; you prepare for it. You gather the right type of information and you use that information properly. The key to the right information is that it needs to help predict something about the future. You don't need information about last week or last year, you need to know what the situation is today and tomorrow.

Jordet calls it Prospective Control. It's an ability to see what is about to happen, though it's only meaningful in practice if it can be linked to action. Things change fast and what's relevant now might not be relevant in three months; or if you're Lampard, in three seconds. Collecting information, updating the overview of your terrain; that allows you to act before others.

It might also help to have a snack before taking an important decision. One study examined more than a thousand parole decisions made by eight judges in Israel over a ten-month period.[11] The judges' days were separated into three distinct sessions: from the beginning of the day until a mid-morning snack break; from the snack break until a late lunch; and from after lunch until the end of the day. Judges were much more likely to accept requests for parole at the beginning of the day than the end. A prisoner's chances of receiving parole more than doubled if their case was heard at the beginning of one of the three sessions. The authors of the study suggest that the judges become mentally fatigued as the number of rulings in a session increase. Once their mental resources are depleted, they are more likely to simplify their decisions.

It turned out that Jordet once had the chance to ask Lampard about his search frequency. He watched a game at Stamford Bridge in which Lampard scored twice in a 5–0 win. Afterwards Jordet coincidentally ended up walking behind Lampard down the stairs as they were both leaving the ground. (He didn't look behind him then.) He saw Lampard again later that night. Jordet was with some colleagues from the Norwegian Centre of Football Excellence; they had gone out for dinner and were in a nightclub in London. Jordet spotted Lampard going into the VIP section and used his psychology expertise to blag his way past the bouncer guarding it. When he reached the bar, the first person he saw was Lampard, surrounded by girls. Eventually Jordet made his way over. He did not know how long he would have with the player he had watched all afternoon, so he got straight to the point.

'I filmed you today and looked at your awareness,' he said. 'Your scanning is really great: how did you get so good at it?' Not much small talk there, but bear in mind the environment was distracting. Lampard looked at Jordet and shrugged. 'I guess I was born with it.'

'Did he say anything else?' I asked. 'Nope,' said Jordet. 'That was the point when some other girls came over.'

They met again at a conference five years later. They were both on stage when Jordet spoke about his findings. Also present was Tony Carr, who had been in charge of the West Ham academy when Lampard was coming through the ranks. The moderator asked Lampard why his search frequencies were so high. 'I don't know where it came from, maybe I was born with it,' he repeated. 'Anyway, it's logical that you scan around because you need to know what's around you.'

This is the problem with asking elite performers how they became so good at something. A lot of the time they say it's natural, or they have no idea. That's no help to people like Jordet, who are trying to learn about the process. Which is why he was so grateful for the intervention from Carr, who had been listening quietly, but then interrupted.

'In the first game Frank played for West Ham, his dad [Frank Lampard Senior] would sit in the stands and shout at his son all the time,' said Carr. 'He'd say the same thing every time: "Pictures! Pictures!" He just wanted Frank to have a picture in his head before he got the ball. That was all. "Pictures!"'

Lampard sat up. 'That's true, he was yelling at me and I did what he said.'

Jordet finally had his answer. Lampard had not been born with it; nor is it particularly logical. Lampard was encouraged to 'take pictures' from a very young age and never learned any differently.

Pictures are what Jordet has been teaching to the kids at Ajax. He shows them two videos. One is of Andrea Pirlo playing for Juventus against Torino in 2012. He is in his final season at Juventus, has grown a thick beard and, aged 35, is even slower than at his peak. But still he looks around before he gets the ball; not quite so prominently as Lampard, but there it is, the look here, the glance there. And then, when he gets the ball, the screen freezes. At the point the ball touches his foot, where is Pirlo looking? Somewhere else entirely. Not his foot. He is already looking for the answer, the next move, the danger pass. He knows the ball is coming, and so he can look somewhere else.

The second video is of players training at a Bundesliga club. There are six players in a square, and three balls. The players pass to each other, and it's simple stuff. Ten metres apart, pass, control, pass, control, pass, control. They do 60 or 70 repetitions of this. The control is perfect, the passes are accurate. But every time they receive the ball, every player looks down at his feet. Pirlo doesn't do that; nor do most other players.

'What they are practising is one of the most common training skills of all, but it rarely happens in the game,' Jordet says. Who has time to look at the ball once it's at their feet? 'They are developing a skill that they do not need. Almost every single player in football, even the ones at the highest level, have hundreds of repetitions of this skill every day, when they warm up and pass the ball back and forth, one to the other. Learning to control the ball without looking at it – now that would be useful. After all, learning something new isn't that complicated.

What's hard is to forget something that you have already learned. To de-learn it.'

Ajax takes their players' VEB seriously. When they played a UEFA Youth League quarter-final against Chelsea in May 2016 (and lost 1–0), their starting eleven all had the highest VEBs in their positions in the entire youth academy.

Jordet said that anything over 0.50 visual searches per second is very high. I sneaked a look at a table of selected players he has filmed at the highest level and saw that Lionel Messi was above that. Others around him included Zlatan Ibrahimovic, Luka Modric and Pirlo.

Cristiano Ronaldo was lower than the others – but there was a reason for that. He times his scans differently, only looking immediately after every touch of the ball from a team-mate. As he sees where the ball is heading, he knows that he has half a second where he doesn't have to look at the ball, and can look around.

One player was so far above the rest it was scary. Xavi Hernandez scored 0.83 in the table. Whenever he received the ball and had not scanned and sampled the information, he played the ball back from where it came. He took no risk when he didn't have the information.

'Think quickly, look for spaces. That's what I do: look for spaces. All day,' Xavi told the *Guardian* in 2011. 'I'm always looking. All day, all day. [He starts gesturing as if he is looking around, swinging his head.] Here? No. There? No. People who haven't played don't always realise how hard that is. Space, space, space. It's like being on the PlayStation. I think shit, the defender's here, play it there. I see the space and pass. That's what I do.'

And was he born with it? No, he learned it at Barcelona, in the system that Cruyff instigated. 'Some youth academies worry about winning, we worry about education,' he said. 'You see a kid who lifts his head up, who plays the pass first time, pum, and you think, "Yep, he'll do." Bring him in, coach him. Our model was imposed by Cruyff; it's an Ajax model. It's all about *rondos* [piggy in the middle]. *Rondo, rondo, rondo*. Every. Single. Day. It's the best exercise there is. You learn responsibility and not to lose the ball.'

I ask Jordet about information overload. Is there such thing as infobesity, receiving too much information? I sometimes get stuck in the pharmacy choosing a shampoo, so how would I cope if I have six players making themselves available to me? He responds with a (hypothetical) question of his own. Say you want to buy a midfielder, and you have narrowed it down to two players. Both are the same technical level but one has an extra pair of eyes in the back of his neck. Which one would you prefer? 'We don't consciously make decisions on each of these pieces of information, but it helps us to be aware of them,' he says. 'And one type of information that's not vulnerable to overload is threats and where they are coming from. That can be just as important.'

As we sit in a hotel bar, Jordet invites me to make some decisions of my own. He pulls out a Virtual Reality headset and puts it on me like a crown. I am now in the centre-circle of a pitch, facing my own goal, with team-mates and opponents making runs all around me. My challenge is to look around – get my VEB score high – and when I receive a pass to my feet, look at which team-mate I want to pass to, and press a button to make that pass. I notice that Jordet has started moving chairs and tables away from me. He says he once did a similar demo with an ex-professional who jumped on his toes throughout and, when the moment came to pass, had a reflexive reaction to kick out his foot at the same time as pressing the button.

For some reason, I am playing at Champions League speed – this can be adjusted depending on the individual being tested – and just as I start looking around for team-mates, the ball comes quickly towards me. I turn to the first team-mate I remember spotting, who now happens to be standing behind an opponent. My pass is intercepted. A score page comes up:

Overall score: 0
*Vision and decision-making is very poor, roll up your sleeves,
there is a lot of work to be done.*
Possession of ball: 0.2s
Team-mates seen: 8
Opponents seen: 4
Time looking away from the ball: 1.5s

I try again and, after a few zeroes, get a few scores in the twenties and thirties. I now understand why Lampard and Xavi look around so much. But I can feel myself improving. I look around more and more before receiving the ball, and spot a few team-mates making decent runs. When the ball comes in, I swivel and play it towards an overlapping right-back. The score page shows:

Overall score: 100
*You showed superb vision and execution on and off the ball,
well done.*
Possession of ball: 1.4s
Team-mates seen: 10
Opponents seen: 10
Time looking away from the ball: 1.3s

My work here is done. This rates among my finest sporting achievements, even if there is only one witness (though I do make Jordet take photographic evidence). I end with a few more zeroes, but quite honestly who's counting now?

This tool works, Jordet says, not just because it improves decision-making the more you do it, but because it's a game simulation tool accessible on smartphones and tablets, so does not necessarily require a VR headset. Jordet has built this product called TEAMTI Football, which is only the first package of a larger suite he is developing in this sphere. Each of the other tools is also related to mental performance, and it's no coincidence that they all give you an edge. Jordet calls it his '11 model of performance psychology' and it includes 'adapt to new contexts, self-regulate learning, manage relationships, cope with pressure, cope with adversity, cope with success'. These are all above-the-shoulder behaviour types to develop an edge, and I have examined each of them, in various ways, throughout this book.[12]

Jordet wants to normalise moments of stress for young players so they are better equipped to cope with them. His tool paints scenarios to enable youngsters to deal with various situations: for example if you are 14 and have been dropped by your coach. How will you respond to that? Or you're in the car on the way back from a game and your dad is asking difficult questions about your performance. 'You will hear him saying something and then get choices to respond and be graded on those choices,' Jordet says. 'And it's gamified so the youngsters playing it get it straightaway.'

This brings us back to those wonderful players who score highly on Jordet's VEB chart. They have all experienced setbacks: they have lost matches, been dropped, suffered injuries. They have felt hopeless, tense, frustrated and worried. This is normal. Jordet is creating tools to cope with it. Brilliant players recover; they show the resilience to cope with it, and make the right decisions, at speed, to succeed.

Playing the simulation tool taught me something else about brilliant players. They don't play a pass without seeing it; the brilliant players look so early that they play the pass before we have even seen that they have seen it's a pass. And it is not about having the best eyesight, but about how you assess the information. As Jordet put it: 'I would have more faith in Xavi's abilities as a CEO than someone whose scores are very low on this.'

Options, options, options. Therese Huston, Faculty Development Consultant at the Center for Excellence in Teaching and Learning at Seattle University and author of *How Women Decide*, advises to always give ourselves three options. Huston gives the example of a company that is thinking about building a parking garage. 'Instead of just should we build a parking garage or not, three options would be: should we build a parking garage, should we give all employees bus passes, or should we give our employees the option to work from home one day a week?'

Once you generate more options, you can take a better decision. Xavi never has two options. He sees things so quickly, and clearly, that he always has at least three, and probably more, to choose from. It's why he makes such good decisions.

HOW TO GET AN EDGE – by GEIR JORDET

1. Hunt for information. The earlier you can get it, the more effectively you can process it, and the quicker and better you can use it to creatively exploit your competitive field.
2. Learn. What's good enough today is not enough tomorrow, and winners are constantly and actively looking for ways to improve what they're already doing, every single day.
3. Cope. Performing on good days is easy, and everyone can do it, so our ability to deliver even on bad days is the key. This comes from individuals' resilience, but equally about how we support each other at those moments.

STEVE LAWRENCE
Beat birthday bias

Relative Age Effect / Montessori in football and business / Drivers of development / The multi-age solution

Steve Lawrence used to take his kids to the local park every Saturday morning. While his wife Lynne had a lie-in, he would read a newspaper with a coffee and his boys, Tom and Jamie, would kick a ball around. They usually ended up near the north-east corner of the park, hoping to attract the attention of older kids who were having a training session there. Both were under five but desperately keen to play in an organised environment. Lawrence, an architect, signed them up to football lessons in a nearby school.

He had no idea how that decision would change his life. Lawrence has ended up writing academic papers, and working closely with Ajax and the Dutch football federation. He has also become a key partner in Cruyff Football. He found an edge, and is now helping others exploit it. This is his story.

Jamie, his younger son, had starting walking at eight months, and Lawrence remembers him significantly favouring his left foot when taking his first steps. He kicked predominantly with his left foot too, but would practise with his dad on his right foot. When Jamie was seven, he was playing in a match in an indoor sports centre around the back of the old Highbury stadium. Lawrence was watching on from a balcony. Another man, who Lawrence guessed was a scout, sidled alongside him and pointed at Jamie.

'Is that your son?' he asked.

'Yes.'

'Nice player. When's his birthday?'

'August the 22nd.'

There was a sharp intake of breath. 'He'll never make it as a professional,' said the man. And then he walked off. Lawrence never saw him again.

What was he talking about? Lawrence had no idea, but he looked up August birthdays online and found a 1985 academic paper called 'Hockey Success and Birthdate: the Relative Age Effect', which pinpointed the issue in competitive sport.[13] The problem comes from having any cut-off date used for grouping children together – in England that date is usually 1 September, while across Europe it is 1 January.

There has long been a historical age bias to 'early-born' players, because they are the eldest in their age groups and so, from a very early age, are used to being bigger, faster, stronger, and for those reasons are seen as better, than their peers. It can become self-selecting: an enthusiastic but December-born six-year-old might come up against players 11 months older but in the same age group and quickly lose interest if they can't keep up.

As Lawrence put it in his academic paper, 'The Age Advantage in Association Football': 'At young ages, team managers and coaches, inadvertently or otherwise, operate a strategy of fielding the oldest possible team within the competition rules. Whilst this strategy achieves the short-term aim of winning the next match, a systemic disadvantage is established in that it simultaneously reduces the available talent pool.'

Early-born players tend to play more matches from a young age, as they are more regularly picked at the expense of late-born players. The knock-on effect of that is late-born players tend to have longer careers, as they have fewer injuries and have more matches left in their tank. Wayne Rooney (October) is early-born, while Harry Kane (July) is late-born.

You can see the Relative Age Effect in action throughout football. Lawrence did a study of over 8,700 matches across nine different Dutch youth competitions and age categories covering seasons 2014–15 and 2015–16. His finding was that the impact of RAE in terms of points per game was similar to home advantage. As he put it: 'Is there a coach who wouldn't choose "home advantage" in a crucial match?' In a study by data company Gracenote Sports of the squad make-up of 22 European and World Cup youth tournaments between 2002 and 2015, spanning over 5,200 players, the results were stark.[14]

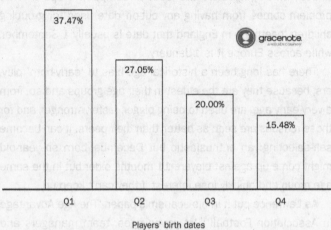

Players' birth dates

Over one-third of all competing players were born in the first quarter of the year, while just 15 per cent were born in the final quarter. At Under-17 level, the results were even more shocking: 44 per cent of the 1,069 players were born in the first quarter, and only 12 per cent in the final quarter.

The same was true of the *Guardian*'s 'Next Generation' feature. In the 2016 edition, 43 per cent of players were born in the first three months (I was guilty of this too: my pick for that year, Malang Sarr of Nice, was born on 23 January). One study looked at RAE in Serie A and concluded that late-born players earned, on average, lower wages – and that the wage gap appears to increase with age.[15]

Academics believe that RAE is a marker for other conditions including ADHD, schizophrenia and obesity, where late-born children are disproportionately disadvantaged.[16] There's even a Chinese paper that identifies disproportionately fewer late-born CEOs in S&P 500 companies.[17] The study, called 'Born Leaders: The Relative-Age Effect and Managerial Success', shows that 29 per cent of CEOs were born in winter (92, early-born) while 21 per cent were born in summer (66, late-born). The other effect was that the late-born CEOs were associated with higher market valuation and better stock performance (that might be because those who do succeed in achieving those positions might be better than early-born counterparts).

Lawrence says that as RAE is so prevalent in education, it is inevitably replicated in the higher echelons of business; and the more competitive the environment, the greater the bias. He claims that there would be higher relative age bias at Oxford University, for example, compared to other universities; and that the business world inherits the age bias that was in that echelon to start with.

This is where he finds his edge. 'If there is a systemic bias, in any system, it means that system is operating below its highest level of efficiency, because it is not making best use of resources available to it,' Lawrence explains. 'My argument is that in order to maximise potential, you have to get rid of the bias in the system. And to do that, you have to go to the point at which it starts, which is age five. If it exists, it goes all the way up. But if you know it's there, then you can exploit it.'

Lawrence's son Jamie was accepted into the Arsenal academy and played with Benik Afobe and Kane in the Under-9s and Under-10s teams. At the age of ten, Arsenal let him go. Lawrence considered it to be the Relative Age Effect in action. 'I have no doubt that if Jamie was early-born, he would be an England international by now,' he told me in 2014.

As an architect used to finding and solving problems, it bugged him. He wrote to the FA, who said that they knew about it but there was nothing that could be done. By now, Jamie was playing in park pick-up games and holding his own against kids three or four years older.

Lawrence's wife Lynne inspired his solution. She had been a talented actress who devoted her career to teaching, working her way up from an assistant at a Montessori school aged 19 to becoming the executive director of the Association Montessori Internationale.

Dr Maria Montessori, the first woman physician in Italy, established the Montessori method in 1907. She devised a 'scientific pedagogy' after being asked to evaluate delinquent children in Rome. The tenets include uninterrupted blocks of time, to develop concentration; freedom of choice over what to play with or study all the time; free movement within the classroom; a discovery model where students learn not from direct instruction; and lessons with multi-age groups.

That was it! Lawrence had found his solution. A multi-age group training set-up meant someone with an August birthday would not always be the youngest in the group, but for one year would be among the youngest, the next be in the middle, and the next be among the eldest.

By now, the whole family had moved to Amsterdam, where the Association Montessori Internationale has its headquarters. Jamie had spent six months in the youth team at Haarlem, a club near Amsterdam that took him on, before Ajax saw him and signed him aged 16. He played in the same team as his neighbour at the time, Christian Eriksen.

The Lawrence family lives in a fourth-floor apartment overlooking the Olympic Stadium. Along the landing are many of his architectural drawings, one of which is an early version of the London Olympic Stadium he was asked to draw up. In the living-room is a giant framed Roy of the Rovers cartoon strip. The apartment's location was a coincidence; but it proved to be not the only connection between the architect, Cruyff and the Montessori method.

Lawrence got to know the people running the Ajax academy while Jamie was there. It turned out Cruyff wanted to install a 'Football Development Centre' and the Lawrence family provided a holistic solution: Lawrence the architect worked on a 'Spatial Development Manifesto' to define the characteristics a new centre would need, while Lynne the educationalist offered her expertise to ensure a 'prepared environment' to accommodate 'dynamic movement' and 'observation'. All three are crucial principles of Montessori. They also appear in the pillars of the Cruyff Plan.

'There is a lot of crossover between the ideas of Cruyff and Montessori,' Lawrence tells me over sushi in an Amsterdam restaurant. 'Both were leaders in child development and both had an analytical eye that rethought paradigms after going back to first principles.' The impact of both has been enormous, and perhaps it's no coincidence that, as a child, Cruyff went to schools that were influenced by Montessori thinking. Lawrence is convinced that businesses that share three key Montessori principles can optimise their talent. The first of these components is the environment (for pupils a school, for young footballers an academy, for employees a workplace): the environment has to be conducive to the development of the individual and fitted to that purpose. Lawrence, who designed the Ajax academy, took great inspiration from Google's London HQ. 'It's been designed to give individuals great freedom but also great support, with different places to work, a focus on food and nutrition, an interconnectedness so the flow of ideas is not interrupted by barriers or walls. It's an environment in which an exchange of ideas can take place.'

The second principle is that the individual, whether they are a pupil, academy player or employee, is self-directing and has an inbuilt desire for development. The key to this is to allow the progress of the individual within the business to go at the pace of that individual; and to have them tracked by observation and monitoring rather than testing, as that introduces turbulence into the system.

The third principle is the training of the trainers in the Montessori system: the teachers, academy coaches or workplace managers. This is an essential component and is more of a guiding one than anything else. The guide, as Lawrence calls them, has to start out with the knowledge of what the normalised trajectory of development is likely to be, and then to quietly direct those around the individual to stay on that pathway. Manager is not the best term for this role. Lawrence prefers 'driver of development'. We learned in Chapter 2 that this is how Thomas Tuchel and Didier Deschamps, who constantly observe and rarely criticise, see themselves.

Lawrence knew that multi-age training groups would mitigate Relative Age Effect, and it was to his great delight that Ajax, at the instigation of Jongkind and Jonk, adopted a multi-age group model in 2014. The club developed three broader age groups – 6 to 11, 12 to 15, and 16 to 19 – which allowed for collaboration in training, involving mixed age groups to help peer-to-peer learning, and mentoring programmes. Each player would have a different experience: sometimes being the oldest in the age category with the responsibilities that brings, and sometimes being the youngest. The intake at Ajax shifted from 80–20 in favour of early-born players to something more like 60–40.

By the time the Cruyff Plan was in effect, Jamie was off again. He left Ajax for Sparta Rotterdam and then spent two years at RKC Waalwijk, where he fell out with the coach. He moved to AS Trençín in Slovakia, whose owner Tschen La Ling was a former team-mate of Cruyff's at Ajax. Jamie became a key player in midfield as the team won back-to-back Slovakian League and Cup doubles.

Lawrence did not stop working on solving the issue of Relative Age Effect in sports teams. He developed a way around it, using an average-age rule based not on a cut-off date for individuals but on a team or squad having to meet an average-age target. The oldest player in the squad cannot be more than two years older than the youngest player in the squad. That way, coaches could pick a team across the spectrum with a variety of players involved, as long as they met the Average Age Rule cut-off.

The Dutch FA, also known as the KNVB, was interested in Lawrence's work, and commissioned him to find out how much extra playing time children receive based on their birth month, and how often older teams beat younger ones. 'Are we doing enough to give opportunities to children born in every month?' asked KNVB's football development co-ordinator Lennard van Ruiven. 'We need to find out if this age discrimination is unfair.'

Van Ruiven agreed to pilot a nationwide six-month season of multi-age football at four different age levels, running into 2018, to see if Lawrence's plan of multi-age football can work. Lawrence has also developed a free mobile app, called miTeamsheet, to allow the quick and easy calculation of a team's average age.

Lawrence continued to seek answers from the FA but kept getting fobbed off. He now occasionally resorts to winding up those who work in the FA Talent Identification team on Twitter. But with a solution now in hand, he took his case to the European Commission, claiming that RAE is 'systemic discrimination in breach of the Lisbon Treaty'. As he explained to me, 'It operates globally and advantages one cohort of individuals whilst disadvantaging another. As such it conflicts with basic ethical values of fairness and in particular it conflicts with the fundamental provisions of the Treaty on the Functioning of the European Union. The imposition of universal cut-off dates by the FA establishes systemic relative age discrimination. I have asked the Commission to determine the use of such rules as illegal.

'The European Commission has written guidance in the "Study of Discrimination of Sportspersons in Individual National Championships" which says: "Equal treatment requires abolition of both direct discrimination and *rules* which ... in fact lead to unequal treatment." This is the core of my argument.'

In 2016, as collateral from the fall-out of Cruyff's departure from the club, Ajax dropped Lawrence's multi-age-group concept. Lawrence is sanguine about this: 'It's only a matter of time until they return to it,' he says. 'They were open-minded enough to try it out and found it a bit too difficult, but the desire for competitive advantage will encourage them to try again.'

Ajax's European success in 2017 put the spotlight back on the Cruyff Plan. Ten of the 14 players who played in the Europa League semi-final first leg against Lyon, which Ajax won 4–1, were aged 21 or under; only one was born in the first three months of the year; five were late-born, with birthdays in the second half of the year.

It's hard to avoid the argument that the Cruyff Plan played a key role in this success. Over half the team came through the Ajax academy and played in the multi-age group games insti-gated by Lawrence. The team's average age has gone down – it was the youngest ever to reach a European final – while perfor-mances have improved. 'We are pleased Ajax has been success-ful with a group of players that have benefited from the individual development methodology, the ingrained attacking style, and the training methods tailored to distinct age groups, implemented by the Cruyff Plan,' says Jongkind.

This is where Ajax has found its edge. Another consultant to Cruyff Football, Bob Brouwaeys, instigated a similar method within the Belgian football federation. Since 2012, Belgium's Under-17s and Under-19s have run two sides in parallel: an early-born XI and a late-born XI. This is to ensure that no late-born players fall between the cracks in the development stage. And people still wonder why Belgium, a tiny country of 11 million, have topped FIFA's world football rankings for much of 2016 and 2017.

Jamie Lawrence, meanwhile, continues to develop his career. In January 2017, he signed a new contract with Trenčín, who are building the side around his presence in midfield. His dad remains hopeful that he will one day play for his country.

Lawrence retains close links with the team at Cruyff Football and continues to consult on future projects that involve the Cruyff name. In China, there is an agreement to set up the first Cruyff/Montessori school collaboration. Talks continue over perhaps the greatest legacy of all to the man: a Cruyff Football Club that fulfils the Cruyff vision from top to bottom. 'There was one thing above all else that Johan cared about,' Lawrence says, 'and that was education. Improvement was always more important to him than the result.'

HOW TO GET AN EDGE – by STEVE LAWRENCE

1. Understand your environment; prepare and adapt it for your purposes.
2. Bias in a system represents a waste of resources; identify bias, mitigate it for yourself and exploit it in competition.
3. Derive coherent principles from your analysis of complexity; apply the principles, monitor the feedback and evolve the principles.

TOMORROW'S WINNERS
Develop winning mentality

Halting Dutch slide / Twin Games / Six steps to winners' mentality

Dr Geir Jordet says that when it comes to making the right decisions, the threats and barriers to progress are just as important to understand as the opportunities. That was one of the reasons behind a KNVB conference that took place in Utrecht in December 2014. It was planned long before the national team finished third in the World Cup playing a 3–5–2 system that was distinctly un-Dutch (and therefore hated by Cruyff). The two questions addressed at the conference were simple: What does Dutch football actually stand for? And how do we make that future identity-proof?

It was not only Dutch football's biggest names, Cruyff included, who were involved, but some of the game's leading thinkers. Arrigo Sacchi offered his opinion.[18] And so did Arsène Wenger. 'I believe there are two outstanding things about Dutch football,' the Frenchman said. 'The culture of Dutch football has a sound philosophy of attacking play. And the Dutch have personality. Dutch people are sometimes seen as arrogant because they openly state their belief that the way they are doing something is the only way to do it right. I like that. It simply means you are confident in yourself and your ideas.'

Laura Jonker was paying very close attention. She was head of Research and Intelligence at the KNVB, and it was her responsibility to lead the research into the ensuing report published 18 months later. *Tomorrow's Winners* is a 200-page call to arms to halt Dutch football's slide. 'None of what's in the report is based on guts and opinion, it's all based on solid facts,' Jonker told me over a coffee in Rotterdam. 'The reaction has been positive, and that's because we asked everyone to be involved, so they could never say, "I was not asked to contribute."'[19]

The findings are stark: the average age of players in the Eredivisie, the Dutch top division, is dropping; the league's turnover is static while that of rival nations like Belgium and Portugal grows; the intensity of Dutch games is a long way short of other leagues;[20] and coaches devote far more training time to improving their attack than their defence.

The report says that the 'offensive, dominant and creative football' once synonymous with the Dutch has become universal. It concludes: 'Dutch football is standing still, physically, technically, as well as in terms of tempo, (winner's) mentality, and especially defensively.'

The report took 18 months to put together. Jelle Goes, the KNVB technical manager, conducted interviews with Wenger, Lars Lagerback, Ronald Koeman, Jürgen Klinsmann, Hansi Flick, and many others, for the report. 'The moment you are satisfied with where you are is the moment you start to lose,' he tells me. 'It's a pity we didn't start this process four or six years earlier.' Goes had a point: Holland failed to qualify for the 2016 European Championships and at the time of writing could miss out on a place at the 2018 World Cup.

Not long after I spoke to Goes, the KNVB sacked national coach Danny Blind. On the day that Dick Advocaat was confirmed as Blind's replacement at an antagonistic press conference in May 2017, the KNVB carried out another recommendation from *Tomorrow's Winners*: a keynote speech from a thought leader in the coaching world. They wanted someone who could inspire the next generation of coaches; in fact the current generation, given that the audience included Frank de Boer, Phillip Cocu (PSV coach), John van den Brom (AZ Alkmaar coach) and Mark van Bommel (PSV youth coach). The thought leader they invited was Thomas Tuchel.

'There was a gulf in class between Tuchel and the people in the audience who were listening,' said Michiel de Hoog, a Dutch writer present at the event. 'It's been a while since we heard a Dutch coach talk as eloquently, funnily and lucidly as Tuchel did.'[21] De Hoog had advocated that the role for Holland coach be advertised externally, just as Belgium's federation had done when looking for a new coach. The Belgian FA received interesting applications from around the world and settled on Roberto Martinez. Holland chose Dick Advocaat, who had held the position twice before (1992–94 and 2002–04). 'And we still don't even know what his vision of football is,' sighed De Hoog.

Jonker was particularly interested in *Tomorrow's Winners'* findings on mentality. Her PhD was on self-regulation, and it won a prize in 2012 for the best sports thesis in Holland and Flanders. By then, she was already advising the KNVB on research projects involving grass-roots football, but soon after she was heading up a Research and Intelligence Unit which looks at all aspects of development: increasing player participation, fan engagement, coaching education, with the ultimate aim of improving individual players, teams, coaches and competition infrastructure.[22]

Talk about the spectre of Cruyff and the 1974 World Cup final, though. One passage seems to blame him alone for Holland's collective mindset. 'The Achilles heel of Dutch football (often obscured by the technical and tactical ingenuity) is coming to light: a clear arrogance in the concept of play combined with the inability to outclass and win against opponents at the decisive moment!'

Cruyff, Jongkind and other partners of Cruyff Football contributed to the document. Two of them, Jasper van Leeuwen and Michel Hordijk, had their proposal rubber-stamped as a future recommendation. Van Leeuwen was the Manager of Youth Scouting at Ajax and Hordijk the Technical Manager for Under-6s to Under-12s: they promoted the revival of street football principles by introducing Twin Games for younger age groups on smaller pitches. Instead of 11 versus 11 for Under-6s and above, teams of 12 play in two games of six-a-side, and the scores from both games are aggregated to decide one winning team. They originally piloted this scheme with Ajax's amateur partners in Amsterdam; that was a success, and from 2017–18 onwards, Dutch players aged 6 to 12 will play Twin Games on smaller pitches.[23]

One of the phrases heard most often at the conference was 'we don't train enough winners'. The consensus was that modern players are too pampered, don't take enough individual responsibility, and that 'virtually no professional club has specifically described this theme in the training programme or paid any structural attention to this element'.

These are the recommendations for developing the winner's mentality:

1. Emphasise the malleability of the brain
2. Place more value on commitment rather than the result
3. Encourage a positive self-image
4. Set goals for 'mastery' instead of 'performance'
5. Ensure coaches also have a growth mindset
6. Include a growth mindset/performance evaluation system[24]

It can be no coincidence that some of these sound like the 14 Rules outside every Cruyff Court. There is certainly crossover with the theories that he brought back to the club after the Velvet Revolution. The best hope for Dutch football fans is that the talent developed from the Ajax academy can revive Holland's struggling national team.

HOW TO GET AN EDGE – by LAURA JONKER

1. Always set goals. Set them high, but realistic.
2. Remember the most important questions for learning reflectively: Who am I? What do I want? What am I capable of?
3. Every learning trajectory is unique, so reflection is a unique process and the improvement goals you set are your personal goals. The interaction between player and coach or student and teacher is unique, so don't pretend that one size fits all in learning situations.

AZ ALKMAAR
Create your own future

The Arnhem Group / Ask what talent is / Purpose before outcome / Fighter pilot video games / Your advice, their motivation / Create your own future

The recommendations in *Tomorrow's Winners* cause heated debate in a rented office-space in Arnhem where, every month, nine promising youth coaches based in Holland meet to share ideas. This is where Holland's Tuchels of the future congregate. The space has a bar and they chat in a boardroom with a glass ceiling. A metaphor for their status if ever there was one. They don't agree on everything, but have two pillars of belief that unite them: 1) results do not matter during development stage; 2) talent is not static: it can be trained and improved. One coach gripes that if his team loses even one match, he has to justify himself to a demanding boss who wants to know why.

One of the members of the Arnhem Group is Bart Heuvingh, who is elite lifestyle coach at AZ Alkmaar. He shares an office with Marijn Beuker, AZ's head of performance and development. The pair have made improving mindset a key pillar of the club's training programme. I pay them a mid-season visit at the club's newly built training centre in the peaceful village of Wijdewormer, and the scene could not be more Dutch: beyond the training pitches outside are flat fields, grazing cows and twirling wind-mills. All that's missing are some tulips.

Even before I have taken my seat in their office, Heuvingh laughs uproariously as Beuker gives me a beginner's lesson in growth mindset.

'Raise your hand.'

I lift up my hand above my head.

'Now lift it as high as you can.'

It goes higher, and my arm is now straight.

'Now lift it a bit higher.'

Without thinking, I raise it higher, giving my sore shoulder a good stretch.

'See – we can always do more than we think we can.'

Beuker is a sports science graduate from the Johan Cruyff University. His task is to overhaul Holland's traditional top three of Ajax, PSV Eindhoven and Feyenoord, teams with three times the budget of AZ. He is a fast talker, quick with jokes and does a passable Cockney accent. Heuvingh is younger and evangelical about his role. He has just had lunch with a new signing from the first team. The player had started the season well. 'I asked him, "How can we make you better?" and he was really surprised,' says Heuvingh. 'I don't think he realised that everything can be improved.'

These two came up with the motivational slogans that appear in every dressing-room in the new complex:

'You see the best player in the world. I see room for improvement.'

'I start early and I stay late. Day after day, year after year. That's the reason they call me successful now.'

'Play for the logo on the front of the shirt and they'll remember the name on the back.'

Adorning the walls of the narrow corridor between the dressing-rooms – designed to feel like a tunnel with the first-team training pitch at the end of it – are black-and-white action photos of former AZ first-team players, with the AZ red shirts providing a bright splash of colour. Players include Jimmy Floyd Hasselbaink, Jozy Altidore, Vincent Janssen and Graziano Pelle. One wall shows a row of current first-team academy graduates, with a gap in the middle. Just the silhouette of a player with the message: 'Who's next?'

Their work is about far more than adding positive reinforcements in interior design. AZ won the Dutch academy of the year in 2015 and 2016. This new site, only 20 minutes north of Amsterdam, is likely to attract more talents from the city and give youngsters who would traditionally choose to join Ajax another option. Increasingly, it's one they are taking. This is no place for those who believe talent is static.

'We are the club to come to when a player wants maximum development,' says Beuker proudly. Thirteen academy graduates were in the first-team squad for the 2016–17 season. The team finished sixth and reached the Dutch Cup final. Within two months of its opening in May 2016, Real Madrid sent a 25-person delegation to learn more about their methods.

These two understand that growth mindset is more than a buzzword that praises and rewards effort. For them, growth mindset is a learning behaviour that encompasses hard work, innovative strategies and support from others. They are also aware of 'false growth mindset', which could be just having a positive outlook, or believing in empowerment and innovation until poor short-term results get in the way.[25] Research in growth mindset in business shows that employees feel happier, more empowered and committed (they are 65 per cent more likely to say that their company supports risk-taking), and receive more support for collaboration and innovation. Beuker and Heuvingh are a walking advert for the concept.

Their club's ambition has changed in recent years. AZ was Dutch champion in 2009, when Louis van Gaal coached a young team that contained Moussa Dembélé, Jeremain Lens and Mounir El Hamdaoui to an unlikely league title. Three months later, the DSB bank belonging to owner Dirk Scheringa went bust. AZ's budget, almost overnight, went from €45 million to €21 million. The five-year plan after that was to steady the ship, become financially stable and still compete. They did that, finishing in the top four in three of those years and winning the 2013 Dutch FA Cup. Since 2015, a new five-year plan is in place: to win more trophies, and reach the top 25 of Europe's club co-efficient rankings. (At the time I visited the club, they were number 42. FC Basel, perennial Swiss champions, were number 25.)

The plan, devised by managing director Robert Eenhorn and former technical director Earnie Stewart, is all about having a vision and the patience to see it through. 'The difference with this club is the way we look at the development of our players,' says Beuker. He starts with three questions. 'Answer these, and you can do everything with them.'

- What is talent?
- How do you get the maximum out of people?
- How do you create a winning team?

I have put this talent question to almost everyone I've met while researching this book, and have never received the same answer twice. Every club has a different idea of what talent looks like, and even most individuals within a club have a different idea. The AZ model runs through the club from top to bottom, and it defines talent as the player who has the vision to:

- Understand the game
- Make their own choices
- Be technically and physically in optimum condition
- Be 24/7 focused on performing
- Be strong personalities

Beuker and Heuvingh cannot affect the technical conditioning, which is a standard requirement at all football clubs. But they can, and do, look to develop skills in the four other areas, and often in innovative ways. They don't have the money to compete with their rivals, so they look for an edge elsewhere.

'Understanding the game is not about tactics,' says Beuker. 'Tactics is a strange word here, as for me it means I tell you what you have to do. That means there is no chance for creativity and adaptability. We don't say tactics but we say game intelligence: that is not about what you do, but why you do it. That is a crucial difference. Over the course of the next ten years I think the most important progress will happen with regards to cognitive skills and game intelligence. With this in mind, we want to develop a different kind of player who is capable of seeing spaces and opportunities independently of his position or the team's tactical plan.'

We met Simon Sinek, an expert in managing millennials, in Chapter 1. Beuker points towards a copy of his book *The Golden Circle* on his bookshelf (there are no football books there at all, only leadership books and *Moneyball*, of which more later). The 'Why' is a central part of the book, which starts with the suggestion that every organisation has a golden circle:

WHY = The Purpose
HOW = The Process
WHAT = The Outcome

Most people can explain what they do at work and how they do it. This is the proof of the why. The 'how' is the specific actions taken to realise the why. The why is sometimes harder to pin down. Profit is not an answer, as that's a result. The 'why' is about purpose and cause. What do you believe in? For example, the social capital at Athletic Club de Bilbao. The 'what' is connected to the new-cortex part of the brain, which controls rational thought and language. The 'why' is connected to the limbic part of the brain, which deals with trust, loyalty, decision-making and behaviour.

Sinek uses the example of Apple. Their 'what': we make computers. Their 'how': our products are beautifully designed and easy to use. Their 'why': we believe in challenging the status quo and doing things differently.[26]

Beuker says the most innovative businesses, including football clubs, look from the inside and work their way out. An example: your child is 11 years old and a decent footballer. One of the top three clubs wants him at their academy. So does AZ. The other clubs will pitch themselves with an outside-in argument. They might say: 'We are a good club, we have a great stadium and have won so many Dutch titles. Everyone knows us all over the world; your child should train with us.'

An inside-out pitch from AZ would be more like this: 'We think differently at AZ, we believe in challenging and developing our players and turn them into respectful, curious and self-aware young athletes. We happen to be a football club too. Would you like your child to join us?' Which one do you think is more compelling? Think about your workplace and whether the company is looking outside-in or inside-out. If you can identify the why, then make sure everyone else knows about it too.

This is what accounting firm KPMG did in 2015. One workplace survey – which was not just limited to millennials – showed that working for an organisation with a clearly defined purpose would motivate two-thirds to work harder in their jobs. A similar study showed almost half of the workforce would take a pay cut to work for a company with an inspiring purpose. In response to these, KPMG asked its employees what they did at the company. Bruce Pfau, at the time the vice-chair of Human Resources, explained that KPMG wanted employees to build a stronger emotional connection to the firm, and to look at their work from a different perspective.

KPMG produced a video called *We Shape History*, highlighting its role in historic events, like managing the Lend-Lease Act to help defeat Nazi Germany, or certifying the election of Nelson

Mandela in South Africa in 1994. They encouraged story-telling from the bottom up to reframe the role of their employees, and developed a tool to create individual posters which answered the question: 'What do you do at KPMG?' One woman responded: 'I combat terrorism,' referring to the money-laundering that KPMG helps prevent. Another employee, who works with the credit system to help secure loans for family farms and ranches, wrote: 'I help farms grow.'

KPMG called it the *10,000 Stories Challenge*, figuring if they got that many, they would allow the company two days' extra paid holiday that year. They ended up with 42,000 individual stories.[27] As a result, scores on the annual employee engagement survey rose to record levels, with 90 per cent reporting that the initiative increased their pride in the company. Having a purpose is also central to the way that AZ operates. It's about the 'why'. Always inside-out. As Sinek says: 'Leaders hold power and those who lead inspire us.'

This translates into the other factors that go into talent, explains Heuvingh. 'Making your own choices is about decision-making. We know that the difference between a good player and a phenomenal player is 0.1 or 0.2 seconds in terms of reaction time for the brain to process information. So from a technical point of view, we ask players not to move the ball, but move the opponent.'

AZ uses an Israeli software tool called Intelligym, a neural-tracking originally designed for a fighter pilots game that triggers the same neural pathways as football. It allows the coaches to track and improve visual perception, anticipation, dividing attention and decision-making skills, while the players get smarter at reacting to information connections.[28]

I watch two Under-12 players at their screens. There is a blue team and an orange team, and the player has to switch team whenever the screen tells him. The goal, a small green bar, regularly changes size and position along the side of the screen. The team members look more like Pac-Man figures than footballers. 'The software trains the same part of the brain you need to play football with, but if the software looks too much like football, the wrong perception-actions are being trained,' says Heuvingh. Other tests include firing at dots or bursting balloons.

Each youngster has two half-hour sessions per week with the game. The club haven't worked out if it's more effective for them to play at home or at the training centre, but they know that between the ages of 11 and 14, it improves cognitive flexibility.

A group of AZ players, along with counterparts from PSV, were part of a 2016 academic study conducted by Geert Savelsbergh. Over ten weeks, one set of players used video analysis to identify certain passes and runs, and the other set used Intelligym. Both were then assessed in small-sided games. The skills of the players who had used Intelligym had improved by 30 per cent more than the others.[29]

In the training centre's Mind Room, a Virtual Reality headset similar to the one I tried with Geir Jordet is set up for all the youth players to improve what the coaches call 'their game intelligence on a conscious level'.

Beyond Sports is an Amsterdam-based company that has three products to improve visual perception and decision-making: custom scenarios, to educate players based on the club/coach's preferred tactics; match analysis, which relives specific moments from games played to analyse player performance (the match data can also be used to visualise distance, formations and speeds); and a new fan experience, so you can relive your favourite player's greatest moments through his eyes. Ajax, PSV Eindhoven, AZ and the KNVB have all bought into the system, as have two clubs in the Premier League.

Mark Snijders, a former midfielder who played alongside PSV Eindhoven's 2017 Dutch title-winning coach Philipp Cocu at AZ, is the Beyond Sports sales director. 'I was the guy that made him look good!' he laughs before giving a demonstration of the headset. Beyond Sports is developing similar simulations for American football and cycling.

Their sister company, Beyond Care, is working with post-traumatic stress disorder patients with a VR solution based on eye movement desensitisation and reprocessing.[30] And the product works: a study conducted by the University of Utrecht showed that individuals improve their 'spatial updating' via immersive virtual reality better than through window systems (like laptops) or real-life exposure. Not all clubs have a Mind Room like AZ. The KNVB keeps the system in their medical centre, while PSV has it in the first-team gym. 'We really like that idea,' director Sander Schouten tells me. 'More players use it when it's integrated into the gym environment: they can make a clear link from working on their legs, or their arms, to putting on the headset and improving their eyes and their mind.'

The 24/7 focus makes up the core of Heuvingh's own Top Sport programme. He educates players about nutrition, recovery, social media dangers, visualisation[31] and sleep patterns, so ultimately they can make their own choices. He asks parents of 11-year-old players to allow their child to stay up until midnight on the night before a game, just so they can see how they perform the next day on less sleep than usual. 'We ask them to do it for a couple of days, and by then they understand the experience and take their sleep a lot more seriously. If, after the experience, you give them sleep advice, they will engage it in their lifestyle.'

AZ hired a nutritionist who told the players what to eat and then complained when they ignored her advice. Heuvingh's great strength is in communication. 'A player will come to me and say, "I'm a bad eater." That's not right, though. "No, you eat badly, and that's different." We can change the infrastructure and train will-power to improve that.'

The subtle difference in messaging is crucial; Heuvingh despairs of the coach who times a player's sprint and says, 'Ach, you're slow.' Better for him to say, 'That time was slow, how are you going to develop that?'

'I ask them what they want and where they want to go. If they say, "Barcelona", and most do, then I say that I can help them, if they are willing to take responsibility. The key explanation is how *your* advice fits with *their* motivation.' He asked one age group to WhatsApp him images of their breakfasts every morning for five days. For the rest of the year, that group of players started their days with the perfect meal.

In a team environment, I wonder if too many strong personalities could be disruptive. For Heuvingh, this is about the messaging again: 'By "strong personality" we mean someone with the ambition to work for something that is very difficult to achieve but he still works on it, he delivers in training, in the game – he has mental toughness to go on.'

Stressful situations created by the coaches develop these personalities. The coach may referee a game and deliberately penalise one team for ten minutes to see their reactions. He may ask one player to play in a new position. 'When you know their fears, it's easy to work on them.'

Heuvingh recently took a team to a tournament and, the day before the final, asked which players would be scared to take a penalty if it went to a shoot-out the next day. Five players put up their hand. Sure enough, the game went to penalties. Along with the coach, Heuvingh nominated the same five players to take penalties. They all scored and won the game.

'Winning is important, but we call it learning to win,' says Beuker. 'For successful people, it is about the process and the result. First you look at the required and ambitious end result. Then you ask yourself what has to happen to achieve it and you stick with the process. Players realise that winning is the ultimate goal – but that can only happen if the process is right. We can't only focus on the result. And our choices are not made to win in the short term, it's about the long term.' The coaches like to choose exhibition opponents from a higher age group so the players get used to dealing with failures in their career and learn how to cope with them and recover.

The next question that Beuker answers is: 'How do you get the maximum out of people?' A slide comes up on his office TV screen.

1. Begin with the end in mind
2. Raise the bar (keep high expectations)
3. Always look for improvement
4. Give people responsibility and empowerment of their own development and learning process
5. Stimulate creativity and solution-focused thinking with players and with staff
6. Look for discomfort and challenges. Use FEAR: Face Everything And Respond

AZ is proud to have a learning environment set up to improve staff as well as players. All coaches have an intrinsic motivation assessment – we will be looking at the importance of intrinsic motivation, where process is seen as more important than outcome, in Chapter 5. The difference is that for players, developing is often the opposite of performing. Players train 95 per cent of the time, and only 5 per cent of the time, on match-days, do they perform. In the workplace, we perform for 95 per cent, or probably nearer to 99 per cent, of the time. So we only devote between 1 and 5 per cent to development. There is often no time for it, little infrastructure in place, and therefore our working lives are all match day and no training. Who can possibly improve in those circumstances?

The result of the AZ method is to produce football that is varied, dynamic, with initiative and high intensity, and within a good co-operative organisation. They do not focus on 4–3–3 or any other set formation. 'We want to produce footballers and strong personalities who can play independent of all different surroundings on the pitch,' says Heuvingh.

Beuker fires another question at me. What is a coach? 'Someone who can improve the individuals in his team,' I say, thinking not only of football bosses but also editors and producers I have worked for in the past. 'How you create a winning team is the same for business as in football,' he responds.

He shows me a picture. It's a black-and-white still of a stage-coach drawn by six horses with five cowboys sitting on board. 'It's a way of getting from somewhere now to where you want to be next,' he says. Once again, the messaging is crucial. 'A coach accompanies you from where *you* are now to where *you* want to go. Not where *the coach* wants you to go.'

The next image he shows me is of an iceberg, with the tip just visible above the water's surface. Under the heading 'Make a Personal Profile', Beuker explains that 'What you do', as a player, represents the visible part of the iceberg. Underneath the surface are the words: 'What you think' and 'What you want'.[32] These guys need to know that information to help their players get there. This is why communication is so important. Heuvingh believes that talking off the pitch, in one-on-one sessions but also in groups, brings improved results on it.

AZ trainers and coaches sit with every player in the team – there are 120 across all the age levels – and ask them where they want to go. What do you want to develop? What is your long-term plan? What do you do that you would give yourself a ten out of ten for? That question puts a reference in the player's head, often giving them the end-point for which to reach. They want players to plan for their ideal situation.

Beuker and Heuvingh have defined talent, and identified how to get the best out of people. Get those two right, they believe, and the winning team will not be far off.

To this end, AZ also uses analytics in recruitment. In 2015, AZ signed a striker called Vincent Janssen from second division side Almere City for €300,000. Despite only scoring three goals before November, he ended the season as top scorer and first-choice number nine for the Holland national team. He moved to Spurs for €22 million, a club record sale for AZ, almost equal to the club's annual budget (and more than twice the €10.75 million that the new training centre cost).

Janssen went on a hot streak as soon as 2016 began; he scored 16 goals in the first 13 games of the year, earning his call-up to Holland's first team. He scored on his first start for the national team, a penalty in a Wembley win over England. One day later, *AD Sportwereld*'s front page ran a headline over a picture of Janssen with a quote from the forward that read: 'It can always be better.' This line, according to Beuker and Heuvingh, said everything about Janssen's mindset (which was challenged in his first season at Tottenham Hotspur).

The next challenge for AZ was how to invest the Janssen funds wisely. This is where former Oakland A's manager Billy Beane, the inspiration behind *Moneyball*, and a consultant to AZ, comes in. General manager Max Huiberts has just returned from the USA and there is a buzz around the centre that he has visited Beane. Exactly how involved Beane is remains a mystery. All Heuvingh will say is: 'What he does is help us look at output of players in new ways. And we are looking at other ways of developing talent. Both are important and complementary in our system.'

I ask Heuvingh about his predictors for success. 'Decision-making. Growth mindset. And speed.' He never looks at a player below the Under-18s and decides that he will make it. If he recognises that potential, then he believes it will change his behaviour towards the player. 'I won't name my tips for future talents,' Cruyff once said, 'because it will hinder their performance.'

Beuker and Heuvingh are disrupters, part of a new breed of coaches challenging the traditional authoritarian model. They are about more conversation, more collaboration, more pastoral care. 'We don't copy others, we are critical about our processes and we don't believe in a status quo at a football club, so we are always progressing,' says Beuker. By 2020, he wants AZ to have 75 per cent of its first team developed from the academy.

I wonder where this charismatic duo wants to end up. What are their goals? Heuvingh wants to help the Dutch national team win trophies, 'and not as a trouble-shooter but because they see that understanding, developing mindset and having a professional lifestyle is really important to performance'.

HOW TO GET AN EDGE – by BART HEUVINGH

1. Focus on development with each individual, because current measures of achievement tell you where they are, but not where they could end up.
2. Make individuals responsible for their own development and help them bend their limiting beliefs.
3. Build strong individuals by focusing on prevention, instead of repairing broken ones by fixing their problems.

'My ambition is to have an important influence on the vision, programmes and way of working within a club and with that, win the highest prizes possible,' adds Beuker. 'For AZ, that could be making it into Europe's top 25 and winning trophies here in Holland, but ultimately it means winning the Champions League with a club where nobody expected it to be possible.'

One of his players also has a grand plan. Joey Jacobs is 16 and a member of the AZ youth academy. He is smart, punctual, unfailingly polite and speaks perfect English. He lives in Amsterdam, and has been with AZ from the Under-12s. This season he split off from his peers as he was promoted to play for the Under-19s. He is the youngest in the squad and found it hard to start with but is now settled in the side.

Jacobs could not be more effusive about the set-up at AZ. His decision-making is improving thanks to the combination of training-ground work, Beyond Sports VR goggles, and the Intelligym programme. Beuker and Heuvingh have encouraged him to think about what he eats and drinks, when he sleeps, how to develop his growth mindset – and how to deal with the media. And he's only 16!

The highlight of his seven years at AZ came in 2015. He was voted Player of the Month, and was allowed to choose a first-team player to join for a one-on-one lunch. He picked Jeffrey Gouweleeuw, who in January 2016 moved to Bundesliga side Augsburg. 'I asked him about certain defensive situations, how I can improve my game and what steps I need to take,' he says, his face breaking into a grin. 'It was incredibly helpful and of course inspiring to be with someone who has experienced it all and can offer advice. Now he is in the Bundesliga, which shows his level.'

The long-term ambition for Jacobs is to be in AZ's first-team squad by the time he is 19. He sees the ten players in AZ's squad at the moment aged 21 or under and thinks it's possible. 'Our coach John van den Brom is not afraid to give young players a chance and that is great for us all. It makes us believe we can do this.'

The godfather of Dutch football, Johan Cruyff, would approve of the set-up at AZ. For all his brilliance as a player, coach and innovator, he was above all an educationalist. Jacobs has seen Cruyff's clips on YouTube and understands the debt that Holland owes him.

'All my team-mates feel the same as me, we know how important Cruyff has been in Dutch football,' says Jacobs. 'What a great player! He made the country what it is in the football world and we appreciate that. He always played beautiful football. So did his teams. And he made people think about the game.' The Cruyff spirit of education and development is thriving at AZ. It is a club that doesn't want to predict the future, but wants to create it.

On 25 April 2017, the day Cruyff would have turned 70, Ajax announced that their stadium, the Amsterdam Arena, will change its name to the Johan Cruyff Arena. In a statement, the club said: 'The city council, the management and supervisory boards of Stadion Amsterdam and Ajax … are convinced that this will do justice to the memory of Johan Cruyff and express the hope that the Johan Cruyff Arena is an inspiration for players from all over the world.'

And so, Cruyff's legacy lives on. It goes beyond the Foundation, the Institute, the courts that bear his name and even Cruyff Football, the consultancy that embodies his thinking. His legacy is a conceptual one: that talent can be optimised through individual development. It sounds simple, and it is. Put the individual first – ahead of results – and implement a development infrastructure; the rest will follow.

'He was one of the prophets who came out of nowhere, yet at the same time seemed to fulfil some kind of manifest destiny,' wrote *The Times*'s European football correspondent Gabriele Marcotti.[33] Like many quasi-religious figures, Cruyff had an inner strength to deal with doubters. This inner strength included coping with adversity, with pressure and with success. These behaviours are crucial to finding an edge. When Cruyff died, his great friend Guus Hiddink, also a Cruyff disciple, was in charge of Chelsea. Hiddink stabilised the club after a tumultuous half-season under José Mourinho; then Antonio Conte went on to win the Premier League title in his first season in charge. It felt like Chelsea had rediscovered its edge. My next stop was to Chelsea to learn about resilience – little expecting that one of its staff would tell me about being held hostage at gun-point in Mexico …

HOW TO GET AN EDGE – by MARIJN BEUKER

1. If someone offers you an amazing challenge and you are not sure if you can do it, say yes and learn how to do it later.
2. Choose what FEAR means to you: Forget Everything And Run – or Face Everything And Respond.
3. If you don't want your children to fall into the swimming-pool in your garden, ask yourself: do you build a fence around it to keep them out, or do you teach them how to swim?

RESILIENCE

TIM HARKNESS
Improve your own resilience

Hostage ordeal in Mexico / The resilience algorithm / PIIP and starlings / Confidence 1 and Confidence 2 / Posture and decisions

It's springtime in the well-to-do village of Cobham. Mini Coopers gleam in the showroom next to the train station. Retirees potter in the allotments that back onto the local cricket pitch. Daffodils have popped up in the front garden of the cottages that flank the nearby village hall. Horses from the local riding school munch on grass in a field overlooking the training pitches where some of football's elite players work every day. This is the scene outside the Chelsea training ground, and inside, the mood is just as serene. With good reason: the team is closing in on a first Premier League title under new coach Antonio Conte.

The canteen is quiet today. The coaching staff, wearing training-tops with their initials in fluorescent yellow, are eating lunch: it's salmon or steak with rice or pasta and grilled vegetables. The low hum of conversation is all football: which of the on-loan players look good, how the weekend's fixtures might pan out. Eden Hazard pops in, looks around, and before he has a chat with someone, goes around each table shaking hands with everyone.

The power of small rituals, so beloved by Thomas Tuchel, also exists in Cobham.

I am here to talk to two of the longest-serving members of the Chelsea backroom staff about resilience: what it is, and whether it can be measured and improved. A study carried out by the Cranfield School of Management, called 'Roads to Resilience', stated that resilient companies have better reputations, loyal staff and suppliers, and strong relations with their customers. Resilience, it concluded, should be at the heart of corporate strategy.

My first appointment is lunch with Christophe Lollichon, who joined Chelsea as goalkeeping coach back in 2007. During his time working with Petr Cech and then Thibaut Courtois, Chelsea won two Premier League titles, three FA Cups, a Champions League and a Europa League. It feels like a pretty gentle opening question to ask him if he thinks he is resilient. His response, a story about the time he was held hostage with a gun to his head by Mexican bandits on a bus, leaves me spluttering on my salmon.

It happened a few years ago, when he was on holiday in Mexico with his wife. They were on a tourist bus, driving through the Chiapas region in the south of the country, when they heard gunshots. Five Zapatista bandits burst onto the bus demanding money, passports and electronic equipment. Lollichon was sitting at the back with his wife, a trained nurse, 'which makes her fantastic in emergency situations'. The couple handed over their watches and some money – Lollichon was determined not to hand over his phone, so trapped it between his knee and the seat in front – and the bandits told the driver to take them to the next village. 'We were now hostages,' says Lollichon.

The bandits slapped down any passengers that stood up or tried to confront them. One bandit held a machete that he threatened to use on a man who could not take a ring off his finger. Another went back to Lollichon and demanded more money. He pointed a gun at his forehead. Lollichon vividly remembers seeing the faces of his four children – in chronological order, oldest first – appear in his mind. He did not give them his phone, and the bandits' attention soon turned onto someone else.

This was when another bus pulled alongside the hostages and made it clear that assistance was on the way. The bandits jumped out, and the horror, 'like something out of a movie', was over. Not for everyone: some had nightmares, could not eat and needed counselling. But Lollichon felt nothing. 'Look, I am an emotional guy, but for me, from the next day, it was over. Maybe it is in my subconscious, but I can still get on the bus. I watch a film with a scene like that and it's fine. I was not off my food! Does that make me resilient? What do you think?'

It seemed to be the case, but before I could answer the question with any confidence, I needed to understand exactly what resilience is. Luckily, after lunch I meet with Tim Harkness, a good friend of Lollichon's. Harkness knows. A softly spoken South African who loves cycling, Harkness is Chelsea's head of sports science and psychology. He has been at the club since 2009. Before then, he worked with golf and squash professionals. He also helped Abhinav Bindra become the first Indian athlete to win an Olympic gold medal in an individual event, taking gold in the 10-metre air rifle in Beijing 2008. He has trained dogs, studied baboons and worked with the military. He understands resilience. He has studied it for seven years and he strongly believes that it can be improved; and that we can all develop our emotional lives just as we do our intellectual lives.

Resilience, for Harkness, is 'the ability to accurately assess threats and opportunities and to allocate emotional resources accordingly'. Resilience is not perseverance, or 'keeping on pedalling'. It's an *accurate* assessment, which means it has to be flexible. If you persevere and you continue to get nowhere, then you are wasting energy. 'Sometimes when you fail,' he says, 'you should just give up.'

That's exactly what the Coca-Cola company did 79 days after launching New Coke in the summer of 1985. Its market share had been slipping for the previous 15 years, so the company introduced a new drink that had out-performed the old Coke, now called 'Classic', in taste tests. But there was uproar when the new drink came out; the taste tests did not factor in the bond that consumers felt towards the brand. When the return of the 'Classic' version was announced, it was the front-page story on virtually every paper in the USA. In two days following the return, over 31,000 consumers called the company to thank them. At a ten-year anniversary of the New Coke story, Coca-Cola CEO Roberto Goizueta praised the decision as an example of 'taking intelligent risks'. The company had shown resilience in accurately assessing the threat, or rather lack of opportunity, of New Coke. It was failing, so they gave up.

Harkness remembers that firestorm with a smile. He has developed his model of resilience as a set of steps starting from the premise that resilience is based on skills and not character. One person may be more resilient than the next, not because of their character, but because of their ability to construct, practise and execute these skills of resilience. 'The better we are at executing the component skills of resilience, the more accurate our emotions will be and therefore the more effective our actions will be,' he explains. 'This is not about having less emotion but about having more accurate emotion.'

Why is that important? Harkness points me to the work of Italian neuroscientist Antonio Damasio, who studied people with damage in the limbic system of their brains, where emotions are generated. They were not able to feel emotions, and they couldn't make decisions. Harkness, like Damasio, believes that emotion is an important requirement in decision-making. 'Today this idea ... may not raise any eyebrows *among neuroscientists*, I believe it's still a surprise to the general public,' Damasio wrote in his book *Descartes' Error: Emotion, Reason and the Human Brain*.

Their argument is that accurate emotions lead to better decision-making.

The component skills of resilience make up an algorithm, which Harkness compares to a recipe. He provides the ingredients and it's up to each of us to execute each component (or 'make the cake') as best we can. Some of us might already have these implicit skills; for others it could take longer to learn. The key point that Harkness repeats is that the skills are learnable. This is how we can improve our own resilience, and gain an edge.

It's tough to learn new skills when we are in the middle of a crisis; as Harkness puts it, you don't want to learn to rock-climb while you're falling down a mountain. So as we sit in his office, he in his ergonomic chair and me in a comfortable armchair with a footstool that pops out when you lean back, he patiently explains his component skills of resilience.

1. ABC: Ability to separate adversity from consequence[i]
When we have an adversity, it feels like it leads to a consequence. For example: you stepped on my toe, so I am angry or upset. But there is a belief between the adversity (being stepped on) and the consequence (being angry). So if I'm angry about the toe-stepping, it's because I believe that I'm being threatened in some way. Whatever emotion I have, a belief leads to that emotion. So we need to interrogate our beliefs. Remember: part of being resilient is having an accurate response to threats and opportunities, so we don't waste energy on needless concerns. But how can we know what is an accurate response?

2. Ask three questions: Me? Always? Everything? (or Intent/Frequency/Impact)
There are three questions we can ask to evaluate whether an emotional response is accurate or not. The first: is it me, or was the event intended? There may be a difference between the

impact on me and intention of the other person. In our example, you may not have stood on my toe on purpose. Second question: does this always happen, or is it only happening now? An accurate assessment of frequency – both in the past and in predicting the future – can help devise a correct emotional response. Maybe you always stand on my toe whenever you see me. That might affect my response. The third question: is this everything? If our whole relationship revolves around you standing on my toe, then I might be more upset. This is about the wider context of our relationship, and whether the event affects my opportunity to have a good life, by impacting on my overall well-being. If the answers to these questions are all yes, then a stronger emotional response is more appropriate.

3. Calibrate emotions to external not internal world

Harkness grew up in Empangeni, a small town on the east coast of KwaZulu-Natal in South Africa. His parents kept chickens in the back yard. When he was about ten years old, Harkness would feed them every night. As he walked back through the garden to his house, he was convinced that wolves were ready to pounce on him from behind. He'd try and shake off his anxiety but would end up running home. The running made his anxiety worse. Calibration, as he describes it, is the ability to distinguish between an Anxiety Problem (nervous about the wolves) and a Danger Problem (there really were wolves there).[2] If you treat an Anxiety Problem as a Danger Problem, you don't solve the anxiety. If you treat a Danger Problem as an Anxiety Problem, then you are missing the opportunity to affect it. You may have spotted many footballers cross themselves and say a little prayer before kick-off. But what would happen if they didn't cross themselves? Or rather, can they not cross themselves? They may believe that crossing themselves works, but are they prepared to subject that opinion to an evidence-based test? They might win even more if they don't cross themselves! There is a difference between an Anxiety Problem and a Danger Problem.[3] Calibration is the skill to know which one you are dealing with, as they require different solutions.[4]

4. Ability to doubt

Being resilient is not about being confident but the opposite: to question our emotions, especially our negative ones. At moments of anxiety, you may confirm your physiological response with intellectual thought: if you are anxious, you give yourself reasons why you should be anxious. But if you doubt yourself, you can ask another question: what would change your mind? That requires evidence which makes you an emotional scientist. If you apply a level of rigour to your professional or intellectual life, why not apply it to your emotional life too? The ability to perceive reality objectively and be prepared to learn and change your mind about things is a key component skill in resilience.

I thought back to Lollichon's hostage story and asked myself the three key questions around intent, frequency and impact. Is it always Lollichon? Was the attack intended to single him out? Absolutely not. What about frequency: does this always happen to him when he's on holiday? Again, no. In terms of impact, the wider context of his life, did it affect his well-being? It could have done. But it has not impacted on his holiday plans in the future, considering he intends to climb Mount Kilimanjaro and travel through the Amazon rainforest. So we can assume that he has not been put off by his experience. Maybe the response, for him, was accurate after all. He will tell us more about the particular resilience required by goalkeepers later in this chapter.

Harkness believes that being aware of these component skills, and executing them, can improve resilience. The ability to maintain perspective, through understanding intent, frequency and impact, is an important skill for an elite footballer; as it is for anyone working in any team environment. I have tried to work these component skills into my personal and professional life, and it has helped enormously.

The additional skill comes in calculating how much time and energy to invest accurately into these threats and opportunities. Harkness breaks this down into the mnemonic PIIP, whereby the Probability and Impact need to balance the Influence and Planning. The more probable something is to happen, the more attention you need to pay to it. The more impact it will have on you, again the more attention you should give it. If you are worried that a plane you are about to board will crash, then you need to balance the Probability (highly unlikely) and Impact (great) with your Influence (nothing you can do about it) and Planning (make a will). When you have the right balance of PI and IP, it will reduce your stress levels. This is also part of resilience.

Highly resilient individuals use effective, if implicit, resilience algorithms. The algorithms don't have to be complicated. For Harkness, the secret to having high levels of resilience is making the algorithms simple, even if their execution is not.

He gives the example of a murmuration of starlings; the birds fly together, a collective response to threats and opportunities in their landscape, while also making a beautiful, coherent story. Their algorithm is a simple one: fly close, fly in the same direction and don't bump into any other starlings. Follow those rules and you'll get a murmuration. It's a simple algorithm but hard to execute. 'I believe that many seemingly complex behaviours are the skilful execution of simple algorithms, rather than mediocre execution of complex ones,' he says. Harkness wants to make his algorithms around resilience – based on those component skills – explicit, so we can apply them to our own lives. He has already shared some of his findings with experts in the financial industry.

His comments remind me of what Neil Bath, Chelsea's head of youth development, told the 2014 International Football Arena conference about players of the future. 'As the mental demands placed on players on and off the pitch increases, so will the importance of psychology in football,' he said.

'Clubs are already putting in place mentors or role models for the players. The coach's technical knowledge, as well as his personal skills to manage people, will need to be continually updated – and they will need to get the balance right between letting players express themselves with showing attention to detailed planning in training and games.'

Bath discussed the 'Five Rings' that make up every Chelsea player's Individual Action Plan. It featured Medical, Lifestyle & Welfare, Mental, Technical/Tactical and Physical & Movement Skills. He also shared the six building-blocks of Chelsea's Development Culture. This was in the form of a pyramid, with three blocks along the bottom representing Talent, Trust, Philosophy. The next two up read Ownership and Standards, with the final block, on top, denoting Leadership.

Chelsea's youth teams have been hugely successful in recent years: winning the FA Youth Cup in 2010, 2012, 2014, 2015, 2016 and 2017. The last side to win the competition three years running was Manchester United's Busby Babes in the 1950s. The team also won the UEFA Youth League, the Champions League for Under-19s, in 2015 and 2016. As Bath described the Chelsea vision of football development, it was quite clear that talent is only a small part of it. 'Talent is something that doesn't exist, it's just a construct,' says Harkness. 'What you call talent is totally different to what I might say.'

Harkness questions everything – as you would expect from someone with high resilience himself (after all, he has seen eight different managers at Chelsea) – and sometimes wonders how much resilience actually matters. 'What matters is if I can do my job, or if I come home and love my wife and look after my kids,' he says. 'Resilience is a tool that can impact and improve performance, but as a free-standing entity it means nothing.'

The 'Roads to Resilience' paper looked at the importance of organisational resilience by conducting case studies on the approach to risk management taken by eight companies that have maintained their reputations and balance sheet. The companies were AIG, Drax Power, InterContinental Hotels Group, Jaguar Land Rover, Olympic Delivery Authority, The Technology Partnership, Virgin Atlantic and Zurich Insurance. The principles uniting the companies were that they had exceptional radar, they built strong relationships internally and externally, they had respected and respectful leaders, they could respond rapidly and had diversified resources.

Harkness believes his algorithm of resilience can work in an organisational structure. Just as he thinks resilience is not about *character* for the individual, he says it's not about *culture* in the organisation. Again, it's about the skills. He recommends the following steps: spread the skills through a group of people via a training or educational programme; share exactly the same algorithm of resilience as described on page 175; develop a common language so people can communicate attitudes and ideas to describe their process of evaluating emotions or reflecting on intent, frequency and impact; create an environment of trust where people are comfortable discussing this; divide labour, so it becomes an organisational strength if individuals collaborate to improve resilience. If there's enough trust, this can be a powerful tool, not just effective in the workplace but also in life.

Harkness sometimes pauses mid-sentence to choose his words carefully. He does this during his precise definition of resilience. He takes a similar approach to explaining confidence, which he also feels is commonly misperceived. You can run and kick with confidence, but those terms are the description of something else that produces an outcome. It's the running and the kicking that win football matches, not the confidence.[5]

One of the dictionary definitions of confidence is how likely you think something is to happen. Harkness calls this definition

Confidence 1. Confidence 2 is more important. It's about how you feel about Confidence 1: is that level of likelihood correct and are you okay about that? He gives an example. France played the All Blacks in the 2007 World Cup quarter-final in Cardiff. Before the game, France coach Bernard Laporte had said his team had a one-in-ten chance of winning. At the time it sounded unconfident but it was merely an assessment of the likelihood.

The French felt fine about Confidence 1. If anything, they thought, 'We are better than that.' So they went into the game with a high level of Confidence 2, which is the confidence that produces performance. The misconception is that people try and maximise Confidence 1 – 'I am super-confident that I will win this/overcome this challenge' – but that reduces Confidence 2. The lower you set Confidence 1, the more likely you are to have high levels of Confidence 2. France went on to win the game 20–18.

If your Confidence 1 levels are inaccurate, your performance will be affected. Maybe you will be too submissive (low level) or too aggressive (high level). Talk of these states reminds Harkness about his work on body language. He leaps up to search for a theory that he investigated during his time working with golfers. It's a fascinating one that still holds true in performance culture now.[6] When humans are in conflict or under pressure, there are three social states and therefore three potential body language positions we adopt. One is submission, which is saying, 'There's no point fighting as I will give you what you want anyway.' One is aggression, which has elements of bluff to it, by making yourself as big and scary as you can. The final one is assertiveness, which is a call to arms: 'Let's do this and test our relative abilities.'

The submissive state is a non-athletic position. You are deactivating and disarming your body and you cannot hurt anyone. You can't hurt from the aggressive position as that's a bluff, but you can cause impact through assertiveness.

In golf, you may not be aware of your psychodynamic state, but Harkness identified how those physical positions impact on our ability to execute skills. Submissive golfers, who lack confidence or commitment to a shot, will hook the ball because they can't engage their core and turn into the shot correctly; aggressive golfers, who are trying too hard, will slice the ball as their shoulders, forearms and wrists are too tense; assertive golfers have an engaged core with relaxed extremities, and hit the ball straight.

Physical posture not only affects your ability to think, but also the conclusions you end up drawing. Studies have shown that more comfortable postures can enhance performance in memory tasks,[7] while less comfortable positions can improve reaction times.[8] Increased feelings of power can result from adopting high-power poses for even one minute.[9]

Harkness reminds me of the pencil test: two groups of people were given a pencil and asked to rate how funny they found a series of cartoons from Gary Larsen's *The Far Side*. The first group held the pencil in their teeth. The second group held the pencil between their lips. The group who had the pencil in their teeth thought the cartoons were funnier. Having the pencil there forced them to smile; you can't smile with a pencil between your lips. The hypothesis: physical posture can affect the conclusions you draw about the world.[10]

I sit upright at this point, no longer slouching in the cosy embrace of the psychologist's chair. Too late. Harkness has spotted my change of posture and already reminded me to check out how elite footballers sit. He says you very rarely see them slouch or sit asymmetrically. It's because they are assertive. They are successful. They are resilient. Now, I think I understand why.

I believe my knowledge of resilience, complete with Harkness's four-point resilience algorithm and PIIP formula, gave me an edge as I completed this book. If only I had learned it earlier! Developing skill-based coping strategies is essential for new business owners dealing with fresh challenges all the time. According to research by StartUp Britain, 80 new businesses were registered every hour in 2016. Each one would benefit from this resilience algorithm. My next task was to find a start-up equivalent in the football world, a footballing entrepreneur with a unique approach to resilience. Ralf Rangnick, a German influencer once linked to the job as England coach, was just the man.

HOW TO GET AN EDGE – by TIM HARKNESS
1. Learn from best practice because it is out there.
2. Be prepared to change your mind and use evidence to learn.
3. Seek algorithms that solve recurring problems.

RALF RANGNICK
Believe in your start-up

Hardship of entrepreneurs / Innovate without fear of failure / Can-sellers stun Europe / Rangnick's talent formula / Empowered local innovation / Transformational leadership for Generation Me

The first time I met Ralf Rangnick, it was autumn 2014 and we were both due to speak at the International Football Arena conference hosted by FIFA. He chuckled at the memory of the moment he fell in love with English football. He was a 21-year-old student on a year abroad at Sussex University, as part of his English and PE degree from Stuttgart University. In November 1979, he went to the old Goldstone Ground and watched Brighton & Hove Albion lose 1–4 to Liverpool. 'I remember the Brighton fans singing "Seagulls! Seagulls!" despite the score-line,' Rangnick said. 'And the Liverpool fans responded "Seaweed! Seaweed!" Scouse humour, huh?'

Rangnick famously played for the local non-league side Southwick FC and, before his first away game, against Steyning Town, he turned up 45 minutes before kick-off ready for a warm-up routine. His team-mates warmed up ten minutes before kick-off. After his debut, he ended up in Chichester hospital with three broken ribs and a punctured lung, but even that did not put him off. He played 11 times for Southwick, a short period but one that moulded him as a coach: 'The most important thing for me was the amount of coaching we did on the pitch,' he said. 'There was hardly a situation where we didn't spur each other on, doing some coaching among ourselves or motivating each other. That was totally inspirational for me.'

Nearly 30 years later, Rangnick himself is the inspiration. He has become a specialist in 'start-up clubs', after taking two

German sides from the lower divisions and turning them into successful Bundesliga teams.

I want to ask Rangnick how he does it. The start-up environment suits some people more than others. As Eric Greitens, the former Navy SEAL whose charity, The Mission Continues, helps veterans find purpose through community impact, put it: 'Entrepreneurs *choose* a life of hardship. They *choose* a life that will hopefully be marked by joy, achievement, laughter and satisfaction, but will also inevitably be marked by confusion, chaos, change, fear and disappointment.'

Rangnick embraces it. He is a firm believer in talent above the shoulder. It's what he looks for in his players. And resilience is at the core of his vision of optimising talent. 'The biggest untapped potential lies in the footballer's brain,' he has said. This is how he finds an edge.

His 'crucible moment', the leader's challenge that we spoke about in Chapter 2, came as player-manager of sixth-division side Viktoria Backnang, after losing a 1983 pre-season friendly to Valeri Lobanovski's Dynamo Kiev. Rangnick could not get over the Dynamo pressing game and was convinced they were fielding two or three extra players. That was the basis of his philosophy that continues to this day. It has had a major influence on German football.

The first start-up was Hoffenheim. A ninth-division village club when SAP software mogul Dietmar Hopp bought them in 2000, they were in the third division when Rangnick was appointed coach in 2006. He had already coached, with mixed success, at Ulm, Hannover, Stuttgart and Schalke. Working with a blank canvas suited him perfectly: he had asked for a sports psychologist at previous clubs but was denied one, 'because we have never had them before'. At Hoffenheim, he got one. This is key for the start-up entrepreneur: having the space to innovate without fear of failure.

Rangnick steered the club to successive promotions, and made it to the Bundesliga. Once there, Hoffenheim destroyed

Borussia Dortmund (4–1), Hannover (5–2) and Hamburg (3–0) and were leading the table after 19 games. 'That's the kind of football we want to play one day,' said Borussia Dortmund's then coach Jürgen Klopp. The run of form was not sustainable; during the winter break, top scorer Vedad Ibisevic injured his cruciate knee ligament and the team scored only half as many goals in the second half of the season.[11] Hoffenheim still finished in an impressive seventh place.

The second 'start-up' was two teams owned by energy drinks company Red Bull. Rangnick was having coffee with a friend in the summer of 2012 when he received a phone call from the assistant of (founder and owner of Red Bull) Dietrich Mateschitz. That same day, Mateschitz jumped in a helicopter with Gerard Houllier, Head of Global Football at Red Bull, and paid Rangnick a visit.

Rangnick was persuaded to join as sporting director of two teams, Red Bull Salzburg and RB Leipzig (Mateschitz had also established New York Red Bulls, and teams in Brazil and Ghana). Mateschitz had bought Austria Salzburg in 2004 and changed almost everything: the team name, the stadium name, the colours of the jersey, the badge.[12] They lost fans as a result, but the stadium filled up again when the football improved. Rangnick established Red Bull Salzburg as regular Austrian champions and one of the best talent developers in Europe. We will look at some methods that relate to the Salzburg success story later in this chapter.

The other team was RB Leipzig, which did not even exist before 2009. That's when Red Bull bought the licence to a fifth-division team, SVV Markranstädt, and moved it eight miles east to Leipzig. Again, Red Bull changed the kit, the crest and the team name, although the request to call the team Red Bull Leipzig was rejected by the German football league. So RB Leipzig, with the RB standing for *Rasenballsport*, or 'Lawn Ball Sport', was born.

RB Leipzig was still in the fourth division when Rangnick joined, but straightaway won promotion to the third and then the second division. The next step took a little longer, and it was only when Rangnick appointed himself as coach for the 2015–16 season that RB Leipzig made the final leap, into the Bundesliga for the first time. Leipzig before Rangnick had one promotion; it won three in the following four seasons.

RB Leipzig's debut season in the top flight could scarcely have gone any better. The team was second at the halfway stage and spent the last 22 rounds of the Bundesliga season safely in second place. Incredibly, the team qualified for the Champions League group stages at the first time of asking. I loved the image conjured up by Leipzig-based journalist Guido Schafer: 'It was quite possible that Didi Mateschitz was back on Laucala [a private island in the South Pacific] at the weekend,' he wrote in the *Leipziger Volkszeitung* after another Red Bull win. 'In one hand he has a photo of Ralf Rangnick; in the other hand, a photo of [RB Leipzig coach] Ralph Hasenhüttl; in his third hand, a can of Red Bull – because in the world of Dietrich Mateschitz, nothing is impossible.'

This was also the season when their rivalry with Borussia Dortmund ignited. The German football league (DFL) has ownership rules, known as the 50+1 rule, which guarantees no single investor can gain majority voting rights. This is part of a fan-owned structure that keeps down ticket prices and avoids the kind of calamitous ownership regimes that are *de rigueur* in England.[13]

RB Leipzig has a membership scheme, but with a high joining fee (€800 per year). The club can reject any application. At the 2017 AGM, it was confirmed that the club had 818 active members, of which only 17 have a vote on the board. This is unlike other clubs, where fee-paying fans do have a vote. Borussia Dortmund, for example, has over 400,000 members.

Remember Borussia Dortmund's slogan? *Echte Liebe*. True love. German pundits call them super-traditional and mega-authentic. When they played each other in September 2016, Dortmund fans boycotted the game at the Red Bull Arena. The return match, that one marked by Dembélé's brilliance, was overshadowed by home fans insulting and abusing RB Leipzig fans, pelting them with stones and cans. The Dortmund fans also unfurled banners which read: 'RB! Football belongs to us', 'Red Bull – Football's enemy!', 'Slaughter the Bulls!', 'For the people's sport football – against those who ruin it', 'We are what money can't buy'. Dortmund police filed 28 charges for breaches of the law concerning explosives, assault, dangerous bodily injury, damage to property and theft. The club condemned the behaviour but was fined €100,000 and had to close the south stand for one league game as a result of the trouble.

In comparison to Borussia Dortmund, RB Leipzig is *nouveau riche*, with the emphasis on the *riche*: in summer 2015, RB Leipzig spent more on new players than the rest of the Bundesliga 2 clubs combined. A 2016 study into the top-flight clubs showed that RB Leipzig had the highest net spend of them all over the previous two seasons: €74 million compared with Bayern Munich's €73 million. Rangnick rightly points out that other teams have spent big money and failed to improve; the difference is in how smartly his team invests its money.

RB Leipzig is still derided by critics as just a commercial vehicle. 'You can feel the force of their football – even though it comes from a can,' wrote the *Frankfurter Allgemeine Zeitung*. Another newspaper, the *Berliner Kurier*, published their name as *Dosenverkauf*, German for can-sellers, in a fixture list.

RB Leipzig supporters think this is unfair. Leipzig is a football city built around tradition: the first club to win the German championship, back in 1903, was VfB Leipzig. The new stadium is family-friendly and as vibrant as the football it hosts. And the whole of Germany benefits if a team from the east does well. As one fan put it: 'There's plenty of football tradition in Leipzig, but this is our chance to create a new tradition.'

The clubs may have an ideological disagreement but when it comes to talent, and to finding an edge, Rangnick's attitude is not so different. Don't forget that he was a mentor figure in the early days of Thomas Tuchel's career. Since then, Rangnick has become a byword for tactical influence and talent development in Germany. He has even taken some credit for the national team's 2014 World Cup success. 'His influence on the game is arguably stronger than ever,' wrote Raphael Honigstein in *Das Reboot: How German Football Reinvented Itself and Conquered the World*. 'Rangnick may never win the championship, but he has won the argument. The German top-flight teems with disciples of his ... They all play his football.'

This is why I am excited to hear Rangnick's talent formula to gain an edge. He makes it sound quite simple.

Inherited talent + learned skills × mentality = Talent

'Mentality relates to the effort you put in,' Rangnick tells me. 'Are you hungry? Are you willing to submit everything to get better? Do you want to improve yourself every day? Do you live in a professional way? Are you resistant to things like nightclubs or drinking? Do you need a big car or other things for your ego? If you don't have the right mentality, you can forget about the inherited talent that's in your DNA, and what you have learned from others. It's no use. It doesn't help. It doesn't matter how talented a player is, if the mentality is shit, forget about it.'

This is especially true because of how Rangnick teams play football. When he was at Hoffenheim, he found research that showed the best chance of scoring is within eight seconds of winning back the ball. In training he set out a countdown clock with the target to score within that time. Just as Lobanovski did in Kiev, Rangnick built his playing philosophy around this.

He demands his players win back the ball within eight seconds with aggressive pressing. After winning it back, they are to play direct and vertically towards the opponent's goal, surprising the disorganised opponent to get into the penalty area and shooting quickly. He tells his players to act, not react; to dictate the game with and without the ball, not through individuals; and to use numerical superiority. He also knows that the more sprints a team makes to win back the ball, the greater the likelihood they will score a goal once they have won it back quickly. This was a predecessor to *gegenpressing*, or as Klopp called it, 'heavy metal football'.

During his talk at the conference, Rangnick explained that this style of play suited the Red Bull brand: an attacking, high-pressing, quick transitional football is more attractive to neutrals – and specifically the 16- to 25-year-old demographic that the drink is aimed at – than a defensive, apprehensive, counter-attacking, cautious game. The first thing he did was lower the average age of the squads: at Hoffenheim the average age when they won promotion to the Bundesliga was 21.9, younger than the club's Under-23 team. At Red Bull, he reduced the average age from 30 (Salzburg) and 29 (Leipzig) to 24.

Part of the reason was a practical one: younger players recover quicker than older players, not just between games, but within them. Rangnick wants RB Leipzig to run more, and faster, than other teams in the Bundesliga. The league average for distance run per match is 113 kilometres. RB Leipzig's average in the first half of the season was 115km (it dropped to the average in the second half). The same is true of sprints; Rangnick's target is 250 sprints in total per game. 'We need players who have the stamina but also the mentality to be able to do that.' The team ethic overrides everything.

The cognitive aspect is vital. Rangnick wants players used to a high-tempo game, not the ones who 'can stand on the ball and slow the game down', as the cliché goes. 'We want players with the cognitive ability to learn and improve and the capacity to find solutions in restricted areas under high pressure. For me, resilience is a vital part of having the right mentality.'

That makes sense: if you need a player to react quickly to losing the ball, whether it's the first or last minute, then Tim Harkness's definition of resilience, as the accurate emotional response to threats or opportunities and the appropriate allocation of resources to deal with them, holds true. The longer that RB Leipzig has to work with the talent, and nurture it, the more suited it will become to that playing style. That's why they try and identify them as early as possible. 'The earlier the better.'

Herein lies another ethical dilemma; seven of the players in the successful Bundesliga season were signed from Red Bull Salzburg, which of course plays the same way. Salzburg even has its own nursery club, Austrian second division side FC Liefering. So the pathway for a young talent is clear: from Liefering to Salzburg to Leipzig. Not everyone feels the same. When Austrian defender Martin Hinteregger was ready to leave Salzburg in summer 2016, he rejected a move to Leipzig out of respect for the Salzburg fans. Hinteregger was an outspoken critic of the Red Bull model. 'I think it's a pity how Leipzig has destroyed Salzburg. I would rather be relegated with Augsburg than win the Bundesliga with Leipzig. Leipzig was not an option for me out of respect for Salzburg's fans. Although I might have been better off financially, I am happy that I did not go into the Bundesliga via Leipzig.' So he moved to Augsburg, and ended up scoring a dramatic equaliser in a 2–2 draw against RB Leipzig.

Again, Rangnick shrugs off any criticism with the ease of a man who is used to it. He is executing his personal resilience algorithm just fine. 'To be honest, we don't think about [criticism of the club] that much. We don't have time to do that,' he says. 'We are so convinced about our way, our philosophy. Of course if you do things in a different way – not just football, but in everyday life – if you're looking for new paths that no one has ever done before, then there will always be people who don't like that, because it's different. Whenever you do things in a different way, people may criticise.'

This is resilience the Rangnick way. His method combines strategy with entrepreneurship. 'Strategy without entrepreneurship is central planning. Entrepreneurship without strategy leads to chaos,' wrote Harvard Business School professor David Collis.[14] He cited America's Southwest Airlines as a business that effectively incorporates objective (strategy) and edge (in this case, via entrepreneurship, which he calls 'empowered local innovation').

Southwest is a short-haul carrier in the USA. Its purpose statement is: 'We exist to connect people to what's important in their lives through friendly, reliable, and low-cost air travel.' In one corporate video, Jessica Chatellier tells the story of how her family went to the airport to see off her husband, John, who had been deployed for six months' military service in Kuwait. One Southwest employee, Kelli Evans, allowed the family to go as far as the departure gate so they could have an extra half-hour together. After boarding had taken place, Felix Joseph, another employee, allowed Chatellier and her children onto the plane. The kids were able to run to their father and give him one final hug. 'The amazing part was when the whole plane cheered and clapped,' said Chatellier. John later told her what a great comfort that moment had been for him: it was when he realised that people would be taking care of his family in his absence. The employees were empowered to take decisions that might not have been allowed elsewhere. This has given Southwest an edge.

In Red Bull's case, Rangnick has built an infrastructure of player development that gives players the perfect platform to improve. 'If we compare our players' development to a 1,000-piece jigsaw,' he says, 'we try to offer all of those 1,000 pieces to every player, and it's up to them to use them in whatever dimension they want. We try to have all the relevant aspects of football development in our portfolio. We will never say, "We don't offer this or that." So we want the best possible support staff to develop the players. Everyone's job is vital and they all have a role to play.'

Rangnick sounds like Southwest CEO Gary Kelly, who wants his 50,000+ employees to feel like champions. Every week he gives public praise to an employee who has shown outstanding customer service, and is proud that Southwest is rated as one of the top places to work in the USA. Both men have found the perfect context to combine their strategic and entrepreneurial thinking.

Rangnick has his own personal resilience. He did not waver from his beliefs, but adapted them to a different context, a new club ready to embrace his methods rather than one unwilling to innovate. He believed in the process, and the product. Rangnick has found the right context for his methodology to flourish. Those clubs that did not let him hire a sports psychologist must be regretting it now. Rangnick's skill is in spotting talent – the likes of Joshua Kimmich, who joined RB Leipzing in the third division from Stuttgart Under-19s and three years later was at Bayern Munich, Germany's right-back at the 2016 European Championship, and named in the Team of the Tournament – and providing the infrastructure to improve it. Like Athletic Club de Bilbao, that's how the club (mostly) retains talent.

'Modern-day leadership is about being persuasive and creating a motivational basis so every day the players will want to come in and get better. This is about trust and empathy and human relationships,' he says. Back in his Hoffenheim days, he spoke of a flat hierarchy. He tells me now, with a chuckle, that his leadership style is 'with love and consequence'.

One coach in the audience at that conference had a keen interest in what Rangnick was saying. Fritz Schmid had worked at Grasshoppers, Tottenham Hotspur, FC Basel and with the Austria national team. He instructs coaches on UEFA courses and in his spare time wrote a fascinating book, *From Stories to Questions: A Systemic Approach to Self-Organising Processes and Chaos in Football*, on how cognitive functions can improve football performance.[15]

He agreed with Rangnick that things are changing for modern-day leaders. 'We are seeing a change in coaching styles: a move away from the traditional, "transactional" model – "I give you something, you give me something back" – to a transformational model of leadership, where coaches present players with a vision and inspire them to join the project. This is led by inspiration not direction,' he told me.

'Many leaders have a similar problem with their employees, because the same is reflected in society: there is a growing development of individuality and so we find players who would rather establish their personal brand before they think of the team or the collective. The most important element around football that's changing is the players' personalities and values. We see this social development in everyday life, and the challenge is how to cope with that. Players like Cristiano Ronaldo, Mario Balotelli and Zlatan Ibrahimovic represent this new generation, Generation Me, and other players may look up to them without being as talented.

'Ronaldo, Balotelli and Ibrahimovic don't fall out with their coaches, because those coaches have found the right approach with that type of player. It's not so much about giving orders, but more finding out about their triggers, and what motivates them to sacrifice their qualities for the team. This is where interaction and communication becomes so important: persuading a player not for football reasons but using their own self-awareness and social competence to buy into the project.'

Arsène Wenger understands this transformational shift. 'Players have become millionaires,' he says. 'If you think that the more you pay someone, the more they obey, you're wrong. The more you pay people, the more you have to treat them like millionaires, and explain it to them. You no longer give orders – it's all about convincing, explaining.'

I caught up with Schmid just as he was finishing a three-year spell as technical director of the Malaysia football federation. It was a tough role, especially for an outsider to take, but he was proud of the structural changes he made in improving the development of coaches within the federation. The challenges were familiar ones: building trust, measuring success, developing individuals, but he found solutions to educate a generation of coaches despite the different cultural expectations.

He laughed when I compared him to a salesman trying to make the perfect pitch to convince a sceptical customer. 'That's what coaches are!' he said. 'They now have to give the players a reason to get up for training every morning, and to do that they tap into what drives them as individuals.'

This is what Rangnick understands, and that's why he was a candidate for the job as England coach after Sam Allardyce left the post in autumn 2016. He had turned down an offer to coach West Bromwich Albion, because he knew that their sporting director Dan Ashworth was about to become England technical director (hence the England opportunity). There have been reported approaches from other English clubs, but you wonder whether he might come up against that 'no sports psychologist' mindset again if he moves. The skill of the entrepreneur is to intuitively understand where the ideas will work best.

'I have learned in football to never say never, but it's difficult to imagine somewhere else could make me more happy,' Rangnick says. 'I have so much possibility to develop and create and be innovative here. I don't see anywhere else where it can be better now than in Leipzig.'

Not only did seven members of the RB Leipzig squad that performed so well in the 2016–17 Bundesliga join the club from Red Bull Salzburg. One of the stars of RB Leipzig's season, Naby Keita, reportedly turned down Arsenal so he could follow

Rangnick to Leipzig. I went to Salzburg, home of baroque architecture and the birthplace of Wolfgang Amadeus Mozart, to find out more about the talents they identify and improve.

HOW TO GET AN EDGE – by RALF RANGNICK

1. Find the best possible tutors to develop players in all aspects of the game.
2. There is no space for ego in staff members. Everyone in our staff plays an important role.
3. We need to love our players. If they feel they are appreciated by everyone working with them, it can improve their performance.

VERONIKA KREITMAYR

Respond to success

Speed of stress / Resilience in success / Authentic or hubristic pride / Talent as sacrifice / Perfectionism rising

I am watching Red Bull Salzburg take on Nice in the Europa League on a chilly Thursday night in October. The French side's fans are making all the noise, and with good reason. Nice striker Alassane Pléa scores an early goal to increase pressure on Red Bull coach Oscar Garcia, who is heading for a fifth straight winless game. (The loss of form did not last long. Red Bull Salzburg lost only three matches in the rest of the season as it coasted to another Austrian title success in 2016–17.) But wait: defender Stefan Lainer is clean through on goal, and has a great chance to equalise. Surely he will score! He screws his shot wide. 'Oh no! How could he miss that?' a supporter behind me asks his friend. 'What the hell was he thinking?'

One person in the stadium knew exactly what was going through his mind. She was watching on from the east stand. Veronika Kreitmayr is a former international handball player who spent 11 years working at the Red Bull Performance and Diagnostics Centre in Thalgau, a short distance from Salzburg. It used to be her job to know exactly what he was thinking.

She left in late 2015, and has since set up her own thriving practice, with clients from all industries, including professional sport. She remains friends with many of the club staff, hence her presence at the match. When she first started at the centre, in a building so discreet that you would never know it was there (a rare example of the company *not* branding itself), Red Bull did not own any football clubs. Her role was to assess the cognitive abilities – reaction time, concentration and perception – of its motorsport, cycling, running and extreme athletes. At the time, she was working on her thesis from Vienna University about Alzheimer's disease.

'I knew what it meant to not reach sporting goals, as I never made that last step in my career,' she explains after Nice had secured a 1–0 win. As a handballer Kreitmayr competed in the World Championships with Austria and with her club team, Hypo Niederösterreich, was a bit-part player in winning the European Cup and multiple national league titles. Her coaches later told her that it was not her ability preventing her progress, but her mentality. Kreitmayr can tell me how to find an edge.

She can tell a lot about an athlete's personality by conducting cognitive assessments that focus on flexibility, inhibition (the process of changing behaviour to complete tasks) and working memory. Each one has a clear correlation to performance. 'Flexibility of thought is important for any kind of achiever,' Kreitmayr says. 'If inhibition does not come up in the test, then we are dealing with someone more impulsive who might not be able to block out certain things. Memory is about perception and knowing where your team-mates are; you need to remember things in the short term so you can process the next thing to do.'

Nowadays, Kreitmayr gives her clients personality tests and psycho-physiological assessments. She has put together a 280-question self-assessment personality test that includes questions on empathy, self-confidence, thinking/doing, sociability, sense of health, anxiety and self-discipline.

Remember the self-assessment questionnaire from 2011 at the Premier League club which we looked at in Chapter 2? The only finding was that the best talents had refused to answer the questions. Some scientists disregard self-assessment questionnaires out of hand – a senior figure at one football club told me, 'I'm not interested in their ambition, or what they see as their ambition' – but others feel they are beneficial, as long as their subjectivity is accounted for. The answers are not how the athletes see themselves but how they *want to be seen* as seeing themselves. These tests have a dissimulation scale that compensates for answers conforming to social norms. Younger athletes are often more concerned with how their answers may appear, while older ones tend to be more reflective.

The results of her self-assessment tests make little sense out of context, and that's why the psycho-physiological test is helpful. The test, in which electrodes are placed on the head, measures athletes' brainwave activity when stressed and not stressed, and how fast the levels shift between the two. It also measures the sympathetic nervous system by monitoring breathing times, pulse rates, and skin response, which is the sweating caused by stress rather than activity. 'You can measure the general stress level of an individual through their skin response, so the sweatier someone's hand is, the more stressed they are likely to be,' says Kreitmayr.

One of the most important things Kreitmayr looks for in her sporting clients today is an intangible. She says it is an 'inner strength'. It's a subconscious confidence that comes from knowing you could succeed in any field, built around a support network of good and bad previous experiences. A combination of different characteristics realise this underlying inner strength. Kreitmayr calls it resilience. And she believes that's what gives you an edge.

For her, resilience is not only about coping with adversity or pressure. 'Most of the time, people are preoccupied by the things that go wrong,' Kreitmayr says. 'A coach is often able to talk more about failure than success.'

The irony is that the same environment is unforgiving of mistakes and does not allow a culture of failure to exist. 'You don't know how to win, unless you have lost before,' adds Kreitmayr, echoing the opinion of Michael Jordan. 'Losing is very important to the process and so mistakes are important. I think failure or losing should be equally honoured as winning – but it's not. At most football clubs, you're not allowed to lose. It's not an option.'

This takes the focus away from another important factor in resilience: success. It can be a challenge for a youngster who is suddenly successful – maybe even harder than coping with failure. A study on English development coaches reported that some players' lack of emotional maturity led them to have a 'made it already' attitude that does not help their effective development.[16] Psychologists have drawn out the difference between authentic pride – deriving from a specific accomplishment and often focused on the efforts made for that goal – and hubristic pride, which reflects global beliefs about skills and strengths. This is the path to arrogance. How should a talent cope with success? 'Experiencing authentic pride after successful sports performance is surely not wrong,' explains Geir Jordet, the Norwegian psychologist. 'The problems may start when a player's self-image grows out of proportion and he or she starts to feel entitled to a series of other benefits because of their accomplishments.'

Kreitmayr talks to athletes about goal-setting. She can tell if they are easily satisfied, think they have already made it, or need to be challenged and set tougher goals. 'It's about motivation and that's often linked to what stage of their career they're at. Success brings greater expectations, and if I know how an athlete copes with stress, it gives a marker for how they cope with success as well. It's an important measure to think about – and one that is not always considered.'

There is a reason for this. Studies in social psychology show that the negative effects of bad things affect us more dramatically than the positive effects of good things. So we give more attention to the idea of coping with adversity than we do to coping with success. This can be a problem in any professional environment: we all know someone who became arrogant or entitled after tasting success.

I like the idea that one American law firm had to tell all partners to specifically thank members of staff at moments of success. The results of that became tangible: people worked longer hours and burn-out rates were reduced. Research by Francesca Gino, the Harvard Business School professor of business administration, revealed that showing gratitude results in reciprocal generosity but also increases the likelihood of that employee helping others.[17] And one thing is for sure, in football and in business: if you are successful, you did not do it all on your own.

Kreitmayr measures resilience in all its forms by evaluating stress levels. 'If you go through life always at an elevated level of stress, then that can destroy your body and mind,' she says. 'Your brain won't function as it could, you won't be able to memorise key information, and that's why it's important to have the ability to calm yourself down.'

She recommends developing resilience with simple techniques to keep stress at bay: relaxation, meditation, biofeedback, hypnotherapy or visualisations. 'We need to know ourselves and our strengths better, so we can focus on what we're good at, stay more positive. Sometimes the subconscious destroys the pictures in the brain that help find solutions. We need to open the path to those resources and that can help reduce the stress levels.'

She is clear about the rewards for resilience: 'More confidence. Less stress. More security and self-esteem. Success, probably. A better life, certainly.'

Kreitmayr knows from her own experience that the brain needs to be in peak mode for optimal physical performance. 'It sounds so obvious but the brain is steering everything. If your brain is not working at 100 per cent, the body won't function as you want it.'

Other businesses subscribe to the same view: get the mind right, and the results will follow. Financial institutions have looked at how emotional states can lead to better or worse decisions. Professor Brian Uzzi, of the Kellogg School of Management, examined over 1.2 million instant messages sent by day traders over a two-year period. He found that too much (or too little) emotion affected their success.

One New York-based investment bank conducted a trial in which it gave employees wristwatch sensors to calculate pulse and perspiration to measure emotions. It could also be used in the recruitment process, to find those whose physiology is best suited to risk-taking. According to *Bloomberg Businessweek*, some of America's biggest banks are talking to tech companies about systems that monitor worker emotions to boost performance.

Critics are not sure that this is robust enough: in some cases, a decision is made so quickly that a split-second moment of anxiety might be too fleeting to show up in the physiology monitoring. Rick di Mascio worked in asset management for over 20 years but didn't always know specifically how or why certain fund managers had performed well or not. He set up Inalytics, a company that now has one of the world's largest databases of investment decisions, over 150 million across more than 900 portfolios, to measure investment skill. It's an evidence-based process that calculates which investors have the skill of finding winners and knowing when to sell. Its clients are asset managers, hedge funds and pension funds.

Di Mascio tells me there are clear parallels between fund management and football: both are skills-based activities with definable outcomes (win, lose or draw) and observable decisions. They are also subject to the biases and foibles that we all have. We will look at the significance of bias later in this chapter. Di Mascio knows, for example, that 80 per cent of fund managers do the opposite of what they should do: overwhelmingly, they cut their winners too early and hold on to losers for too long. 'Some of these professionals are superb at identifying the right stocks, but sell at the wrong time,' he says. The equivalent is the winger who dribbles around the defence, beats the goalkeeper, but can't put the ball in the back of the net.

Inalytics identifies the links between fund managers' process and performance, and from that can determine what governs behaviours. Di Mascio was able to show one particular client pure data-led evidence that his decision-making deteriorated during certain market conditions. Together they identified those conditions – a volatile market – and the fund manager adapted his behaviour. The next time there was volatility, he sold the vulnerable stocks that he would previously have held onto. As the client put it, 'I panicked fast, and I panicked hard.' That change in decision-making was worth a fortune. Di Mascio derives great pleasure from seeing how data changes people's behaviour and can help them successfully cope with stress.

Kreitmayr says that in sport there is a clear link between stress and injuries. 'We noticed that athletes who were highly stressed get injured very often. Even with injuries like ligament breaks, stress was often a trigger.'

At her practice in Salzburg, Kreitmayr carries out cognitive, psychological and psycho-physiological tests on her clients. The process takes three hours, and then comes her favourite bit: talking through the results, discussing areas to improve, and solutions for doing so. Her sporting background helps athletes open up to her, while her engaging manner, ready smile and disarming use of pauses in conversation usually reveals more truths.

Kreitmayr is now working with other football clubs but will not confirm if any of her tests are built into a player's medical before they sign. I suspect they might be. It seems to me that they should be a prerequisite.[18] The only employees on the sporting side who do not seem to be tested, ironically, are the coaches – arguably the ones who might benefit the most.

It always comes back to one magic word: talent. 'When you look at the derivation of the word from Greek times, it was a coin you paid with,' she says. 'That's exactly it! What are you willing to pay? What are you willing to give of yourself? That is talent.[19] So put people in the positions they are good in, and the talent, what they are prepared to put in, will flourish.'

Most of the individual athletes Kreitmayr works with request personal development programmes as a matter of course. When it comes to team sports, the figure is less than 50 per cent. 'Team players want to improve but I think they still see psychology as something scary,' Kreitmayr says. 'I think they don't really understand that you can improve mental abilities without being mentally ill. But this is a form of training like anything else.'

Kreitmayr also sees differences between male and female athletes. Female athletes tend to place higher expectations on themselves, are more stressed, more reflective about their development and more performance-oriented. Why? 'Because they have a lot more to prove than the male athletes,' Kreitmayr says. She recognised herself in those results. She was the same.

Red Bull Salzburg continues to find top talent from around the world. In July 2015, they bought a young French centre-back called Dayot Upamecano from Valenciennes. He grew up in Evreux, the same French town as his childhood friend Ousmane Dembélé. I didn't know that when I picked Upamecano for the *Guardian*'s 'Next Generation' feature in 2015. In January 2017, Salzburg sold Upamecano ... to RB Leipzig. In summer 2017, Red Bull Salzburg Under-19s won the UEFA Youth League, dispatching Manchester City, Paris Saint-Germain and Atlético Madrid in earlier rounds before coming from behind to beat Benfica 2–1 in the final. Hannes Wolf, an Austrian midfielder, could be the next star to emerge. It may be frustrating for fans losing talent to its German partner, but the future is still bright in Salzburg.

Kreitmayr has now worked for over 13 years with professional athletes. Worryingly, she has noticed a change in their approach during that period. There is an increased desire for perfection. 'As there is an increased focus on the details, athletes feel they have to be perfect,' she explains. 'You can see it when you talk to them and they are stressed when something is not perfect. But perfect doesn't exist. This is a message that comes from society and social media as well. We need youngsters to know – not just in sport but in business and in life too – that the concept of "perfect" is a false one, and it's not a healthy aspiration to have. Because you will never attain it, and therefore will never be happy.'

The highest rate of perfectionism that Kreitmayr noticed is in the goalkeepers she works with. Lucky, then, that my next appointment is with one of the best goalkeeper coaches in the world.

HOW TO GET AN EDGE – by VERONIKA KREITMAYR

1. Own your goals: being motivated means making your goals personal and not just based on the environment.
2. Maintain low stress levels: people who are highly stressed mainly focus on not making mistakes.
3. Manage expectations: it can be stressful if you can't reach your own high standards, or don't believe your work is good enough.

HANS LEITERT
Challenge unconscious bias

Benchmark, time and strategy / Transfer and near-post bias / Seven goalkeeping principles / Feedback, problem-solving and reflection

As pre-match talks go, this was probably one of the more memorable that young goalkeeper Ramazan Özcan had heard. 'Approach today's game like you would good sex!' Hans Leitert, his goalkeeping coach, told him. 'You can show and do everything, let yourself go. But keep your emotions under control. The final whistle will be the exclusive climax!'

It was just before Özcan played for Austria Under-21s against England Under-21s in a 2006 European Under-21 Championship qualifier at Elland Road in 2005. The Austrians had never won before in England. Leitert noticed during the warm-up that his player was over-motivated, and struggling to control his adrenalin level. He thought he might become 'irrepressibly euphoric' during the match and took him aside for a chat. As it was, Özcan was outstanding as Austria won the game 2–1.

Leitert is too modest to say his words made a difference. A former goalkeeper himself, he may be one of the most impressive coaches you have never heard of. He spent five years as Head of Goalkeeping across the Red Bull clubs in Salzburg, Leipzig, New York, Ghana and Brazil. He oversaw 17 goalkeeping coaches responsible for 70 different goalkeepers.

He has a lot to tell me about the dangers of unconscious bias in talent identification. He believes that resilience can make the difference for a professional goalkeeper. He talks about how best to solve problems, the importance of openness to feedback and realistic goal-setting in a goalkeeping and business context. He draws clear parallels between the two.

Leitert was a goalkeeper in the Austrian top flight in the 1990s for Austria Vienna and VfB Mödling, and was an Under-21 international. In 1995 while training he broke his scaphoid, a bone in his hand, and that ended his career. By then, he was already thinking about how goalkeeper performances were analysed: he would get wound up when Austrian newspaper *Kronenzeitung* said he played badly when he thought he had played well; and was just as annoyed when it said he had played well, and he thought he had not. He would challenge his feedback from coaches, which created some tense relationships. 'Maybe it was a sign that I should be doing something else,' he admits.

He devoted his time to looking into ways of assessing goalkeeping performance and, after completing a sports science degree, worked as goalkeeping coach at Rapid Vienna, Austria Under-21s, Recreativo Huelva, Panathinaikos and Tottenham Hotspur. He then spent five years with Red Bull.

One of his tasks during the 2012–13 season was to recruit a goalkeeper with a unique profile for Red Bull Salzburg. The club wanted a new goalkeeper for the following season. The overall group strategy was that RB Leipzig would be a Bundesliga side in the next four years (they were in division four then, but as we know, made it to the German top-flight for season 2016–17). So Leitert needed to hire a goalkeeper who could play at the top level in the Austrian league and in the Europa League for at least two years – for Red Bull Salzburg – and then would be ready for the Bundesliga, where the average goalkeeper is around 28 years old and worth around €5–6 million. Salzburg's strategy was to find a goalkeeper in his early twenties, who could peak in his late twenties; its budget to find this player was under €1 million.

He looked at Red Bull's partners in the USA, Ghana and Brazil but their best goalkeepers were not quite good enough. So he pooled his 17-man coaching resource and analysed every Under-21 national team goalkeeper in Europe. They eliminated those who were too expensive and settled on Peter Gulacsi, a Hungarian goalkeeper on Liverpool's books. He fulfilled all the performance analysis criteria, and ticked the due diligence boxes. 'Red Bull has a sophisticated scientific approach when they recruit talents and have specific environments to test out lots of things,' is how Leitert describes the diagnostics centre in Thalgau.

The player was a good pick. Gulacsi won back-to-back league and Cup doubles with Red Bull Salzburg in 2014 and 2015, and he moved to RB Leipzig in summer 2015. He played a significant part in RB Leipzig's promotion-winning season in 2015–16 and was superb as the team finished second in its Bundesliga debut season.

Leitert breaks down the challenges of talent development into three key parameters:

1. *Benchmark:* If I know where the elite competitors in my field are, then I know what I need to do to bridge the gap. Every job has to be defined by performance benchmarks – in the case of goalkeepers, as we speak it's Manuel Neuer and David de Gea – so I need to know exactly what I'm looking to achieve with this talent.

2. *Time:* How much time do I have to develop this talent within the academy system? Will I be able to work with them for two years or four years and get them ready for the first team? That will help inform a decision on their suitability.

3. *Strategy:* What type of training can I provide to the player so they can develop? It's the coach's responsibility to regulate the load stimulation (heavy training) and provide the right amount of rest.

He adds a kicker, perhaps the most important one of all. It's about measuring the talent in the first place, which, as he says, 'requires an open mind and a look beyond the traditional ways to develop'. Leitert hosts educational courses for FIFA, where he talks to the goalkeeping coaches of tomorrow. He asks a simple question. 'What is an efficient way to measure goalkeeping talent?' Here are some of the answers he gets back:

- Size of goalkeeper
- Passing ability
- Save percentage
- Technical execution of dives
- Peripheral vision
- Safe hands at crosses
- Bravery in one-versus-one situations
- Ability to learn fast
- Communication skills
- Authentic confidence
- Ability to get over mistakes
- Fast reaction times

It's all of them, of course, yet none of them in isolation. The first answer he always hears, size, is a particular bugbear for Leitert. 'Many people interested in football see height as the only measurable and therefore logically understandable property,' he says. 'But I think it's absolutely irresponsible to rate a goalkeeper on the basis of a component that cannot be affected. I always hear, "He's too small, he'll have problems with crosses," but I never hear, "He has problems with crosses because he has not had specific training in anticipation." Saying that a goalkeeper who is 1.79m won't perform as well as one who is 1.82m is like a bad joke. Do you judge the performance of your car by its engine output or its body?'

Leitert is talking about unconscious bias, the assumptions we make about people and talent without even realising it. Our brain fills in the blanks about people based on background, cultural environment or personal experiences. And that can prevent us from making the best decisions.

Leitert was at a meeting where the merits of two goalkeepers were under discussion. One was 1.92m, the other 1.85m. Most of the people in the room preferred the taller goalkeeper. Leitert was not convinced. The goalkeepers did a test; each standing with his back to a wall and raising both arms up as high as possible. The shorter goalkeeper had longer arms, and more flexibility in his shoulder. The seven-centimetre difference between the two became only two centimetres. Next they did a 'jump and reach' test, measuring the highest point at which each goalkeeper could claim a ball. The shorter goalkeeper out-reached the taller one by eight centimetres.

This may come as a surprise in England, where the average height for a Premier League goalkeeper is 191.2cm, the highest of the top 31 divisions under the UEFA banner. Shortly behind is Czech Republic, 190.8cm, and Germany, 190.7cm. At the other end of the scale are Israel, 186.5cm, France, 186.7cm, and Spain, 186.8cm. The average for all goalkeepers across Europe is 188.8cm – by contrast, midfielders come in at an average of 179.1cm.

Unconscious bias is around us all the time in the workplace. Google, who in 2014 promoted an initiative to counter unconscious bias, named all the conference rooms in a new building after male scientists and only changed it after someone pointed it out. The same company represented men in 83 per cent of its 'Doodles' on every Google homepage across the world, with only 17 per cent honouring women and only 5 per cent women of colour. A 2017 campaign called Dads4Daughters called on fathers in the workplace to pledge to achieve greater gender equality in the future workplaces of their daughters by calling out unconscious bias when they see it.

In another example, one academic study gave participants job applications for the role of police chief. The candidates were similarly qualified, though one had more education and the other had more experience. When no names were on the applications, the participants selected the candidate with more education. When male and female names were attached to the same applications, participants overwhelmingly preferred the male candidate, even when he had less education.

'Stereotypes led to a shifting of the very criteria that was deemed important,' explained Stanford University sociologist Shelley Correll.[20] 'Because stereotypes led participants to expect to see a male in the role of police chief, they unconsciously shifted their evaluation criteria ... in order to justify hiring the male candidate.'

A 2004 study sent fictitious CVs in reply to help-wanted adverts placed in newspapers in Boston and Chicago and found that candidates with traditional European names like Emily and Greg were 50 per cent more likely to get called for interviews than those with African-American names like Lakisha and Jamal, despite having identical CVs.[21]

'Subtle assumptions we make about people can have a lasting effect on who we are promoting, who we are hiring, and putting in leadership positions,' said Nathalie Johnson, a People Scientist at Google. Megan Smith, US Chief Technology Officer at Google, took this one step further: 'If you're not conscious of the biases you have, you're just not contributing at the level you could and not innovating at the level you could, so your products won't be as good and your results won't be as good.'

How do we avoid unconscious bias? In the hiring process we can create clear criteria for candidates before evaluating their qualifications, and standardise the interview process so that each candidate answers the same questions. In its efforts to increase diversity in science, technology, engineering and mathematics (STEM) and develop a world in which studying and working in science is open to all, the Royal Society suggests that we deliberately slow down decision-making, reconsider our reasons for decisions, question cultural stereotypes and monitor each other for unconscious bias. 'We cannot cure unconscious bias but with self-awareness we can address it,' said the Royal Society's Professor Uta Frith.

I always wondered if there was a transfer bias in football; whether teams might be more likely to sign someone who had played well against them in the past. I had heard plenty of coaches say, on signing a new player: 'He caused us all sorts of problems when we faced him,' or words to that effect. I still find that strange: why sign someone who was good against *your* team when now, the only team he *won't* play against, is that very team? My Soccernomics colleague Stefan Szymanski (University of Michigan), working with Christian Deutscher (University of Bielefeld), came up with a way of calculating whether transfer bias exists. They examined 70,000 ratings of Bundesliga players from *Kicker* magazine over ten seasons (from 2005–06 to 2014–15), looked at their average rating, then compared that to players up against a team they would be employed by in the future. The findings, in the first five years of data, were clear: those playing against future employees did receive higher ratings. 'The rational explanation is that teams hired players who play well against them,' Szymanski tells me. The bias has disappeared in recent years, probably because since 2010, clubs have improved their scouting network by using software companies to provide video footage. But it was there.

Leitert agrees that unconscious bias can get in the way of accurately judging talent. He gives another example: 'Everyone remembers when a goalkeeper is beaten at his near post [the post nearest to where the ball has been struck] but no one seems to care if the goalkeeper is beaten at the far post or even in the third of the goal nearest that post.' He believes that most goalkeepers over-protect the near post to avoid criticism from conceding there. He is interested in protecting the whole goal, not just a part of it. A goalkeeper not so obsessed with his near post might concede two more goals there if he changed his starting position; but he might save an extra five goals at the far post by doing so. 'Sometimes we look for the obvious thing to see and we believe we know it all,' he says. 'We have to be very careful with how we judge. We all need to know about our own unconscious biases.' And as long as we are aware of the bias, then we are less likely to fall into the trap.

Leitert demands that his coaches look beyond the obvious. He encourages them to ask better questions and make better judgements. He broke down what he sees as the key aspects to the role and published them in a fascinating book called *The Art of Goalkeeping, or the Seven Principles of the Masters*. Those principles are:

- Optimal positioning and distance
- Balance
- Ready in time
- The correct beginning
- Actively towards the ball
- Courage
- Controlled focus

Put together, they produce a goalkeeper who has a strategy; who doesn't depend on luck; who has a plan for complex situations, can read triggers and adjust his tactical response accordingly; and who has charisma, or presence. Leitert calls the whole package the 'intangible spirit'.

I ask if he could identify this – and spot the difference between 'real confidence' and 'acted confidence' – just by watching a goalkeeper on television, or even live. Not with total confidence, he says, but I'm sure he'd do better than most of us. So after all the performance analysis is done, the only way to fully assess the individual is to spend time talking with them. Leitert always wants to know: 'Why do you choose to play in goal?' There is no right or wrong answer, but understanding deeper motivation is important. Some young players say it's because of an idol that they admire, some don't know, and some say they want to be the one who decides the game, who wants to take on the responsibility.

He likes to ask his goalkeepers a provocative question. 'It's the most important game of your life[22] and you have two options: either your team wins 3–2 but you make two bad mistakes. Or your team loses 1–0 but you have made ten world-class saves. What do you prefer?' Leitert prefers his players to say they would rather lose the match. 'If you deal with players who care about performance, you will gain much more than just the result,' he explains, 'as that result is only a consequence of performance. Coaches want players who care about their performance.'

He asks about previous performances, best moments, worst moments, tough challenges and inspiring or difficult coaches. 'It's a very quick way to find out if you are talking to someone who reflects on their performances and thinks about what they're doing,' he says. 'Are they giving answers based on deep reflection or are they just not aware of anything? The goalkeeper position is exposed. You can't hide. That means reflection is important, as it helps you deal with mistakes and setbacks. If you know why you made a mistake, you can continue with the game, but if you don't know, then it's hard to get out of this fear of it happening again.'

This is where resilience is required. 'It's a very crucial skill for a goalkeeper, but he needs to have certain characteristics within himself, and one of the most important is authenticity,' says Leitert. When he talks to a goalkeeper the day after he's made a mistake, he checks the response: how is the goalkeeper dealing with constructive feedback and is he ready to have an open dialogue? 'It's very easy to criticise goalkeepers, but we have to remember that development includes lots of failures.'

Christophe Lollichon, the goalkeeper coach who told me about his Mexican hijack horror when we met in the Chelsea canteen, agrees that motivation, reflection and openness to feedback are key to understanding goalkeepers. 'Why do we want to become a goalkeeper in the first place?' Lollichon asks. 'We wear gloves, a different shirt, we have some rules that other players cannot have. To become a goalkeeper is to have the ambition to be a saviour. You need to like taking responsibilities and helping others. You have to have a certain ego, because when the light is not on you, it can get very dark. These are reasons why the talent is different: but we cannot separate this person from the team. He has to be part of the group; he is an important football player. He just has particular skills.'

Lollichon is keen to bust the myth that goalkeepers are crazy. If anything, it's the opposite. 'You need to have courage, to sacrifice yourself for the team, to stay lucid under pressure. And most of all, if you make a mistake, you need to be resilient,' he says.

Lollichon worked closely with Petr Cech at Rennes and at Chelsea. When I first met the pair, they were having an intense discussion about Bahrain's human rights record. They each brought out the best in the other. 'If every young talent has a tank and the coach's job to fill it up, you need that talent to be open to the learning process,' he says. 'Petr was always asking about everything. He wanted to learn all the time, and not just about football. He has courage, and everything else you need to succeed in life: resilience, yes; adaptability, yes; decision-making, top, top; but also teamwork and this sense of the team.'

He admits that Cech taught him a great deal too. 'His mental strength was unbelievable and he has definitely taught me what it takes to get to the very top. You need to be aware of what is needed: the ability to be assertive, to control the pressure, it's all a form of resilience.'

Lollichon is a huge fan of Differential Training. All his goalkeepers play head tennis, basketball and *peteca*, a Brazilian sport which is like badminton with your hands. He wants to improve their agility and co-ordination by working with circus trainers and classical dancers. He has learned from the France national handball team's goalkeeper Thierry Omeyer about how best to protect the goal. He is also working with an ophthalmologist, who he believes might improve goalkeepers' peripheral vision by 1 per cent.

Cech moved to Arsenal in 2015, but they are still working together. They have teamed up with another Lollichon alumnus, Mikael Landreau (who made a record 619 appearances in Ligue 1), to establish an international goalkeeping school in France for 14- to 18-year-olds. It will be called The sKool (capital K for Keeper) and the trio hope it will develop goalkeepers of the future. 'But it won't be football, football, football,' Lollichon says. 'We will give them multi-activities so they have a wide capacity for education. We want to develop their adaptability, their knowledge, their decision-making and their resilience. You don't do that just by putting them in goal and firing shots at them.' He wants to improve them as human beings too.

And so, resilience is not just about openness to feedback. Leitert also connects it to self-belief. If you have self-belief, then you are more likely to be resilient when faced with big obstacles. You can cope with the threats and opportunities. He sees this as different to confidence, which is short term, comes and goes, and is more susceptible to ups and downs. Rangnick spoke about the importance of the cognitive aspect of his players. Finding talent with self-belief rather than confidence is crucial to the Red Bull success story.

Two other aspects of resilience fascinate Leitert: problem-solving and goal-setting. Any mistake, he says, is the last consequence of a chain of events that led to that mistake. If a goalkeeper failed to catch a ball, for example, it's not that he's bad at catching balls; maybe his timing was off, or he started in the wrong position. Perhaps his vision is faulty and not as sharp under artificial lights – this was found to be the problem with one of his goalkeepers, who made more errors under floodlights, had corrective surgery and improved. The mistake is the final part of a whole chain. 'You need to make the individual aware of the source of the problem, and then he can become more in control of his performances. It's a long-term solution: more control means more consistency which means less criticism.'

Goal-setting is also important, but it has to be realistic. Here's a problem Leitert often faces: an 18-year-old goalkeeper plays for his country at Under-19 level. He gets called up to his club's first-team squad and goes on tour with them. He plays one half against a local side in pre-season. He is still on his youth-team wages but is now mixing it with the first-teamers who play international football and have lucrative endorsement contracts. The goalkeeper coach likes to take three goalkeepers to away games in case someone gets injured, so the youngster even does pre-match warm-ups with the first team on match-days. The coach thinks this might give the rookie a great experience, getting a taste of what it means to be included, but a wrong signal could also be triggered. He may begin to feel like he's made it already. But he has not – not by a long shot.

Leitert has calculated the qualitative difference between academy-level football and the Premier League. It's vast. If there is a 10 per cent increase in development every year, it will take between four and six years for that teenage talent to be ready for the top flight. So he tells them this: 'You are not ready yet. Now is the time to learn your trade in senior football. It could take you six years of education, in which there will be failures, setbacks and pressure. You will learn to deal with it and hopefully, if your development path continues, you will make it as a number one goalkeeper.'

The average age for a Premier League goalkeeper is 29.1, the oldest in Europe. So while teenage outfield stars like Ousmane Dembélé are not uncommon, a goalkeeper doesn't peak until his late twenties. In this case, the talent needs to be patient and accept the reality of the goals. 'If he has the right expectations, and if they are realistic, then setbacks will not be so hard to deal with, and they can cope with it better,' said Leitert.

Once again we come back to the idea of reflection as important for the talent's development; also required is a cool head from the manager's side. 'Our job is to avoid the trap of emotion and to remain logical,' he says. 'We also have to ensure that our player is guided through the week so he can peak on match-day.'

Leitert uses the ploy of provoking a player by setting up exercises that will only give him a 50 per cent success rate. As match-day approaches, that number will increase to between 80 and 90 per cent to improve the player's confidence. The period of optimal learning, according to Leitert, is between 70 and 80 per cent. 'That's the sweet spot where you need to provide the right amount and type of feedback – without overloading on information.'

Leitert is adamant that his pillars of performance have the same impact in a workplace environment. 'Every job is defined through performance, whether it's number of sales, profits or click-throughs; whatever the performance parameters, you need to know where you are trying to get to. And you need to know the time-frame you have to get there, whether it's a six-week internship or a two-year contract to get from here to there. When it comes to strategy, that is just defining how you are going to take the first two elements and make it work. That's the how element. But in football, like everything else, the most important question is why. Not, "how shall we train today?" but "why should we train like that?" Development happens when we ask why and not how.'

As well as coaching coaches, Leitert works as a consultant for the Spanish FA and for a top-half Premier League club, which he doesn't want to name. He is still tweaking his performance analysis model to predict future goalkeeper performance: for example, how might Manuel Neuer fare if he played for, say, Sunderland? On a more realistic level, his model looks at a target player and assesses future performance within the framework of the purchasing club. 'It would depend on the club requirements, but this is the aim – and to determine whether a quick fix or a long-term asset will gain you more points depending on what you need right now.'

I wonder if Leitert will stop once he finds the perfect goalkeeper. 'No!' Leitert laughs. 'I have been studying this for over 20 years and the one thing I know for sure is that the perfect goalkeeper doesn't exist. There's no such thing.' And he looks genuinely happy about that.

I find Leitert, and Lollichon, inspiring because their quest to find an edge leads them on interesting journeys (and I don't mean Zapatista areas of Mexico). They are at the forefront of talent development in a position that is constantly evolving. They are always looking for answers, and open to creative solutions. In the next chapter, we will examine the best ways to unlock creativity. My first step was a return to France; this time, to a café in Paris ...

HOW TO GET AN EDGE – by HANS LEITERT

1. Mistakes are the final consequence of a chain of problems, so treat the source and not the symptom.
2. Understanding the basic principles of any role will allow you to self-regulate decisions and result in more consistent performances.
3. Don't just ask what and how but always ask why too.

CREATIVITY

CLERMONT FOOT 63
Innovate through diversity

The reluctant, sexist, innovator / Diversity drives innovation / Women need champions, not mentors / Menstruation matters

The man who just walked into a downtrodden Paris café in Boulogne-Billancourt does not look like a pioneer. He does not even claim to be a pioneer. You could show his picture, or mention his name, to most football fans in France, and they would not know who he was. That's how he likes it. But Claude Michy, an understated events manager with a love of motorsport, is unique in modern-day football. He is the sole owner of his local football club, Clermont Foot 63, who play in France's second division, Ligue 2. And in summer 2014, he found a brilliant way to get an edge. He appointed a female coach to lead the team.

The night before I meet Michy, Corinne Diacre has just coached her hundredth game in charge of Clermont. It was a 1–1 draw against Brest. That she is still there nearly three years on is to Michy's great credit; not because he might have sacked her, but the opposite. In September 2016, the French football federation asked Diacre to coach the France national women's side. She said no, out of loyalty to Michy – she felt she owed him that.

Over the next few hours, Michy will tell me how Diacre brings an edge to Clermont. Their story is not about female empowerment, or bringing a more empathetic management style to the club. It's about creativity; how Michy, best described as a reluctant innovator, wanted a female coach for his team, and found the right one (eventually). He has gone against the grain of football orthodoxy. He has taken a risk. His innovation is not granting creative freedom, but granting creative freedom to a woman in an industry where hardly anyone else has dared do the same.[1] And it has worked.

Studies on women in business suggest that a female team coach would be successful. Professor Kathleen O'Connor, an organisational psychologist who studies negotiation and teamwork at Cornell University, tells me that women demonstrate different behaviours to men in a negotiation process; that women will fight very hard on behalf of a group, but are less effective when it comes to representing themselves. And that women in general use more collaborative skills with teams. The 'command and control' form of management is outdated, she says, only required in crisis situations and tends to be used by those, usually men, who feel threatened.

There was some symmetry to the timing of my visit. Clermont faced the same opponent, Brest, the previous night as in Diacre's first game in charge. Before that match, Brest coach Alex Dupont presented her with a bouquet of flowers.[2] She kissed him and smiled politely. Brest won 2–1.

Last night, there was no bouquet for Diacre. That seemed significant to me, as I will explain later. Brest was top of the table. Clermont, in fifteenth place, frustrated them. It was a freezing night and the stadium was not even half-full – just over two thousand hardy souls turned up. But Diacre has been successful. Clermont has the seventeenth lowest budget in the division, and finished twelfth (2015), sixth (2016) and twelfth again (2017). Diacre over-achieved with the squad she had. The risk paid off.

'It was no risk for me,' says Michy. 'At least, it's exactly the same risk as if I've hired a man. I chose someone based on their competence. Okay, she's a woman too. But I've not chosen a woman. I chose someone who played 120 times for their country [Diacre was a centre-back for France's women's team] and spent five years as assistant coach to that team. So there's no great risk there. I don't see myself as doing a great service for diversity for bringing in a female coach. It surprises me when I hear that. There are women who are team managers in Formula 1. There are female prime ministers in Germany and the UK. So when people question the appointment of Corinne as a woman in the men's game, it's a little bit reductive, don't you think?'

Michy is being disingenuous here. Diacre was only appointed after his first-choice as coach, Helena Costa, walked out a few days after her appointment and before she had even taken one training session. Neither coach was his idea; both came from agent Sonia Souid, who first convinced Michy that Costa, a Portuguese who had been in charge of the Iran women's team, would be a good replacement for Régis Brouard.

Michy tells me that Costa walked out because her mother was ill in Portugal, and it was only once she arrived in Clermont that she realised things would be difficult. Costa tells another version: that players had been signed and pre-season matches arranged without her knowledge. Sports director Olivier Chavanon had signed players she didn't want, refused to reply to her requests for information, and when he did reply said he was 'fed up with her emails'.

Before Costa's departure was publicly announced, Michy spoke to the players in the changing-room. 'I said, "I want to know, all of you in here, who has *never* been dumped by a woman? Lift your hand if that's the case." And no one lifted his hand ... "So now we are all on the same team, because Helena Costa is leaving."'

To me, this reeks of everyday sexism. Michy, to his credit, does not disagree. 'I think I have a sexist side, it's a tendency for people of my generation.' He is 67, and his reported comments after Costa's departure certainly support that case. He said: 'She's a woman so it could be down to any number of things ...'

Michy, then, is a self-confessed sexist appointing women to senior jobs. His main business, which is to organise motor-shows, *Grands Prix*, ice figure-skating and boxing, also has senior women in charge. Is this admirable, or worrying? He is filling the positions with women, but not changing (his own) attitudes – even though he tells me that women are smarter than men.

It feels like a misnomer to describe gender balance in the workplace as a diversity issue. After all, 60 per cent of graduates entering the workplace are now female, and women make 80 per cent of consumer decisions. 'The question should not be why, but why not?' asks Aviva Wittenberg-Cox, a gender balance expert who sits on a committee focused on redressing the balance in French football.

Wittenberg-Cox makes a compelling case for women in football: she says that companies that are more gender-balanced in leadership outperform their peers; and those who are better at promoting women are happier places to work. She identifies three barriers for most organisations: that the leaders are not aware or skilled at leading the change; that the culture unconsciously excludes female talent; and that the systems underwrite those behaviours with unconscious bias impacted into the existing talent management system. 'We'll only really have equality when lousy women get promoted as much as lousy men,' she jokes. We're a long way from that at the moment. She sees her role as changing the dialogue around gender balance: it's not about human resources, unconscious bias, or even a strategic goal. It's simply a cool business opportunity with a clear economic case in its favour.

HOW TO GET AN EDGE – by AVIVA WITTENBERG-COX

1. Gender balance is not the ultimate goal. Identify what the goal is and use gender balance to help you get there.
2. Reframe everything you say to be 100 per cent inclusive.
3. Promote all the people who make the best balance and fire those who don't.

Michy seems to have grasped this fact. I like that he could have chosen a man after the Costa experience, but he didn't. 'When you want to try something, you have to go through with your ideas, that's what I think.' So without telling me, it's clear he did want to have a female coach in charge. It was not just a PR stunt, especially as Michy himself prefers to stay under the radar. He talks of other French club presidents who are constantly in the media. He is not.

Instead, he felt that his (original) decision to be innovative, to be different and, yes, to be creative could give Clermont an edge. So he approached Diacre, the first woman in France to receive her coaching diploma, after getting her number from the former France women's coach, Bruno Bini, whose assistant she had been. In fact Bini wanted the job himself. Michy offered Diacre the same salary as the previous coach. She said yes.

'I said yes because I could not be sure the opportunity would come again,' Diacre said in an interview with FIFA's official magazine *FIFA Weekly*. 'I had sent my CV to lots of teams in women's football and had not received any responses. I asked myself: "Should I go there?" The fact it was the men's game made little difference. I took some advice and everybody said, "Go, go, go!" I just didn't know if the opportunity would come again. I couldn't say no. I knew that by saying yes, I would be seen as the woman in a man's world, but it became the only thing people said to me. From my point of view, Clermont Foot needed a coach, and signed me to be coach. The media talked about me more as a woman than a coach.'

Michy went back to the dressing-room and asked the players another question. 'You all told me you have been dumped by a woman. Which of you has *never* found a new woman after that?' No one lifted a finger. 'Same here,' he said. 'I have found a new woman and her name is Corinne Diacre.'[3]

Diacre was surprised at just how non-stop the narrative became. 'Every question I was asked was about being a woman more than being a coach. It was the only thing people had to say to me.' At a press conference a few months after her appointment, she was so fed up with the constant questions about her gender that she snapped: 'The first! The first! The first! Can we please talk about football now?'

She was particularly wound up by the question about when and whether she would go into the changing-room. She had never heard Bini, or any other male coach of a female team, asked the same question. She felt certain people wanted her to fail, so they could say, 'I told you so.' She said in a rare interview: 'One thing seems certain: the global narrative is that if I fail, it will be because I'm a woman. I am not the only person around who has had critics, but I think I have had to be brave in the face of many factors.'[4]

Diacre always had a natural authority. When she played for France, she was the most vocal of her team-mates. 'You need that personality in the men's game,' she said. 'You could not cope without authority. My management style always involves the players, but being a leader is natural for me, it's in my DNA.'

There were issues inside the club. One player, one of the most talented in the squad, was unhappy at having a female coach, so he was sold. There was also a power battle over new signings with Chavanon, who left the club the following summer. 'Some members of my staff put roadblocks in the way,' she later said. 'Some of them didn't want to work with me. As a club we had to decide which way we were going to go and the president backed me. [Football] is a hostile environment. When I arrived I was judged before people knew me, purely because I was a woman. That surprised me. Why make such hasty judgements, be so suspicious?' Diacre has since taken control of all signings and has proved very canny in the transfer market.[5]

Michy explains that whenever Clermont lost in that first season under Diacre, the story was: 'Diacre lost ... Diacre loses again ... another defeat for Diacre.' When the team started winning: 'Victory for Clermont Foot ... Clermont win again.' It was tiresome for both coach and owner. Michy never put Diacre under pressure, or made her fear for her job.

'I am not a football man but I know we cannot win every game,' Michy continues. 'You, me, we are not at 100 per cent every day. We ask professional players to be at 100 per cent all the time. But they are human beings, and sometimes they have ups and sometimes they have downs. Most of the time, when there are downs, the coach is sacked. But that's not how I do things.'

He is more of a hands-off leader, then. 'At Clermont, the coach is the boss. I have no expertise in football. So if the coach says, "I want a new player, I'm not happy with this one," I would say, "That's fine, let's do it." I trust them. My job is to make the coach understand that you have no doubts about them, that you support them totally. Everyone has their own job, their own skills. Mine is to hold the purse-strings.'

This makes him different from other owners in France, many of whom have been super-successful in business. He tells me about Jean-Pierre Caillot (Reims), Jean-Michel Aulas (Lyon), Michel Seydoux (Lille), Louis Nicollin (Montpellier) and Jean-Raymond Legrand (formerly of Valenciennes). 'They have all succeeded in their own business, but in their football club, it is the opposite. They made profits in business but not in football. It is very strange.'

I ask why no other clubs have followed Michy's model and hired a female coach. He doesn't know, but accepts that there might not be many female candidates who have the requisite coaching qualifications. Michy is also sole owner of the club, and his board consists of himself, his son Philibert and a friend. So there are fewer barriers to a decision like this. 'I can imagine at another club, the discussions might be long.'

Cindy Gallop is not so generous. A former chair at advertising company Bartle Bogle Hegarty, she is now an equality campaigner who set up a website called MakeLoveNotPorn to quash the myths of hardcore pornography and begin a dialogue around how real people have sex. She is pushing for more diversity in the workplace. And she has a sharp tongue quite in contrast with her cut-glass English accent.

'At the top of every industry there is a closed loop of white guys, talking to white guys, about other white guys,' she tells me from her apartment in New York. 'Fuck that shit! Seriously: fuck it! The problem is, we see no change, because the white men at the top, sitting pretty, have absolutely no desire to change. That closed loop is actively closing ranks and keeping them out. It's not unconscious bias but conscious bias.'

She tells me about a cartoon in web-comic *XKCD* that has stayed with her. There are two images, one of a man doing maths sums on a blackboard and getting them wrong; the other is a woman doing the same. 'Wow, you suck at maths!' is the caption under the male image. Under the female image: 'Wow, women suck at maths!'

'Men are hired and promoted on potential and women on proof,' Gallop continues. 'And then they are held to a different set of standards. Has she done the job before? Did she do it well enough, or for long enough? I am sick to death of talking about this because I find myself having to say the same thing over and over again. Fuck talking about it, fucking do it.'

Gallop's language seems a conscious effort to reclaim the 'swearing space' usually acceptable for men but not for women. The words are shocking not because they come from a 50-something executive in a smart suit, but because that executive is a female. She forces us to confront our own biases. Are you shocked by the language, and if so, why? Would you be more or less shocked if a man had said the same thing?

I tell her that Michy has fucking done it. Football's diversity issue is there for all to see. In France, in the 2016–17 season, there were two black coaches in the top division, and in the second division, more women (one) than black coaches (zero).[6] In England in the 2016–17 season, there were three black coaches across all 92 league clubs.[7]

There is a similar issue among coaching appointments in the USA. There have been two black coaches in the 21-year history of the MLS, while the number of black and Latino coaches at the start of the 2017 season, five out of 22 teams, is only one more than in 1998 and 2008; this despite an initiative in 2007 requiring teams to interview candidates from diverse backgrounds. Fernando Clavijo was born in Uruguay, played for the USA national team, and coached New England Revolution and Colorado Rapids in the 2000s. He is now FC Dallas technical director.[8] He sounded like Diacre when talking about his opportunities: 'I always thought that for me to get a job I knew I needed to be better than, not equal to, anybody else.'

'I refuse to believe that the best people and best professionals are mostly white males,' added Chicago Fire general manager Nelson Rodriguez. 'I would find that an incredible set of coincidences.' Hugo Perez, a former USA youth national team coach, worries that this lack of diversity will leave the nation behind the rest of the world. You need those types of coaches to bring something different in order for us and for our players to be able to compete with the rest of the world,' he told the *Guardian*. 'If you don't, you're going to be the same thing you've been for the last 20, 25 years.'

Lillian Thuram, a former France defender who now runs an anti-racism organisation called the Lillian Thuram Foundation, believes unconscious bias stops black players trying to become a manager. 'Sometimes black players ask themselves, "Should I become a manager?" But then they think, even if I get my qualifications, who's going to hire me?' he said. 'I think that, in the collective unconscious, we have trouble imagining a black manager ... A black man in charge of the team? That is something people have much more trouble conceptualising.' He urges black players to continue to get their qualifications, and those making the decisions to question their own biases.

'Football is missing out on a huge opportunity to galvanise, to energise, and to reinvent the future of the sport,' Gallop says. 'Diversity drives innovation. Female coaches bring completely different perspectives and insights to the table. Football leaders are missing out on this totally when they do not embrace a gender-equal scenario.' Gallop told a Sydney conference in 2016, 'Women make shit happen, women get shit done. Want to do less work and make more money? That's the answer ... working with women and "people of colour" is uncomfortable because we are "other". But out of that will come extraordinary insights and perspectives.'

HOW TO GET AN EDGE – by CINDY GALLOP
1. Female lens.
2. Female lens.
3. Female lens. That's your edge right there.

This diversity is also lacking in women's football. Only seven of the 24 national teams to compete at the 2015 Women's World Cup had female coaches. Yet teams coached by women often do better: women were in charge of three of the last four women's World Cup-winning teams, including Jill Ellis's USA side in 2015.[9]

It's a similar story in the women's domestic game. In the top two divisions of the FA Women's Super League, there are five female coaches out of 20 teams. The 2015 league and FA Cup winners, Chelsea Ladies, were coached by Emma Hayes, who might just be best-placed to replicate Diacre's achievement in the British game. Not that she expects it to happen anytime soon.

'For me, it's absolutely ludicrous to think that Premier League teams, who hire expensive management and backroom staff teams to manage the psychology of the dressing-room, have no women in senior coaching positions,' Hayes tells me. 'Having gender balance in the dressing-room could have a significant impact on performance. Balance is critical in all areas of our life. But it's almost like [football clubs] negate the importance of women in their lives. I'm astonished that to this day there are still so few females working in the men's game.' She cites the rise in mental health awareness after former England winger Aaron Lennon was detained under the Mental Health Act amid concerns for his welfare in May 2017. Ryan Giggs and Jamie Carragher wrote in their respective newspaper columns that they had seen psychologists during their playing days. 'There is too much pressure for men, and for me this is another reason why women in a male dressing-room is crucial,' she says.

Hayes was assistant coach at Arsenal Ladies when the Gunners won the quadruple of Premier League, FA Cup, League Cup, and UEFA Cup in 2007. She then worked in USA, coaching at Chicago Red Stars and Washington Freedom, before returning to Chelsea in 2012. Since then, the team has never finished outside the top two.

So would she be prepared to work as a coach in the men's game? 'Of course I'm open to it because, for me, coaching is coaching. I wouldn't have any issue with that. But I don't see this issue as something changing quickly, even if it is beneficial to have different people around. If I was in charge of a football club, or a business, it's something that I would drive.'

Hayes is an eloquent speaker on the subject, even if she gets frustrated (her word, polite for bored) at being described as a role model for women's coaches. 'Everyone tells me that's what I am, but I'm a professional coach first and foremost. We don't mention it enough: female coaches are always role models, but what are male coaches? This is the language around our game, as though it's inferior, even though we are more engaged with our fan-base.'

She looks for the same qualities in her players as some of the teams, like Athletic Club de Bilbao and RB Leizpig, that we have already met: how they deal with setbacks, what their idea of success is, what their motivators are, how receptive they are to learning. Like Thomas Tuchel and Didier Deschamps, she is a relentless self-improver. She says it's harder for coaches to get the same level of feedback as her players. 'I want more open paths to feedback, as I have to make sure that my performance is improving too.'

Hayes agrees with Gallop's theory that women have mentors and men have champions, far more prepared to stick out their necks in the boardroom when it matters. 'No one else is championing these women, so you need to,' urges Gallop. 'Strike mentor from your vocab, inherent in the term is a touchy-feeliness. Fuck the mentor and find the champion! Then go out on a limb for them. Women don't have champions and they need them.' Hayes believes women are more likely to champion a male coach simply because they are used to one. She is quick to champion other impressive female coaches, the likes of Emma Coates (Doncaster Belles), Gemma Grainger (FA Under-15s coach) and Kelly Chambers (Reading Ladies).

When I speak to Hayes, who was awarded an MBE for services to women's football in 2016, she has recently returned from an off-season in Japan. While there she lectured coaches (95 per cent of whom are male) on the challenges of the menstrual cycle in the women's game. She is putting the finishing touches to a paper on the subject – she has been researching it for over two years – and she is scheduled to deliver talks on best practice around the world in 2018.

'The majority of women, let alone men, are completely uneducated about periods, what they are and what they do. So it's hard to optimise your performance when you have an unspoken subject that could be affecting you physiologically or psychologically in one out of every four weeks.'

Hayes says that periods can affect reaction time, neuromuscular co-ordination, manual dexterity, blood-sugar levels, aerobic capacity and muscle maintenance in differing ways. Coexist, a community arts organisation based in Bristol, has created an official 'period policy' to allow women to take time off, in the hope that the workplace will become more efficient and creative. Women tend to be more creative, for example, in the spring phase of their cycle, days 6 to 12, which is just after their period. This is due to a rise in the hormone oestrogen to help the body prepare for ovulation.

'This subject is pushed away like a taboo but it's important,' Hayes continues.[10] 'I can help achieve best performance and avoid risk and help women live and prosper with something that can be very painful and hard to do. People will think I'm crazy but when they talk about specialists, like coaches for forwards, or nutrition coaches … if I had unlimited resources, I would hire someone to manage my players' menstrual cycles. This is a value-added benefit that is clearly applicable outside of sports too. It all depends on how creative you want to be.'

Understanding the menstrual cycle is not 'touchy-feely', as Gallop might say. It relates back to Geir Jordet's visual frequency searches: the more information you have coming in, the better the decisions that you can make. Hayes is learning about physiology and psychology because she wants to win. This is her way of getting an edge.

HOW TO GET AN EDGE – by EMMA HAYES

1. Teach people well enough so they can leave, but treat them well enough so they don't want to.
2. Make sure you have five mirrors looking back at you, and demand feedback.
3. Share success, shoulder blame.

Michy, the Clermont president, might not be ready for a menstrual-cycle coach just yet. But he reminds me that at Clermont, with its low budget, he needs to be smarter than those with a lot of money to spend. So he finds creative solutions. Football remains a mostly conservative world. Who makes brave decisions? When companies are under pressure, the notion of threat rigidity tends to surface: hierarchy, and a focus on the one thing that company does well, takes over. Sometimes this can work, as in the example of Total, the French energy company, who had hoped to get into gas production in America, but ended up grateful it missed out. Another French firm, Kering, sold off brands like Printemps, Fnac and Conforama, and now focuses on more lucrative luxury goods.[11]

So is it cowardly or lazy not to look at more female options in football? 'I think most people adopt the cautious approach we like in France, which to my mind is an intellectual madness,' says Michy. 'I'm not a pioneer. Hiring a woman as a coach has not changed my daily life. The sun still rises in the east. I don't feel like I'm an innovator, just because I hired someone with the competence and the skills to do a job. That's not innovation.

Results on the pitch are nothing to do with me. I leave that to the coach and I trust her. When you have the right coach with the right qualities, they can improve the players and make them grow. That coach could be a man or a woman.'

Diacre always said that she would not think past her daily work at Clermont. And there was a reason for that. She knew that her only chance of coaching in Ligue 1 would be if she went up with Clermont. She did better than expected there, and was accepted by players, fellow coaches and the media – *France Football* magazine voted her Ligue 2 coach of the year in 2015. But as Gallop suggested, there is no Michy equivalent in Ligue 1. No one else would give her the trust, patience, time and space to succeed. No one else would champion her, or have the creativity and innovative instinct to appoint her.

In August 2017, after three seasons at Clermont, she took the job as coach of the France women's team. But it would have been nice had she got Clermont promoted to Ligue 1 before that. Just so she could have stuck two fingers up at her critics, and that player who wrote her off when she joined.

The lack of flowers at her one hundredth game told a story of its own. Men don't get flowers before landmark matches. Why should she be treated differently? Her adaptability was complete. By the time she left Clermont, Diacre was one of the longest-serving coaches in Ligue 2. Michy ignored the conscious bias in the football industry and made a creative decision to hire a coach who would give his team an edge. We could all learn from that.

Michy is more hands-off in his running of Clermont Foot 63 than any other owner I have met in football. That is part of his skill. Later in this chapter, I will learn that stepping back and not interfering in the process is one of the best ways to allow creativity to flourish. At least, that works for one of the most talented youth coaches in football today. I am heading back to England, to meet the Liverpool academy chief whose job is to find the new Steven Gerrard.

HOW TO GET AN EDGE – by CLAUDE MICHY

1. Hard work is seen as a rude word now. There are no miracles. If you work harder than those with more talent, you will be more successful.
2. Keep the people around you motivated at 100 per cent, not 60 per cent, otherwise someone else will take their job.
3. Don't let work affect your personal life. That can be contagious to others.

ALEX INGLETHORPE
Allow creatives to flourish

Creatives need principles / Adapt and Recover, or Die / Intrinsic motivation and the Creativity Maze / Lessons from maverick Townsend / Woodburn and interference factor

As you walk past the main pitch outside the entrance of Liverpool Football Club's youth academy (address: The Liverpool Way), there are banners of former players affixed to each lamppost. The first you see is Jamie Carragher, next Jon Flanagan, then Steven Gerrard, whose picture is closest to the main entrance, and finally Raheem Sterling. All four came through this academy. They are constant reminders to the youngsters who come here – from age five upwards – of what can be achieved.

In the past, this academy has been a battleground between its head coach and Liverpool's first-team manager. In 2007, Steve Heighway, the former Liverpool player who played in their glorious era of the 1970s – winning four league titles, two UEFA Cups and two European Cups – was ousted as academy manager after falling out with then-coach Rafa Benitez. Since then, Piet Hamberg, Pep Segura and Frank McParland have all come and gone as Liverpool's academy manager.

The role has become a political hot potato, not helped by the fact that the Kirkby site, next to a David Lloyd tennis centre on the outskirts of the city, is a ten-minute drive from the first-team training ground at Melwood. As one Liverpool-based writer put it: 'The quest for absolute control or the protection of fiefdoms has ultimately prevailed at the cost of productivity.'[12] Jamie Carragher, more bluntly, said: 'When personalities don't like each other, they hope the other person doesn't do well. Do I think Rafa wanted Liverpool to win the FA Youth Cup? Probably not. Did people at the academy really want Liverpool to be flying under Rafa? Probably not. When a relationship breaks down like that, the club suffers.'

This is the context behind the role that Alex Inglethorpe took when he was appointed academy manager in August 2014. Those four banners mean his job is far more emotive than the title. He is looking to identify, nurture and develop players for the first team. In short, his job is to find the next Steven Gerrard for Liverpool. No pressure, then.

Inglethorpe is suited to the task. He is thoughtful and reflective, takes notes during our time together and admits he doesn't have all the answers. Even if you might remember Thomas Tuchel saying the same thing, this is still a rare admission for people who work inside football clubs. He enjoys having his ideas challenged.

During our wide-ranging conversations, he explained his methodology behind unlocking creativity, motivating millennials, communicating with digital natives, and the importance of promoting authenticity, empathy and happiness in the workplace.

One of Inglethorpe's first moves was to bring Heighway back into the fold (and another former youth coach, Dave Shannon), while it was lost on no one that Liverpool coach Jürgen Klopp spent his first full day in charge of the club watching an Under-18s match from the balcony overlooking the main pitch at Kirkby. In spring 2017, it was confirmed that the senior team would train on the same site as the youth structures. Inglethorpe was also involved in the decision to bring Steven Gerrard back to the academy to start his coaching career. Who better to help him find the new Gerrard than the original one? The former Liverpool captain speaks highly of Inglethorpe, who has told him about the importance of his body language and his coaching voice, which he wants to carry the same power as when he was Liverpool captain. 'He has been honest and straight with me,' said Gerrard. 'He's been first-class.'

Inglethorpe's three years in charge of the academy are beginning to bear fruit. In the 2015–16 season, Klopp's first at the club, nine academy graduates were given first-team debuts.[13] In 2016–17, there were another four, three of whom – Trent Alexander-Arnold, Ovie Ejaria and Ben Woodburn – have made the move to Melwood full-time.[14] This is a ringing endorsement of the work done by Inglethorpe and his academy staff.

Many coaches in England develop talent as a stepping-stone, part of the process, to becoming a senior first-team coach. Inglethorpe is different. His was a proactive decision to focus on development rather than be a head coach. He had played for Watford (for whom, bizarrely, he once scored a pre-season goal against Östersunds FK, the Swedish team we met in Chapter 1), Leyton Orient and Exeter City. His coaching career began at Leatherhead, and he was in charge of Exeter City when they drew 0–0 with Manchester United in a 2005 FA Cup tie. He turned down offers from MK Dons and Brentford to be their coach. He would have got more money and more prestige, but felt he was better suited to developing talent.[15] Instead he moved to Tottenham Hotspur and worked under academy head John McDermott. He describes it as 'my Harvard education'. That decision encapsulates him. He knows his strengths. He thinks before he speaks. He doesn't waste words. He has an unflappable quality about him.

And he is honest: whether it's admonishing one of the better Under-16 players in front of his team-mates for making a lazy foul in the last minute that could have led to a goal, or announcing to a packed dressing-room that an Under-15 triallist would be given a contract (normally that happens in a quiet meeting with parents present, but he felt the emotional contagion from the good news would infiltrate the squad, and it did).

He does not expect the players to like him. Respect is far more important; and he measures that by former players who have made it to Premier League level and who still keep in touch.

Those who played in the 2016–17 Premier League season include: Adam Smith (Bournemouth), Jake Livermore (Hull City), Ryan Mason (Hull City), Danny Rose (Spurs), Harry Kane (Spurs), Andros Townsend (Crystal Palace), Tom Carroll (Swansea) and Harry Winks (Spurs).

His definitions of talent and creativity provide the perfect starting-point for our discussion. Like Ralf Rangnick, he defines talent as a mathematical equation:

Potential + time + opportunity – interference = Talent

Creativity, as he sees it, is deviation from the norm. In his words: 'An ability to go off script.' When he watches most matches, he can see where the best pass *should* go, or would normally go, but once in a while, a player will come along and not follow the script. 'Sometimes that can leave you thinking, "Where did that come from?"'

'The danger with that level of creativity is that it can be stifled at a young age,' Inglethorpe says. 'It can be coached out of you if you're in the wrong environment.' The coach draws a line between the need for rules, a rigid structure that takes away options and makes the game-situation less complex, and the need for principles, which relate to behaviour, approach and work ethic. He talks to his coaches a lot about this difference; which players and staff need rules and which need principles. Creative talents work better with principles rather than rules. 'We are very wary, as we do not want to be a limiting factor to talent. We do not want to be a hindrance.'

This sense of freedom is vital for the creative. Ed Catmull, head of Pixar Animation Studios, wrote as much in a business article that was a precursor to his 2014 book *Creativity Inc*. A strong believer that talented people trump great ideas, he demands an environment 'that nurtures trusting and respectful relationships and unleashes everyone's creativity'. Pixar's operating principles (not rules), he continued, were that everyone must have the freedom to communicate with anyone; it must be safe for everyone to offer ideas; and to stay close to innovations happening in the academic community.[16]

Inglethorpe draws me a diagram of the people that were around Michael Owen when he broke into the Liverpool team aged 16 back in 1996.

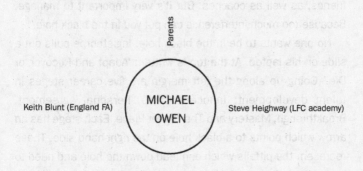

Alongside that, he draws a circle of a highly rated 16-year-old currently playing for a rival club.

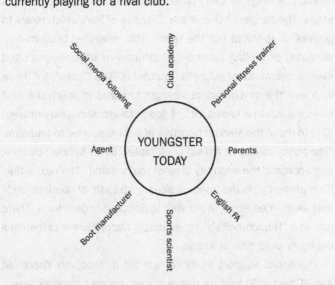

'Look at all that information he has coming into him!' Inglethorpe says. 'It's from different people, with different agendas, all wanting different things. How is he going to be able to concentrate on football without that consistency of message? Or at least, how much energy is he going to devote to sifting through all that information? And most of all, how will he be able to enjoy it? The interference can come from other parties, like agents, parents, friends, as well as coaches. But it's very important to manage. Because too much interference can put you in the black hole.'

No one wants to be in the black hole. Inglethorpe pulls out a slide on his laptop. At the top is written: 'Adapt and Recover, or Die.' Going up along the left margin are five career stages in talent development: Innocent Climb, Personal Agreement, Breakthrough, Mastery and The Higher Plane. Each stage has an arrow which points to a black hole on the right-hand side. These represent the pitfalls which can lead down the hole and need to be avoided. As we go through each one, the names of players pop into my head of those who fell along the way.

The challenge for every player is to adapt and recover at each stage. The dangers? One is the 'Disease of Me', which refers to players' inability to put the team first: resenting team-mates' success, or feeling paranoid, frustrated or under-appreciated even at moments of success. Another is 'The Choke', for those who lack the psychological strength required to reach the next level. Inglethorpe knows lots of good players who have not been able to make the step up because of their response to pressure. 'The ability to play at Anfield is ultimately down to how you think and approach the enormity of what you're doing.' The next pitfall, 'Complacency', is the 'made it already attitude' of hubristic pride that we learned about in our visit to Salzburg in Chapter 4. There are also 'Thunderbolts': unpredictable factors like a career-ending injury or long-term illness.

The social support study carried out by Nico van Yperen at Ajax (Chapter 3) told us that a strong support network was a predictor of success. But *too much* influence can have the oppo-site effect. The Chelsea psychologist Tim Harkness explained to me what he felt was a key difference between elite performers and the rest: 'One of the differences is that successful people just have more energy. They are still hungry and driven to succeed. The other is their ability to manage the circumstances that influence your motivation. Some people are hungry. Some people are strategically good at managing their influences. A very small number are good at both. If you want to be an elite foot-baller you have to be good at both, that's what can really sepa-rate you from the pack.' It's a way of getting smart with the motivation resources that you have.

Inglethorpe makes it his business to understand the players' triggers for optimal performance. 'I need to know what buttons to push for every single one of them.' That's a lot of information to take in, given there are 170 players in the academy (this figure has come down from 240 when Inglethorpe took over, as he is looking for quality over quantity).

He tells me about one of his Under-18 players, who was strug-gling for a time last season. It was obvious to see and the coach brought him in for a chat. The youngster always had a ball in his rucksack, and was under-performing because he had stopped playing his favourite game, which was two-on-two football with his best mates in a tiny garage near the block of flats where he grew up. As a creative player, he was able to learn, improvise and practise moves in such small spaces. It was also football as pure enjoyment, not work, and away from the homogenised atmosphere of an academy environment.

Over a period of several conversations, Inglethorpe under-stood this was at the core of the player's blockage. So he suggested that he carry on playing his two-on-two. 'Your head says that if a player is this talented and 18 years old, you should not let him play garage football. The sports scientists would say no, the medics would say no. But you need to be intuitive and sometimes just understand what's best for the individual. This is not based on a performance model, it's a development model.'

It was also a calculated risk. Inglethorpe wanted the player to remember what made him unique, and encouraged him to tap into his own authenticity. It's similar to the 2015 Converse 'Made by You' advertising campaign, which showed over 200 portraits of Chuck Taylor sneakers personalised by creative customers worldwide.[17] Some had been coloured with rainbow stripes; others had hearts or messages painted on the toes; others were scuffed in an original way. All were celebrating individualism. Inglethorpe likewise wanted this youngster to celebrate his own individualism. The player went back to his garage game. The confidence boost was immediate and, not long after, he made his debut for the Liverpool first team. He is now a regular with the Melwood group.

There are a few factors going on here, so let's break them down. The first is interference. Inglethorpe understood instinctively that giving the player autonomy in the development process would help his creativity. Second, the coach also showed empathy, simply by spotting that his player needed assistance and offering it. By making that first move, he showed that he cared. Third, he communicated his message in a clear and concise way. Now for a closer look at these factors.

First, interference: we have explored the difference between process and outcome in Chapters 2 and 3. Thomas Tuchel wants his team to represent a certain spirit regardless of the result. The AZ Alkmaar coaches tell their players which mountains to climb but not necessarily how to climb them. A clearly specified goal can aid creativity, but too much interference can be harmful.

Harvard professor and creativity expert Professor Teresa Amabile sums this up by explaining the Creativity Maze. There is a reward in the middle in the maze. Someone outcome-oriented would rush through the maze as quickly as possible, maybe taking obvious paths that have been used before, to get the reward. This approach is based on *extrinsic* motivation, a reward that is outside of the individual. It could be money, status, or even just avoiding the sack. The *intrinsic* motivation approach is about the process. It will probably lead to more errors. It may take longer. But the route in the maze would be more interesting, and the ultimate solution more creative.

'People will be most creative when they feel motivated primarily by the interest, satisfaction and challenge of the work itself – and not by external pressures,' says Amabile. Creative people have stronger intrinsic motivation. Albert Einstein described it as 'the enjoyment of seeing and searching'. Michael Jordan loved basketball so much that he had a clause in his contract that he could play a pick-up game whenever he liked.

Other companies are taking note. A study by the University of Warwick asked 700 participants to add a series of five two-digit numbers in ten minutes.[18] Some were then shown a ten-minute film based on comedy routines performed by a British comedian; or they were treated to free chocolate, drinks and fruit. The film, and the free snacks, succeeded in raising reported happiness levels of those who saw it, and improved their productivity. They found that happiness led to a 12 per cent spike in productivity, while unhappy workers were 10 per cent less productive.[19]

One Brighton-based conference business set up a Happiness Index for its employees with three buckets and a load of tennis balls. At the end of each day, everyone would take one ball and put it in one of two buckets: H marked happy or U marked unhappy. Not exactly sophisticated: but the results were collected every night and over a period of months, the company's collective emotional temperature was taken. It turned out that Tuesdays tended to be a bad day.

Inglethorpe gets it. His staff love what they do so much that he has to beg them to take more time off. 'The best places of work are the ones where you don't see it as work,' he says. That is intrinsic motivation. He has it, and it's important that the creative talents also have it. They need it the most.

Intrinsic motivation is the main reason behind Liverpool's decision to cap salaries for first-year professionals (i.e. for 17-year-olds) at £40,000 per year. They believe this policy of 'delayed gratification' will benefit the players in the long term. Southampton and Spurs do the same, while other Premier League clubs have reportedly offered contracts to 16-year-olds worth over £500,000 per year.

'Think back to when you were 17 and how you would have handled a huge salary, plus a lot of time on your hands, *and* getting recognition from people around you. Would that have helped you fulfil your potential?' Inglethorpe asks. (Thinking back, I struggled at that age without any of those things.) 'We are trying to limit certain parts of the equation to help the player fulfil his potential.' The lower salary should weed out athletes with extrinsic motivation who could earn more money elsewhere.

Inglethorpe has also learned from experience. His period working with Andros Townsend at Spurs informed his response to this particular Reds youngster. He remembers Townsend fondly as 'an off-the-chart maverick in his approach'. Townsend was single-minded and obsessive in his approach to self-improvement. He would ignore advice to rest from sports scientists. He would hide a ball in the bushes behind the training pitch at Spurs and then play for another two hours with Tom Carroll and Jon Obika. He was stubborn and had no fear of failure. But he also had extremely high levels of intrinsic motivation.

'He taught me a valuable lesson,' says Inglethorpe. 'He needed to get it wrong more than he got it right, and that approach worked for him. Andros got the best out of his talent, and he showed me there is more than one way to do that.'

It was not just the lack of interference that helped Townsend. (Of course Inglethorpe knew about the ball in the bushes, but he never took it away or forbade Townsend from playing.) It was also empathy, as the coach also provided an emotional support to allow that fearlessness to remain. Even if senior Spurs players like Dimitar Berbatov and Robbie Keane would get frustrated when he didn't pass, Townsend was never afraid to fail with a dribble. A few days before Inglethorpe told me this story, the winger had scored a goal for Crystal Palace that summed up this attitude: running from inside his own half to score in a crucial win against Middlesbrough. 'Maverick talents take more risks so there is more chance of them failing,' he adds. 'But the upside is always greater.'

This is about care. Caring for the body gives a player an edge. But care from managers, particularly in the form of emotional support, is a huge driver in performance. The presence of a caring environment allows you to take risks and innovate without fear of failure. Geir Jordet also believes that helping a team-mate during a game can take your mind off your own pressure and so enhance your performance

Anthony Knockaert would agree. The Brighton winger was devastated when his father died in November 2016. Two days later, captain Steve Sidwell celebrated scoring a goal from the halfway line by running to the touchline and holding up Knockaert's shirt (Knockaert was absent on compassionate leave). The next week, coach Chris Hughton and 14 of Knockaert's team-mates crossed the Channel to pay their respects at the funeral near Lille. 'When one of our team hurts, we all hurt,' tweeted goalkeeper David Stockdale with a unique team picture: the whole squad wearing black suits outside a church. Knockaert was blown away: 'When I say it was the best moment for me in my life, I hope you know what I mean,' he told *The Times*. 'My family were so proud, they realised how good this club is, the best I've been at.'

This is also becoming a priority in business. The Empathy Business rates companies that successfully create empathetic cultures based on their ethics, leadership, company culture, brand perception and public messaging through social media.

The rankings correlate empathy to growth, productivity and earnings per employee. Those companies with high rankings also have high retention rates, environments where diverse teams thrive, and are the most financially profitable. In 2016, Facebook, which had recently established an 'Empathy Lab' devoted to building accessibility features into the site for blind, deaf or otherwise disabled users, topped the Empathy Index.[20]

I notice a similar level of care in the smallest exchanges at the Liverpool academy. During a short walk from Inglethorpe's sparsely equipped office overlooking the training pitches to the canteen, he greets every youngster he sees by name.[21] He expects the same in return. He sees a 15-year-old from Spain about to eat, and asks him how he's getting on. 'Good,' says the boy. 'What's on your plate?' asks the coach. 'Rice, vegetables and, um ...' 'Those are prawns,' says Inglethorpe. 'Well done. Your English is getting a lot better. Great stuff. Enjoy your meal.' The boy beams and tucks in.

The third factor, after interference and empathy, is communication. Didier Deschamps told us about the art of listening in Chapter 2, but managing millennials is no easy task. Jens Lehmann once told me about his brief spell with Arsenal's reserve side as a 40-year-old back in 2011. In the team coach on the way to a game he was surprised by the total silence. 'No one was talking,' he said. 'I thought, "Has everyone gone to sleep?" But then I looked around. Everyone was on their phones, typing away on Twitter or Facebook. They were all hanging on their devices and I think this has a major impact on communication.

'These kids are not used to quick language commands and all their time on the phone makes them incapable of quick commands on the pitch. They text instead of talk and that means they are not quick thinkers any more. I really do think this is influencing the games now: we have to teach them how to communicate on the pitch. I know of some players who have been told to get off Twitter as they are addicted.'

One coach told me that his goalkeeper spends so much time looking down at his device that it is actually affecting his spine. He fears that the player will decline much quicker than other goalkeepers as a result.

Social psychologist Sherry Turkle, author of *Alone Together*, argues the muscles in our brain that help with spontaneous conversation are getting less exercise than ever before, and therefore our communication abilities are declining. One 18-year-old boy came up with something she found interesting. 'Some day, but not now, I'd like to learn how to have a conversation,' he said. 'Why not now?' she asked. 'Because it takes place in real time and you can't control what you're going to say,' he said.

'Our devices are so psychologically powerful they don't change what we do but who we are,' Turkle said. 'It matters because we set ourselves up for trouble in how we relate to each other and how we relate to ourselves and our capacity for self-reflection. Our devices give us the illusion of companionship without the demands of friendship ... If we don't teach our children how to be alone [without devices], they will only know how to be lonely.'

Liverpool deals with this problem by telling all players in the Under-18s and above to hand in their mobile phones when they arrive, and they can only pick them up after they leave. 'They have to learn to communicate,' says Inglethorpe. He draws a crucial distinction. 'It's only harder for leaders to communicate with them if you choose for it to be harder. They are a different generation in the way they communicate *with each other*, but if you are prepared to make the time to sit down and have a chat, I don't know a single player that would not appreciate that. It's wrong for us to assume that generation do not want an old-fashioned face-to-face chat. They do want it and respond well to it.' Smartphones are kept out of sight, as they are in coaches' meetings as well. This is a lesson out of the Deschamps's playbook. Both recognise that having devices out of sight leads to more fulfilling interactions.

Dr Sherylle Calder, a South African vision specialist who has worked in American football, golf, motor racing, rugby, and in the 2016–17 season with the Bournemouth goalkeepers, advises that less screen time improves players' decision-making.[22] 'When you look at your phone there are no eye movements happening and everything is pretty static,' she says. 'In the modern world the ability of players to have good awareness is deteriorating.' She argues that we develop instinctive natural skills by climbing trees, and walking on and falling off walls. Spending time on devices weakens those skills. 'If you don't see something, you can't make a decision. One of the skills we work on is being able to see, or pick up, something early. The earlier you see, the more time you have to make a decision.'

I am reminded of a picture that, ironically enough, went viral minutes after Argentina had beaten Venezuela 4–1 in the 2016 Copa America semi-final. Argentina, who had not won a major trophy since 1993, was one game away from ending this 23-year drought. It was taken by Argentina defender Marcos Rojo and posted by team-mate Ezequiel Lavezzi on Instagram, with the caption: 'You've just finished playing a game and ...'

There are seven of them, sitting on the dressing-room bench. All have their boots off, some have taken off their socks or their shirts. Collectively, they could make up one of the finest five-a-sides (plus two subs) in history: Lionel Messi, Sergio Aguero, Lavezzi, Gonzalo Higuain, Javier Mascherano, Jonatan Maidana and Ever Banega. Not one of them is looking at anyone else. No one is speaking. They are all looking down, at their phones. In their own world; together, but miles away; present, but absent. 'This is the national team 2.0,' joked one newspaper, *Olé*, while a writer in *Clarin* pointed out: 'If phones are our full-time companions today, why shouldn't they be for footballers too?' The only people who weren't happy with the picture were Venezuelan fans, as some of their players' shirts can be seen strewn on the dressing-room floor. Lavezzi was happy: his picture got 147,000 likes. Argentina went on to lose the final, on penalties, to Chile.

Another image from a game in November 2016 sticks in my mind. Liverpool had just beaten Leeds United 2–0 in the League Cup quarter-final and two players are walking off the pitch, smiling at each other. There is an ease in their movements, comfort in their company; each one is chuffed for the other. There is nothing lonely about this moment. Communication does not seem to be a problem.

These two might be the next players whose image will be on the lampposts overlooking the academy main pitch: one of them is Trent Alexander-Arnold, the 18-year-old right-back whose whipped cross from the flank set up Divock Origi for the opening goal.[23] Ben Woodburn, the other player, is even younger. He was making his second appearance for the first team and scored a goal at the Kop end, where Liverpool's loudest support sits. At 17 years and 45 days, Woodburn had just become the youngest ever scorer in the club's history. It was an incredible moment. 'Roy of the Rovers stuff,' says Inglethorpe, who watched the match with the Under-18s team at the stadium. 'It was wonderful to be around them when Ben scored.'

I had first heard of both players a few months earlier, sitting in that academy canteen with Inglethorpe and his colleagues. As we all ate pea soup, they were talking about players with talent. 'But do they have an edge?' I asked. The answers were unanimous. Woodburn, particularly, seemed destined for the top. They spoke of his quiet determination. His will to win. Cool under pressure. Ice in his veins. Reacting well to team-mates losing the ball, or when he misses chances. He had been fast-tracked through the club: at 15 he had played for the Under-18s and then as part of the Elite Youth Group that trained with the senior team at Melwood once a week. Now he trains there every day. He doesn't want that goal to be the defining moment of his career.

A few months after that goal against Leeds, he was called up to the senior Wales squad.

'You're more nervous around a highly talented boy, so the best thing is to give him the freedom to develop,' says Inglethorpe. 'The skill of a coach is to know when to push and when to provoke. Sometimes the best way to manage a creative talent is to leave them to it.'[24]

In the cases of Woodburn, Alexander-Arnold and Ejaria, this is no longer a choice for Inglethorpe. They have moved on to Melwood. They are all one step closer to their dreams. Inglethorpe is one of the coaches who helped make it happen, and he will still be there for them, if they need him. He certainly still cares. There's also the next generation to consider, which includes an exciting teenage creative talent called Rhian Brewster. He has a long way to go. As long as Inglethorpe is running the academy, he is in good hands: with a specialist who understands how to give young talent an edge.

Inglethorpe is coaxing the best out of potential but what about the manager who is dealing with established talent? I wanted to ask someone who has been part of a team that contained a genius talent how best to unlock creativity. I knew just the man: a World Cup winner, former team-mate of Diego Maradona and a successful coach with Real Madrid. My final appointment on this quest for an edge was with Jorge Valdano.

HOW TO GET AN EDGE – by ALEX INGLETHORPE

1. Everyone has to feel engaged in whatever they're doing.
2. Accept no compromise in standards.
3. Enjoy work, have fun: the best workplaces are where you don't see it as work, but as a meaningful part of your life.

JORGE VALDANO

Make room for the maverick

Progressives reject mainstream / Football reflects life / Conditions for talent growth / Team as state of mind / Optimistic leadership and **The Happy Film** */ The connectivity curse / The genius transaction*

Jorge Valdano tells a neat story about Diego Maradona's second goal against England in the 1986 World Cup quarter-final. Maradona dribbled from inside his own half past a series of lunging England defenders and stroked the ball past the goalkeeper, Peter Shilton, to secure a famous victory. It remains one of the greatest goals ever scored, and Valdano had the best view of it.

Valdano was Maradona's Argentina team-mate at the time, and was running alongside Maradona waiting for him to pass the ball. 'Why didn't you pass to me?' he asked Maradona after the game. Maradona told him he had wanted to, and was watching Valdano while skipping beyond each challenge, but the defenders kept coming, and before he knew it he'd beaten them all and scored. Valdano couldn't believe it. 'While scoring this goal you were also watching me? You insult me. It isn't possible!'[25]

Valdano's moment of glory came in the final. He scored the goal that put Argentina 2–0 ahead against West Germany. At that point, he realised the enormity of the moment, and started watching the game like a fan. Before he knew it, the score was 2–2. As Argentina kicked off to restart the game, José Luis Burruchaga turned to Valdano and Maradona and said: 'We're feeling good, aren't we? No problem, this one's in the bag.' Two minutes later, Burruchaga scored the winning goal.

Valdano played for Real Madrid at the time. He had been

voted Overseas Player of the Year for that season. The team, five of whom were developed in the club's academy, won five league titles in a row from 1986 to 1990. The pick of the bunch was the charismatic Emilio Butragueno, whose nickname *El Buitre* ('The Vulture'), spawned the team nickname *La Quinta del Buitre* ('The Vulture's Generation'). Valdano added experience and goals to this mix.

Valdano later became Real Madrid coach – giving a debut to a willowy 17-year-old called Raúl – and, twice, sporting director of the club (from 2000 to 2004 and from 2009 to 2011); he was in charge when they bought David Beckham, Zinedine Zidane and Cristiano Ronaldo. Although Real Madrid is still identified with General Franco and considered a right-wing club, Valdano, a former law student who is now a columnist, commentator, author and management consultant, is proudly left-wing, although he prefers the term 'progressive'.

'A progressive approach rejects the mainstream belief that organisation takes precedence over freedom, that the collective counts for more than the individual,' he once said. 'It rejects the notion that the coach's ideas outweigh those of the players, and fear neutralises attacking instincts.'[26]

This is why I want to ask Valdano about talent and creativity, and how he finds an edge in rejecting 'the mainstream belief ...'. Take his first-ever game as a coach, in charge of relegation-threatened Tenerife: his first-choice defence, all four of them, were unavailable (injured or suspended). The club owner, a local gynaecologist called Javier Perez, offered to buy Jorge Higuain (Gonzalo's dad) to shore things up at the back. Valdano said no. Instead, he fielded two wingers at full-back, and two attacking midfielders at centre-back. Tenerife won 1–0.

That team had looked doomed when Valdano took over with eight games left to play. 'It was crazily unwise by me,' he admitted later. 'It could have compromised my career as a coach and my credibility as a commentator. I had everything to lose but also wanted to be a coach and had the conviction that I could adapt my ideas to the characteristics of the team.'[27]

Tenerife were safe before the last day of the season. Final-day opponents Real Madrid needed to win to be crowned champions, and were 2–0 up at half-time. Valdano told his players that they would be the centre of the football world if they turned it around. They did, and won the game 3–2 – which meant that Barcelona won the title. The rest of Spain declared Tenerife true champions.

'The coach de-blocked us mentally,' said Tenerife's attacking midfielder Felipe Miñambres. 'He taught us to dare, to no longer have fear, to take risks. We would have followed him anywhere. We believed everything he said. He made us feel invincible.'

The same thing happened the very next season: Tenerife beat Real Madrid on the last day, helping Barcelona win the title.[28] Tenerife also qualified for the UEFA Cup. After Tenerife beat Real Madrid in the Copa del Rey semi-final in the following season, the capital club had had enough. They hired Valdano as coach. He won La Liga in his first season in charge.

Valdano explains that he was a coach who always looked for greatness. 'It was based on my desire for efficacy, courage and beauty – even though I wasn't judged on those factors, but was actually judged on my results.'

He remains a romantic. For him, process outweighs outcome. He loves the art of improvisation. Creativity matters. Mavericks *should* succeed. That's why he wrote a column in *Marca*, Spain's best-selling newspaper, bemoaning the goalless 2007 Champions League semi-final between Liverpool and Chelsea as 'shit hanging from a stick'. His view? 'The extreme control and seriousness with which both teams played the semi-final neutralised any creative licence, any moments of exquisite skill ... Such extreme intensity wipes away talent, even leaving a player of Joe Cole's class disoriented. If football is going the way Chelsea and Liverpool are taking it, we had better be ready to wave goodbye to any expression of the cleverness and talent we have enjoyed for a century.'

He also fully agrees that the business world has a lot to learn from football. 'The analogies between the sport and business are fairly obvious. Companies need to earn money and achieve their targets. But the world we live in is full of frustration, anxiety and stress, all of which subverts these goals and strategies. In my view, football can offer solutions. Football helps us understand who we are. It reflects what is happening in our cities: the commercialism and the competition, the ugly and the beautiful aspects. And why is it so compelling as a metaphor? Because it is a world of exaggeration, of excess. It produces powerful images, images we can all relate to.'

Valdano is in a privileged position to teach us about getting an edge. He even set up a company, called Makeateam, which advised how to manage talent and discover the motivations within a team to optimise performance. Rather like this book, its aim was to improve businesses by offering real-life lessons from the football world.

As a player, team-mate, coach, sporting director, columnist and author, he has stuck to his view of football as an art form. Like Thomas Tuchel, he believes in the aesthetic (now there's a conversation I would like to listen in on). It takes courage to think, to play, to coach and to write the way he does. When he said he could never have scored Maradona's solo goal, but he can describe it better than his team-mate, he was establishing a difference between narrative intelligence (his own) and footballing intelligence (Maradona's). 'The first has more prestige but the second has more complexity.' This is why his nickname, *El Filosofo* ('The Philosopher'), is not meant ironically.

Before he tells me how to unlock creativity, I ask how he defines talent. 'It's a gift that chooses us,' is his response. 'A special facility that, cultivated properly, can distinguish us professionally. We know there are many ways for us to shine. The intelligence needed for painting is not the same intelligence needed for solving a maths equation or for playing football. And talent needs a proper environment. That cultural force pushes talent like no other force can. 'Talent,' he continues, 'needs certain conditions to flourish:

- *Opportunity:* talent grows relative to the difficulties it has overcome.[29]
- *Training:* training for eight hours a day with passion is the best way to honour talent.
- *Other talents nearby:* because to be in touch with other talents will strengthen your own.
- *Confidence:* maybe the only thing that takes your talent to the frontier of your possibilities.'

Wherever he works, Valdano makes sure the people around him are confident. His job is to enhance his colleagues' belief that they can perform beyond their expectations. It's a mental trick that relates to one of his more famous quotes: 'A team is a state of mind.' What does that mean?

'A team is a state of mind. That definition can be applied for any team: sports team, business team, political team, academic team … For example, I believe that a football coach needs to know about football but also about human beings. Knowing about football makes you value the knowledge, while knowing about human beings makes you value the emotions. In a technology company, the equation is the same: you need to know about technology but also about human beings. It's the same in any organisation. A positive state of mind can work miracles in the performance of a team; a negative state of mind too, but the other way around.'

We have seen that businesses can improve results by improving the happiness of their employees. Optimistic leaders can also boost production by focusing on opportunities, finding solutions, and enabling collaboration and innovation.

The best form of optimism is what business leaders call 'realistic optimism'. One study had a psychologist interview obese women in a weight-loss programme about how confident they were about reaching their goals. Those who were confident lost an average 26 pounds more than the self-doubters. The other difference was in who had 'realistic optimism' about their efforts. The women who believed it would be difficult to reach their target lost 24 pounds *more* than those who thought it would be easy. Optimism is one thing, but it has to be realistic. The psychologist behind the study, Gabriele Oettingen, found similar results applied to other areas of life: students looking for jobs after college, old people recovering from hip replacements, singles looking for love. The realism associated with the task led to higher success rates.[30]

Valdano has his own version of optimism. The best teams, he says, need passion; people who believe strongly in what they are doing. 'People with such outstanding qualities that the realm of the team's possibilities becomes as wide as possible. I say that because people normally look for faults first and choose those who don't have any.' Valdano prefers to focus on the positive. 'I choose the outstanding quality [first] and normally I fall in love with that because that gives you the enthusiasm to help those around you to improve.'

Valdano also warns that you need time to work on state of mind. He recommends a change of scenery. To aid his creative thinking, he takes proper time off from football every three or four years and it does him the world of good.

He is not the only one: Stefan Sagmeister, a double Grammy-winning New York-based designer who has made album covers for the Rolling Stones, Jay-Z, and Talking Heads, makes everyone in his design studio Sagmeister & Walsh take a year off every seven years as a way to enhance their creativity. During one such break, he was designing furniture in the Balinese town of Ubud. A friend joked that all he had to show for his amazing experience was some beautiful chairs – and so what? Sagmeister asked himself the same thing.

Sagmeister, a controversial figure in the design world, wondered if he could train his mind to be happier.[31] He wanted to take time to really explore what can make us happy, and even change his personality to become a better person. He made a film about his quest, which turned into a seven-year odyssey that, as he put it, 'attracted every possible catastrophe I could imagine. Working on *The Happy Film* made me profoundly unhappy.' The result was an ambiguous, funny, sad, sensitive and honest picture of a man trying to be a better person.

It was also a success. *The Happy Show*, originally conceived as an extension of the film, has become the world's most visited graphic design exhibit, showing in nine different cities.[32]

Sagmeister is an optimistic leader in the Valdano mould. He recently argued with his older sister over who was the more optimistic. (His nieces broke it up and said they would be the judges. It was a tie.) His method of unlocking creativity comes from the philosopher Edward de Bono, who suggests starting to think about an idea for a particular project by taking a random object as point of departure. Sagmeister gives the example of a pen, and looks around his Japanese hotel room for a random object. 'Bed spreads! So, bedspreads are ... sticky ... contain bacteria ... ah, would it be possible to design a pen that's thermo-sensitive, so it changes colours where I touch it. That would be nice, and not so bad considering it took me all of 30 seconds. This works because the method forces the brain to start out at a new and different point, preventing it from falling into a familiar groove it has formed before.' This is Differential Learning, by a different name.

Sagmeister is a fair-weather Bayern Munich fan, only because his great friend Bobby Dekeyser was briefly on their books. Dekeyser became a successful entrepreneur himself, his luxury furniture brand DEDON making him millions and selling to the likes of Uli Hoeness, Michael Ballack, Brad Pitt and Julia Roberts. 'We invented the outside living-room,' he said. The secret to his success was 'The Bobby Principle', of keeping his employees happy. He offered free health care and travel to work and a sports instructor every night for different tuition. He also engaged employees in his social purpose, among which is to help people on the Philippine island of Cebu build sustainable lives.

The main purpose of Sagmeister's sabbaticals is to make sure that the work remains a calling, 'and does not deteriorate into a job'. I ask him if we are too connected to be truly creative. With smartphone addiction filling up spare moments, those opportunities for inspiration become increasingly rare. Who has ever had a great idea while checking emails in a restaurant, clicking on cat memes or watching a Donald Trump gif?

'The problem itself is not that I am too connected, the problem is that I use this available connectivity as an excuse for being too busy to do real work,' Sagmeister replies. 'It is just so much easier to answer a couple of emails, do some Skype calls and reply to texts, than it is to sit down and actually, properly, think. The problem is not the technology, the problem is me.' Given that around 75 per cent of Americans use their phone in the bathroom, and 25 per cent of Brits let their device interrupt sex, I suspect he is not alone.

HOW TO GET AN EDGE – by STEFAN SAGMEISTER

1. Take a train trip and work while looking out the window.
2. Move into a new place for a month.
3. Start thinking about an idea using a word in the dictionary that has nothing to do with that idea.

Thomas Tuchel took a sabbatical in 2014 after his five years at Mainz and before he joined Borussia Dortmund. At the start, he felt under pressure to travel the world in a camper van, but he soon enjoyed a slower and less scheduled way of life. He booked a two-week family holiday in Italy and ended up staying for eight weeks. He was able to enjoy other cultures: going to gigs and, on the recommendation of an 80-year-old he met at the local swimming-pool, visiting Vienna's Kunsthistorisches Museum to see the work of Pieter Bruegel.

'I had the time to discover artists and musicians and to get to know different people,' Tuchel says. 'Also my neighbour – to sit and have dinner and listen to his ideas about books or other things. That can help keep things fresh in your mind and allow you to think about your talent, your destination and your journey.' So would he take another sabbatical in the future, if required? 'For sure, 100 per cent. And this time I would switch off for longer, and not think about the next job too early.'

Not everyone is in a position to take time off work to recharge, refresh and reinvent. But even *some* quiet time can help. Luciano Bernardi, an Italian doctor, discovered that our muscles and breathing are more relaxed by silence than by relaxing music. A 2013 study of work environments in the *Journal of Environmental Psychology*, based on a survey of 43,000 employees, concluded that the noise and distraction disadvantages of open-plan offices outweighed the anticipated, but unproven, benefits such as raised morale and productivity boosts from spontaneous interactions.[33]

Valdano believes that space and freedom allow creativity to flourish. 'You put a limit on the possibilities of a child's development if you cut their needs of expression.' Like many South Americans, in football terms he believes 'the street' is the best teacher. In football schools, there is homogeny and an obligation to follow a model of learning. That leads to kids all running and playing in a similar way. Fine for the average ones. But for the special ones? 'It's terrible. The street respects spontaneity and doesn't hold back those ones who are different.'

So how does a leader get the best out of a maverick talent in the workplace? 'You need to be someone who first recognises the talent, but is also within a team who can live with a different personality. Geniuses aren't always easy people to live with, but their contributions produce such a jump in quality that they deserve the collective hard work and support. That will put us in front of a true team, which is the one that strives for excellence starting from the collective intelligence. Some environments, like the world of technology, tolerate genius types much better than others. They perfectly understand that you cannot have adventure without risk.'

Argentina learned to tolerate its own genius. Before the 1986 World Cup final, all was quiet in the Argentina dressing-room. The biggest moment in the players' lives was close. Everyone was nervous. Then Maradona started to cry out to his mother. 'Tota, come and help me! I'm afraid, I need you to protect me!' Maradona was sending a message to his team-mates: 'Don't worry if you're afraid. I'm Maradona, and I'm afraid too.' It worked – but Burruchaga's realistic optimism also played a part.

Valdano is often asked how many geniuses you can realistically fit in a team environment. By definition, a genius is an exception. How many exceptions can you have inside your team? Maradona had his own whims, caprices and eccentricities. But it worked within the Argentina team. Why? 'There is a transaction between the genius and the team,' Valdano explains. He and his team-mates had to ask themselves if they were willing to accept someone so special. The answer was yes. In this case: 'This genius will make me better and help me win a World Cup.'

Mavericks make others uncomfortable. They create conflict. They struggle with routine and, as we learned earlier, can be better suited to principles than rules. The chief executive we met in the Prologue, who runs his media business along the lines of his favourite Premier League coach, empowers his mavericks. 'I've never met anyone truly talented who is easy to manage,' he said. 'I don't tell them how I want them to work, but I tell them what success looks like.'

This can also cause issues. Another chief executive told me that managing the maverick is not always the problem; that just as much time needs to be spent managing the attitude of others towards the maverick. 'Others will be constantly frustrated by them, so you need to help them see what the mavericks bring and that they are worth the pain and aggravation.'

Managers can intervene if the maverick upsets colleagues, to remind them of the shared goal; they can offer the empathy and communication that works for Inglethorpe at Liverpool; they can create an environment that welcomes risk and bravery. But Valdano's method is much simpler: agree to the transaction, accept that the maverick will take the team to a better place, and it might even be fun, if a little scary, along the way.

Valdano urges discipline, professionalism and, above all, humility from those around the genius. There is no shame in *not* being the exceptional talent. Many people don't even get to be part of a team with one. So if you are lucky enough to be in that position, says Valdano, be pleased and be humble.

I have learned that this also the best way to get an edge. It cannot come just from within. We all need support along the way, whether it's from family, friends, colleagues, specialists – or mavericks. Our above-the-shoulder behaviour types can help maximise our talent and that of those around us. The football experts I spent time with during the course of writing this book have taught me that much; they have helped me, in different ways, develop my own edge. But none of us can do it on our own. 'Ego interferes in the pursuit of collective success,' Valdano reminds me. 'You always need other people to succeed.'

HOW TO GET AN EDGE – by JORGE VALDANO

1. Be passionate, as without energy it's impossible to be competitive.
2. Be humble, because vanity is corrosive.
3. Find a seductive idea. The leader's job is to spread this idea.

EPILOGUE

Even I was surprised at how well Ousmane Dembélé has done since I picked him for the *Guardian*'s 'Next Generation' feature back in 2014, before he had made a first-team appearance for his club Rennes. I still love watching him play: the languid ease with which he dribbles past opponents, combined with the ferocity and accuracy of his crossing, makes football look so simple.

I think my pick says more about the deep talent pool in French football than about my abilities as a great spotter of talent. After all, the other names on my original 2014 shortlist have hardly slipped back into playing Sunday League. They are all Ligue 1 professionals, and represent France at youth level: Issa Diop is a regular centre-back at Toulouse, Lucas Tousart a squad player at Lyon and Enock Kwateng plays in defence for Nantes. Jean-Kévin Augustin, who also made the cut, stayed at Paris Saint-Germain, where he was a substitute, stuck first behind Zlatan Ibrahimovic and then Edinson Cavani in the pecking-order. Then, in summer 2017, Augustin joined RB Leipzig on a five-year contract.

But none have reached the level of Dembélé, and I doubt they ever will. In France, locals talk about where Dembélé first played football, on the Ludoparc in the city of La Madeleine in Evreux, northern France, in reverent terms. The same hushed tones are used to describe Buenos Aires's Potrero Villa Fiorito, where Diego Maradona first played, Rio's Valqueire Tênis Clube, where

Ronaldo started out, and the concrete slab of Castellane, Zinedine Zidane's first pitch.

From an early age, Dembélé responded well to the challenges he faced. His coach for Evreux Under-13s, Grégory Badoche, would substitute him off, telling him, 'Just because you're Ousmane, you're not guaranteed to play.' Dembélé, who even then would strike corners equally well with either foot, took it well.

When he moved to Rennes at 13, his mother Fati moved the whole family to be with him. We saw in the work of Dutch academic Nico van Yperen how important social support is to success; Liverpool academy head Alex Inglethorpe and Chelsea Ladies coach Emma Hayes also told me that the influences around a talent are an important marker of success.

His decision-making, and not just on the pitch, would make Dr Geir Jordet blush. Borussia Dortmund was not the only option he had after ending his first season in 2015–16 as Ligue 1's Young Player of the Season. Liverpool, Manchester City, Arsenal, Bayer Leverkusen and Juventus were all interested. This was a critical point in his career. Make the wrong choice, and opportunities become limited, development stalls and dreams are put on hold. He made the right call. It's hardly a coincidence that his best form has come under the care of Thomas Tuchel and Didier Deschamps, two emotionally intelligent managers who believe in the individual player paradigm and understand how behaviour drives performance.

'On one side, Ousmane had a great education and the perfect support from his family system; on the other, he has an ego and pride because he is conscious of his talent,' said another former coach at Rennes, Julien Stephan, in an interview with So Foot magazine. 'Talents often have this profile, both determined and unpretentious. He can also ignore the context, so can pull off the same moves in front of 50 people, or 50,000 people, as he does not suffer from inhibition or tension.'

So far Dembélé has adapted positively to all of his challenges: being the best at Evreux; moving to Rennes; respecting his opponents; continuing to work hard; not thinking he'd made it already; staying hungry; moving to Dortmund when bigger deals were available. He even played well when *L'Equipe* reported that his agents had fallen out in an ugly row over commissions following his move to Germany. His latest challenge is to replace Neymar at Barcelona. This is his form of resilience: whatever the context, his response is impressive.

'He has an incredible talent ... if his development continues, "Ous" has no limits,' said Borussia Dortmund chief executive Hans-Joachim Watzke. This is surely true, whatever your definition of talent – and we have seen that everyone has a different idea of what talent actually is. Ignacio Palacios-Huerta, the head of Talent ID at Athletic Bilbao, said it was 'ability × commitment'. Thomas Tuchel called talent 'an extraordinary gift that comes with a responsibility and an obligation to improve'. Ralf Rangnick described talent as 'inherited ability + learned ability × mentality', while Didier Deschamps put it more succinctly: 'The confirmation of potential.'

But this is where the confusion ends. All the experts I spoke to in researching this book – the coaches, sporting directors, psychologists, heads of talent identification, heads of academy, club owners, academics, and even the cultural coach – agreed on one thing: we can all get an edge by developing our behaviours above-the-shoulder.

It might be by using Athletic Club de Bilbao's different measure of success, Ben Darwin's internal hiring recommendations, or Graham Potter's cohesion development concept. It might come from Thomas Tuchel's measure of motivation, Professor Wolfgang Schöllhorn's Differential Training, Tynke Toering's self-regulation analysis, or from Didier Deschamps's lessons in leading and listening.

It might be by using Cruyff Football's individual development paradigm, Dr Geir Jordet's decision-making programme, Steve Lawrence's Montessori principles or AZ Alkmaar's holistic mind-set. It might be by memorising Tim Harkness's resilience algo-rithm, Ralf Rangnick's start-up suggestions, Veronika Kreitmayr's principles on reacting to success or Hans Leitert's proposal to overcome unconscious bias.

It might come from Claude Michy's belief that diversity breeds creativity, Emma Hayes's knowledge of menstrual cycles or Cindy Gallop's passion for the female lens. It might be taking Alex Inglethorpe's non-interference strategy based on intrinsic moti-vation, Stefan Sagmeister's recommendation for space, freedom and train trips, or Jorge Valdano's demand for humility.

Whatever it is, football can be a prism through which we can all develop. At the elite level, the game is full of experts who can teach us important lessons in our own personal growth. They can teach us how to optimise our own talent; how to improve our own performance; and yes, they can teach us how to gain an edge. Jorge Valdano was right: 'Football helps us understand who we are.'

And if Dembélé does go on to win the *Ballon d'Or*, as many are predicting he might, please remember where you heard about him first.

NOTES

1. Cohesion

1. The previous managers of the club had also been English: from 1903, a Mr Shepherd, replaced in 1914 by Billy Barnes and then, in 1920, a Mr Burton, before Pentland's appointment. This period of Athletic's history is charted in more detail by Rory Smith in his excellent book *Mister: The Men Who Gave the World the Game*.

2. Lieberman, M. and Eisenberger, N. (2008), 'The pain and pleasures of social life: A social cognitive neuroscience approach', *Neuro Leadership Journal*, 1, 38–43.

3. Valverde has long understood the significance of having a social purpose. A keen photographer who studied at the Institut d'Estudis Fotografics de Catalunya, in 2012, while in charge of Olympiakos, he published a collection of black-and-white images in 2012. The proceeds went to social projects in Athens.

4. Those two clubs are Lyon, in France, and, ironically, Real Sociedad. The report shows that 52 per cent of Lyon's first-team squad are academy-trained, while La Real's figure was 53 per cent. Athletic came in at 42 per cent. Another 27 per cent was free transfers, which shows the recruitment is working too. This is set against the global context of a regular decrease in the presence of club-

trained players: from 23 per cent overall in 2009 to 19 per cent in 2016. In parallel, the level of expatriates reached a new record high in 2016 of nearly 39 per cent, over twice the club-trained number.

5. Kahneman, D. & Deaton, A. (2010), 'High income improves evaluation of life but not emotional well-being', *PNAS*, 107(38), 16489–93. This backs up the findings of the 2010 Princeton University study that showed having a higher income increases happiness until you reach the figure of $75,000 per year. After that, other factors take over.

6. He found that the decision-making period activated neural activity in the bilateral pre-frontal regions, especially in the left inferior pre-frontal cortex – the greater the activity, the more successful the player was. And for randomisation of choices, he found greater neural activity in the contralateral right inferior pre-fontal region.

7. Externally shared experience only takes into account the on-field/game and training relationships, so an away-day 'bonding' trip would not count in this measurement.

8. Berman, S.L., Down, J. & Hill, C.W.L. (2002), 'Tacit knowledge as a source of competitive advantage in the National Basketball Association', *Academy of Management Journal*, 45(1), 13–31.

9. Gerrard, B. & Lockett, A. (2016), 'Team-specific human capital and performance', *British Journal of Management*, ISSN 1045–3172.

10. Groysberg, B., Sant, L. & Abrahams, R. (2008), 'When "stars" migrate, do they still perform like stars?' *MIT Sloan Management Review*, 50(1), 41–6.

11. Heffernan talked about the Muir experiment in her TED talk, entitled 'Forget the pecking order at work'.

12. This is measured by a test called 'Reading the Mind in the Eyes'. It's considered a test for empathy. You are shown

36 sets of eyes and given a multiple choice of four options of what emotion is being shown. Examples include: friendly/horrified/guilty/dominant to joking/ashamed/confident/dispirited. The average score is around 26 out of 36.

13. This was not about having equal numbers of men and women, but simply having more women. Woolley said this was explained by the fact that women, on average, were better at 'mind-reading' than men.

14. 'The club represents about 45,000 *socios*, and more importantly the wider population, both male and female,' one director says. '*Socios* perceive it as a sign of current more modern times. I think it generates a source of greater respect for people.'

15. The pair were connected by Kindberg's friend Graeme Jones, a former team-mate of Potter's at Boston United, who was assistant coach to Roberto Martinez at Wigan, Everton and Belgium.

16. Kindberg has turned ÖFK into the closest thing a football club can have to a holacracy: a type of flat-management peer-to-peer organisational structure where everyone has a say. Potter still picks the team, but in a holacracy, people fill several different roles, authority is distributed and decisions are made locally, each individual team organises itself and everyone is governed by the same transparent rules (so less 'office politics').

17. Kraus, M.W., Huang, C. & Keltner, D. (2010), 'Tactile communication, cooperation, and performance: An ethological study of the NBA', *Emotion*, 10, 745–9.

18. Bolin, the culture journalist from Sverige Radio, interviewed Ngozi Adache and she sent a message to the Swedish club. 'Hello, this is Chimamanda and I'm going to start by trying to speak Swedish and pronounce your name properly: Östersunds Fotbollsklub. I'm very impressed to

hear about your dabbling in culture and that you produced a play and have read my novel. I think that literature and football go very well together, because we have many ways of telling our stories. Football is one of them, and reading is another. Bye!'

19. This was holacracy in action: I asked Kindberg who had the idea for the LGBT support and he was not sure: but he has empowered his workforce to implement ideas that fit the values.

20. Other integration projects have also succeeded in the city, including Hej Främling! (Hello Stranger!) a charity that organises community runs for refugees. 'The goal for Hej Främling! is inclusion for different groups of 'outsiders' in society,' said its running coach Martin Machnow. 'Integration is about people meeting people – connecting into a wide network into the society where the refugees will build their future.'

2 Adaptability

1. Gilbert added: 'You get the sense he puts so much pressure on himself that it becomes unbearable for him. He is an idealist, always in danger of failing to live up to those ideas.'

2. Modern football demands that its full-backs often play higher up than in the past, but their job is still to be part of a back four, even if at times it may feel like a back two.

3. Tuchel means creating well-rounded human beings, but this is still interesting. When I mentioned this to someone at another club, he snapped that the coach's job is to improve football skills – running, kicking, passing – and not life skills. The fact is that Tuchel sees the two as inextricably linked.

4. You don't have to be in a small company to be a rule-breaker. As Tom Goodwin, of Havas, put it: 'Uber is the

world's largest taxi firm but owns no cars; Facebook is the most popular media company but creates no content; Airbnb is the world's largest accommodation provider but owns no property.' These are today's rule-breakers, the companies pushing boundaries in a changing, VUCA-inspired business world.

5. Didi Hamann revealed that Rafa Benitez did something very similar at Liverpool in 2004. He complained about cliques at mealtimes and told his players to never sit next to the same person twice. He also said no one could get up until the last person had finished. 'It's about respect,' he said. Hamann ended up sitting with Harry Kewell and talking to him. They had been team-mates for a year and never spoken. 'I'm not saying that's the reason we won the Champions League, but Rafa started a thought process in everybody that day,' said Hamann.

6. The German press like to call the table that shows as the '*Tuchel-Tabelle*'.

7. I was feeling the *Echte Liebe* when I walked past the club shop and saw a woman cycling past with a pot of black-eyed susans, yellow-and-black flowers, in her basket. Talk about living the brand.

8. 'He is very grateful that the coach gives him the opportunity to play regularly,' said his father Mark. 'Borussia Dortmund is the perfect club for him. It's the best fit.'

9. Watzke also felt that there had been an implicit criticism of Dortmund's senior officials for agreeing to UEFA's plan.

10. Gumbrecht wrote about how fans consume sport in his book *In Praise of Athletic Beauty*.

11. He felt better when he came up against Heynckes in his first season at Mainz and the veteran was incredibly nice to him. 'Wow, what a lesson in respect he gave me. What a guy, so warm and generous.'

12. This normalcy is a theme for Tuchel. He tells a story of when he went to watch the Madrid derby with a friend. He saw that Radomir Antic, 74, and Bora Milutinovic, 69, two highly experienced coaches, were in the same area watching the game. He introduced himself as a young coach from Germany. They responded: 'Oh, we are young coaches too.'

13. In some cases, this unique foot pressure could also identify the individual's emotions, fatigue level, and even what type of music they might be listening to. Albrecht, S., Janssen, D., Quarz, E., Newell, K.M. & Schöllhorn, W.I. (2014), 'Individuality of movements in music – finger and body movements during playing the flute', *Human Movement Science*, 35, 131–44, and Janssen, D., Schöllhorn, W.I., Newell, K.M., Jäger, J.M., Rost, F. & Vehof, K. (2011), 'Diagnosing fatigue in gait patterns by support vector machines and self-organising maps', *Human Movement Science*, 30(5), 966–75.

14. Repšaité, V., Vainoras, A., Berškiené, K. & Sendzikaité, E. (2015), 'The effect of differential training-based occupational therapy on hand and arm function in patients after stroke', *Neurologia i Neurochirurgia Polska*, 49(3), 150–5.

15. Toering, T. & Jordet, G. (2015), 'Self-control in professional soccer players', *Journal of Applied Sport Psychology*, 27(3), 335–50.

16. I liked the view of Antoine Mestres, who wrote in *So Foot*: 'Didier Deschamps was pretty much the finished article before he'd even reached adolescence. Answering how he imagines himself aged 60, Deschamps replied: "That's too far away. In my head I've always stayed 32, the age I stopped playing." But on the inside he's still that 11-year-old boy, watching his friends play football. A boy who already had a 60-year-old brain.'

17. In Chapter 4, we look at the importance of being aware of our own unconscious bias. While it might be fashionable to accuse millennials of being difficult to manage, others believe that the term 'millennial' itself is meaningless. 'I would no more refer to anyone on this planet as a "millennial" than I would call someone from my parents' generation geriatric,' said Peter Mead of advertising company Abbott Mead Vickers. 'It can never be right to categorise people, real people, according to the year in which they were born and then claim that as a result they exhibit behaviour and display attitudes that are entirely the same as each other and completely different to anyone else.'

18. Sinek explained this theory in his 2016 interview with Tom Bilyeu on *Inside Quest*.

19. Zenger, J. & Folkman, J. (July 2016), 'What great listeners actually do', *Harvard Business Review*.

20. Misra, S., Cheng, L., Genevie, J. & Yuan, M. (2014), 'The iPhone Effect: the quality of in-person social interactions in the presence of mobile devices', *Environment and Behavior*, 10, 1–24.

21. The American essayist David Foster Wallace, writing about John McCain's campaign for president in 2000, defined a real leader as: 'Somebody who can help us overcome the limitations of our own individual laziness and selfishness and weakness and fear and get us to do better, harder things than we can get ourselves to do on our own.'

22. Bill Gates said the same: 'Success is a lousy teacher. It seduces smart people into thinking they can't lose.'

23. Before the second leg, Deschamps invited film-maker and actor Jamel Debbouze to Clairefontaine to screen his new film, *La Marche*, about a peaceful march in 1983 that was a key event in the fight against racism in France. It struck a

chord with the squad, and Debbouze admitted to laughing and crying with the players after the screening. The players agreed that it had a positive impact. 'It was about pushing your own limits towards a common goal, which was a better way to convey the message than the manager writing "Together" on a chalkboard,' said *L'Equipe* football writer Vincent Duluc.

24. Bennis, W. & Thomas, Robert J. (Sept. 2002), 'Crucibles of leadership', *Harvard Business Review*.

3 Decision-Making

1. Besides the Cruyff Courts in the city, there are many more local football clubs. Two are less than ten minutes away from the Olympic Stadium. I walk past one, ASV Arsenal, on a Thursday morning in term-time and the five pitches are packed with children enjoying organised sessions.

2. Kuper, S. (March 2016), 'Johan Cruyff revolutionised Dutch football', espnfc.co.uk.

3. This was the tournament at which Cruyff showcased his 'Cruyff Turn' to the world in a game against Sweden. He faced his own goal and side-heeled the ball behind him and his marker, whom he ran past to continue his dribble. The defender he beat, Jan Olsson, later called it the proudest moment of his career. 'I thought I'd win the ball for sure, but he tricked me. I had no chance. Cruyff was a genius.'

4. This includes two people watching different movies in the same cinema; choosing which character's point of view to a watch scene from; an immersive experience of say, rain-drops on your head in a rainy scene, or a splash of perfume in a scented one; or even a dating algorithm connecting viewers who registered similar emotional responses during the film.

5. Van Yperen, N.W. (2009) 'Why some make it and others do not: Identifying psychological factors that predict career

success in professional adult soccer', *The Sport Psychologist*, 23, 317–29.

6. Ericsson, K.A., Krampe, R.M. & Tesch-Römer, C. (1993), 'The role of deliberate practice in the acquisition of expert performance', *Psychological Review*, 100(3), 363–406.

7. That figure dropped to 72 per cent once you took out variables like the coaches' assessments of the players' performance levels, the players' social situations (i.e. ethnic origin, parental situation and number of siblings), and the number of extra hours that players practised away from the club.

8. England's successful rugby coach Eddie Jones backed this up, with the *Guardian* reporting that he likes to select players whose parents divorced when they were young. 'I talk to them about their backgrounds and you get a pretty good idea ... All the world's best players have some sort of massive desire to do something.'

9. Groysberg, B. (Jan. 2014), 'Headhunters reveal what candidates want', *Harvard Business Review*.

10. The Zidane film focused purely on Zidane during a league match between Real Madrid and Villarreal in April 2005 and was filmed in real time using 17 synchronised cameras. In the last few minutes of the game, Zidane was sent off for fighting. Film critic Peter Bradshaw wrote in the *Guardian*: 'This movie is a must-see for everyone interested in football ... That final foul shows that somewhere in Zidane's massive, imperious hauteur, there is a reckless, ugly side that will always surface. Surreally, he achieves the status and presence of a Coriolanus, a martial hero of uncontrolled severity and anger.'

11. Danziger, S., Levav, J. & Avnaim-Pesso, L. (2011), 'Extraneous factors in judicial decisions', *PNAS*, 108(17), 6889–92.

12. Jordet's 11 model was an inspiration in the planning stage of this book. The other behaviour types are to relentlessly pursue performance, prospectively control game dynamics, regulate total load and innovatively advance the game.

13. Barnsley, R.H., Thompson, A.H. & Barnsley, P.E. (1985), 'Hockey success and birthdate: The relative age effect', *Canadian Association of Health, Physical Education, and Recreation Journal*, 51, 23–8.

14. This research was conducted by Gracenote Sports and gathered data from the Under-17s World Cup and European Championship (both 2013, 2015), the Under-19s European Championship (2013, 2014, 2015, 2016), the Under-20s World Cup (2005, 2007, 2009, 2011, 2013, 2015) and the Under-21s European Championship (2002, 2004, 2006, 2007, 2009, 2011, 2013, 2015)

15. Fumarco, L. & Rossi, G. (2015), 'Relative age effect on labor market outcomes for high skilled workers: Evidence from soccer', *Birkbeck Department of Management*, 1–51.

16. There are many academic papers on how RAE starts in school, some of which are listed in the Bibliography below.

17. This is an index of 500 stocks that is seen as a leading indicator of US equities made up of companies selected by economists.

18. Arrigo Sacchi, an innovator who won three European Cups with AC Milan in the 1990s, said: 'It can be said that they opened the eyes of the others. Dutch football has always been progressive, revolutionary and positive, and it has produced some truly great players. But now the revolutionary element is missing. Dutch players are only trained to attack and build up the play. Other teams can easily set themselves up for this, so you create difficulties for yourself … When I am scouting for players, I look for three things: winner's mentality, discipline and intelligence. All talented players have to deal with adversity in some form; I look for

players who can best handle it. Playing well makes players better. The Dutch footballer should be more specific about wanting to improve himself and wanting to win.'

19. There is one notable omission in the credits section of the book: Louis van Gaal. The national team coach who reached the 2014 World Cup semi-finals, he was asked to take part but declined as he wanted to focus on his new job at Manchester United.

20. This was calculated by the average distance and number of high-intensity runs made in the Eredivise compared with other leagues. Eredivisie players ran 501 metres per game at high intensity, compared to 567 in Germany, or 548 in England.

21. De Hoog was amused that top-level Dutch coaches were asking questions of Tuchel, a coach their own age but with years of extra coaching experience – and knowledge – already behind him.

22. Jonker did not stay long in the role. By the time Tuchel was speaking at the KNVB, she had set up her own business specialising in measuring optimal teaching environments through self-regulated learning, goal-setting and feedback in sports, education and business.

23. This is straight out of the Montessori model: objects and furniture in a classroom are proportioned to a child's body so books and materials are easily accessible. The prepared learning environment may be a classroom or a football pitch, but it needs to allow the children to participate in the best possible way. Six-year-olds playing eleven-a-side on a full-size pitch clearly does not do that.

24. The KNVB are working with Nico van Yperen on an educational programme for coaches which involves classes on resilience, self-efficacy and self-regulation.

25. The pair are devotees of Carol Dweck, the professor of psychology at Stanford University who coined the term

'growth mindset' and whose ground-breaking research into learning behaviour has impacted training in education and sports. 'Organizations that embody a growth mindset encourage appropriate risk-taking, knowing that some risks won't work out,' Dweck wrote in the *Harvard Business Review*. 'They reward employees for important and useful lessons learned, even if a project does not meet its original goals. They support collaboration across organizational boundaries rather than competition among employees or units. They are committed to the growth of every member, not just in words but in deeds, such as broadly available development and advancement opportunities. And they continually reinforce growth mindset values with concrete policies.'

26. Sinek's example is significant, perhaps, because in an interview with the *New York Times*, Beuker described AZ as 'the Apple of the football industry'.

27. Pfau, B.N. (Oct. 2015), 'How an accounting firm convinced its employees they could change the world', *Harvard Business Review*.

28. PSV also use these tests. They believe if a player scores low on the tests, they tend to leave the club at a low level, while those who score high leave at a high level.

29. Smith, R. (5 March 2017), 'To put ball in net, Dutch club shoot space aliens first', *New York Times*.

30. This is called EDMR: a patient recalls a traumatic memory, then follows a moving object with their eyes only at the same time. The dual task of memory recall plus eye movement taxes the working memory, causing the traumatic memory to become less clear and vivid. The idea is that after many repetitions of this, the memory loses its ability to trigger intense emotional responses.

31. The AZ Under-16 coach Kelvin Duffree tweeted a video of his team before a match. They were sitting in the dressing-

room with their eyes closed, as the strains of 'Zadok the Priest' – also known as the Champions League music – filled the room. The team was visualising the game ahead. Critics sniggered at the video, but AZ beat FC Twente 5–0.

32. The iceberg is clearly a regular visual management tool. The more popular image is *The Iceberg Illusion*, drawn by Sylvia Duckworth. Again, the top of the iceberg is visible with the word 'Success!' on it. An arrow denoting 'What People See' points to it. Below the surface is 'What People Don't See'. This is where you have Persistence, Failure, Sacrifice, Disappointment, Dedication, Hard Work, Discipline.

33. Marcotti, G. (24 March 2016), 'Johan Cruyff was one of football's greatest trailblazers on and off the pitch', espnfc. co.uk.

4 Resilience

1. The ABC is a classic Cognitive Behavioural Therapy technique. Harkness is happy to acknowledge this. In fact, he is rather down on psychology as a profession as he knows everyone is interested in the behaviour of other people. We are all psychologists. One of his key lessons is that psychology boils down to best practice: 'I may have a theory of how to calm a person who feels he's been disrespected. But through sheer force of numbers, there will be a best practice out there that's better than my technique. My job is to try to find that and use it myself.'

2. On further consideration, Harkness remembered that his neighbour had the pelt of a lion on the floor of his house that had been shot in the vicinity a couple of generations before; there was also a serial killer who terrorised the town for a while who turned out to be living two doors down from the Harkness family, with his front door around 50 yards from the chicken coop. But he still thinks his fear of wolves was irrational.

3. Harkness tells me that people who suffer from OCD often confuse an Anxiety Problem for a Danger Problem and vice versa.

4. Harkness suggests the solution for an Anxiety Problem would be to calm yourself physiologically or engage in an effective cognitive appraisal of the threats and opportunities. Performing a repetitive ritual, or having a behavioural tic, is not necessarily the best way of managing anxiety: it may give temporary relief but it's not a real solution, and it's not best practice. The solution for the Danger Problem? 'Run!'

5. Harkness talks about motivation in a similar way. He breaks down motivation into three areas: the size of the reward, the size of the task, and the confidence level which, put together, produce motivation.

6. As Harkness brings it up on his screen, a picture flashes up of him standing next to Tiger Woods on a putting green at the 2007 Open at Carnoustie. He claims he was just photo-bombing Tiger, but the picture seduces you into thinking he's advising the former number one on his technique.

7. Lipnicki, D.M. & Byrne, D.G. (2005), 'Thinking on your back: Solving anagrams faster when supine than when standing', *Cognitive Brain Research*, 24, 719–22.

8. Vercruyssen, M. & Simonton, K. (1994), 'Effects of posture on mental performance: We think faster on our feet than on our seat. Hard facts about soft machines – the ergonomics of seating', in R. Lueder & K. Noro (eds), *Hard Facts about Soft Machines*, London: Taylor and Francis, 119–31.

9. Carney, D.R., Cuddy, A.J.C. & Yap, A.J. (2010), 'Power posing: Brief nonverbal displays affect neuroendocrine levels and risk tolerance', *Psychological Science*, 21, 1363–8.

10. Strack, F., Martin, L.L. & Stepper, S. (1998), 'Inhibiting and facilitating conditions of the human smile: A nonobtrusive test of the facial feedback hypothesis', *Journal of Personality and Social Psychology*, 54(5), 768–77.

11. Other reasons given for a second-half decline were that some players believed their own hype and others were courted by rival clubs.

12. Rangnick told the International Football Arena conference: 'Had I been there then, I would have persuaded them to do it more moderately. We know that football is an emotional business and supporters identify themselves through those things ...'

13. The DFL makes exceptions to 50+1 in cases where tradition can be proven. For example, Bayer Leverkusen is a factory team founded by workers at the Bayer pharmaceutical group, as is Wolfsburg (with the local VW plant). If an investor or company has been involved in the club for 20 years or more, they can plead a case with the DFL to circumvent 50+1.

14. Collis, D. (March 2016), 'Lean Strategy', *Harvard Business Review*.

15. The German title, *Vom Sager zum Frager*, is a play on words, literally translated as 'From someone who speaks to someone who questions'. In the context that Schmid intended, maybe 'From instruction to empowerment', or 'Leading with questions' works better.

16. Mills, A., Butt, J., Maynard, I. & Harwood, C. (2012), 'Identifying factors perceived to influence the development of elite youth football academy players,' *Journal of Sports Sciences*, 30(15), 1593–1604.

17. Grant, A.M. & Gino, F. (2010), 'A little thanks goes a long way: Explaining why gratitude expressions motivate prosocial behavior', *Journal of Personality and Social Psychology*, 98(6), 946–55.

18. A director at one of the Premier League's biggest clubs told me of the conversation his board had before signing an international player they all knew was a difficult character. 'He costs a lot of money, but will he produce for us?' 'He is capable of scoring goals but we've heard he's got a fragile mentality and is a bit of a head-case, do you think that matters?' 'We need some good players here, let's buy him anyway and I'm sure he'll be fine.' It didn't work out like that at all. The move was not a success.

19. The derivation of talent comes from the Greek word 'talanton' which referred not to a coin but to a weight of money used as the basis of monetary exchange. It came to mean sum of money but the word 'talent' meaning 'special natural ability, aptitude, gift committed to one for use and improvement' had developed by the fifteenth century, from the parable of the talents in Matthew 25:14–30.

20. Fisk, S. (11 April 2013), 'Leveling the Playing Field', The Clayman Institute for Gender Research.

21. Marianne, B. & Mullainathan, S. (2004), 'Are Emily and Greg more employable than Lakisha and Jamal? A field experiment on labor market discrimination', *American Economic Review*, 94(4), 991–1013.

22. Leitert says 'most important game' rather than 'the World Cup final' because every keeper can relate to it. Only a few goalkeepers will ever get to play in a World Cup final. For others, the most decisive game may be a Cup semi-final or a relegation decider.

5 Creativity

1. In Hong Kong, the coach of Premier League title winners Eastern is a 27-year-old woman called Chan Yuen-ting. Her success landed the team a spot in the Asian Champions

League. According to reports, Chan has rejected a job offer to coach a second division side in Europe.

2. It was also her fortieth birthday that day.

3. Diacre had earned her diploma to coach in a youth academy in 2010. Normally you need to have played 30 games as a professional, but the women's game was not professional in France. Because of her playing career, her application was accepted and two years later she earned the diploma.

4. One journalist based in France made a point of reading Clermont's local paper *La Montagne* before and after every game. He was struck by how little was made of Diacre's gender or lack of experience at this level. Her predecessor Régis Brouard was more often criticised for being flashy. At national level, this reporter was surprised how little interest there was in her. After the initial spike in interest there was very little coverage, although this could be down to her reluctance to do one-on-ones with the media. She refused my requests for an interview.

5. She signed Famara Diédhiou who in 2015–16 scored 21 goals, was voted Ligue 2 Player of the Year and earned a call-up to the Senegal team. He publicly thanked Diacre: 'She has helped me get the best out of myself.'

6. Franck Passi at Marseille, then Lille, and Antoine Kombouaré at Guingamp.

7. This was also noticeable in my research for this book. The lack of people from BAME backgrounds in senior positions in football, not just coaching, was overwhelming. It's important to note that Gallop's opinions on diversity in the workplace are not just limited to women.

8. In 2014, Clavijo hired former Colombia midfielder Oscar Pareja as head coach and, like Clermont, the team has over-achieved since the appointment.

9. Ellis's side was notable as the players in the side who were mothers were allowed to bring their children to

training camps, friendly matches and certain tournaments. The US Soccer federation paid childcare expenses, including nannies and travel and accommodation. 'It shows how much respect the female athletes have over here,' Ellis told Anna Kessel, author of the excellent book *Eat, Sweat, Play*. Compare this to Katie Chapman, one of England's best midfielders who missed the 2011 World Cup because she couldn't afford childcare. The English FA's maternity offering has since improved and Chapman played in the 2015 World Cup.

10. In *Eat, Sweat, Play*, Anna Kessel writes of how women, female athletes among them, are consistently shamed into hiding their menstrual cycle. One athlete said she was much more likely to get injured in the week before her period. Another told her: 'It feels like male coaches have no idea what to do, to be honest.'

11. Schumpeter (7 May 2016), 'What do the Foxes say?', *The Economist*.

12. Hughes, S. (18 Oct. 2015), 'Liverpool vs Manchester United: Why English football's greatest rivals are struggling to produce local talent', *Independent*.

13. Cameron Brannagan, Pedro Chirivella, Ryan Kent, Joe Maguire, Sergi Canos, Danny Ward, Connor Randall, Sheyi Ojo and Kevin Stewart.

14. The other is Harry Wilson.

15. We looked at Maslow's hierarchy of needs in Chapter 3 and the idea popular in Holland and Germany that being a development coach is an end in itself rather than a means to an end. The prevailing attitude is that youth coaches are responsible for stars of the future, and need to be paid commensurately. In England, that does not seem to be the case.

16. Catmull, E. (Sept. 2008), 'How Pixar fosters collective creativity', *Harvard Business Review*.

17. 'We got to the idea that Chucks are a work of art. We're really lucky with Chucks that it's a product that people love when they're worn,' explained Ian Stewart, vice-president of global marketing at Converse.

18. Doward, J. (11 July 2010), 'Happy people really do work harder', *Guardian*.

19. Oswald, A.J., Proto, E. & Sgroi, D. (2015), 'Happiness and productivity', *Journal of Labour Economics*, 33(4), 789–822.

20. Facebook also works with competitors such as LinkedIn, Yahoo and eBay to talk over how they all work to make their sites easier to use.

21. The whiteboard on his wall has six pitches on it with magnetic circles with players' faces on them. Each pitch represents a different group: Loans, Under-15, Under-16, Under-18, Under-21 and Melwood (the first team). Inglethorpe used to think that a player needed between 70 and 100 games at a lower level, either youth or loans, before he could break into the Melwood group. Liverpool coach Jürgen Klopp has made him question that view. 'It's like having a youth-team coach manage the first team, as he believes in the players,' says Inglethorpe.

22. Austin, S. (8 March 2017), 'Bournemouth pioneer use of Sherylle Calder's EyeGym', trainingground.guru.

23. The last time Liverpool played Leeds in the League Cup, back in 2009, Alexander-Arnold was ten years old and the Liverpool mascot being led out by captain Jamie Carragher at Elland Road.

24. The team behind INSEAD's Management Acceleration Programme, Jennifer and Gianpiero Petriglieri, agree that being labelled a star can be a curse, adding pressure and encouraging 'bland conformity, risk-averse thinking, and stilted behaviour'.

25. Valdano has some good stories about Maradona. I particularly like the one he told *Der Speigel* in 2006: 'We

spoke recently, as a matter of fact. He had tried to call me several times. When he finally got through he said, "Jorge, you sure are hard to get hold of. Who do you think you are? Maradona?"'

26. Gorris, L. & and Huetlin, T. (30 June 2006), 'The pitch is a jungle', *Spiegel Online*.

27. He sounds like an old-school Gary Neville: a top pundit shipped in to salvage a struggling Spanish side. Neville's time at Valencia ended in ignominy, but Valdano's was different.

28. This game is still controversial in Spain, as Real Madrid's flight to the Canaries was cancelled, and so they drove for 14 hours in a coach with no air-conditioning. The game was played at five o'clock in the afternoon, and Madrid blamed their poor performance on the travel and humid playing conditions.

29. This is a typically poetic phrase from Valdano: he means that the more difficult the challenges faced over time, the quicker the talent evolves.

30. Oettingen, G. (2000), 'Expectancy effects on behaviour depend on self-regulatory thought', *Social Cognition*, 18(2), 101–29.

31. He announced his business partnership with 25-year-old Jessica Walsh by posing naked with her in his office. He was wearing only black socks and she was perched on several magazines to reach his height.

32. Philadelphia, New York, Chicago, Los Angeles, Toronto, Vancouver, Paris, Vienna and Frankfurt.

33. Kim, J. & de Dear, R. (2013), 'Workspace satisfaction: The privacy-communication trade-off in open-plan offices', *Journal of Environmental Psychology*, 17(36), 18–26.

BIBLIOGRAPHY

Books

Ansari, Aziz & Klinenberg, Eric. *Modern Romance*, Penguin Random House, 2015

Beilock, Sian. *Choke: The Secret to Performing Under Pressure*, Constable, 2011

Calvin, Michael. *Living on the Volcano*, Century, 2015

Coyle, Daniel. *The Talent Code: Greatness Isn't Born, It's Grown*, Arrow, 2010

Cruyff, Johan. *My Turn*, Macmillan, 2016

Damasio, Antonio. *Descartes' Error: Emotion, Reason and the Human Brain*, Vintage, 2006

Duke, Vic & Crolley, Liz. *Football, Nationality and the State*, Routledge, 1996

Harford, Tim. *Adapt: Why Success Always Starts with Failure*, Abacus, 2012

Heffernan, Margaret. *Beyond Measure: The Big Impact of Small Changes*, Simon & Schuster, 2015

Honigstein, Raphael. *Das Reboot: How German Football Reinvented Itself and Conquered the World*, Yellow Jersey, 2015

Jonker, Laura. *Self-regulation in Sport and Education*, University Medical Center Groningen, 2011

Katwala, Amit. *The Athletic Brain*, Simon & Schuster, 2016

Kessel, Anna. *Eat Sweat Play: How Sport Can Change Our Lives*, Macmillan, 2016

Kuper, Simon. *The Football Men*, Simon & Schuster, 2012

Kuper, Simon & Szymanski, Stefan. *Soccernomics*, HarperSport, 2012

Leitert, Hans. *The Art of Goalkeeping*, Onli Verlag, 2009

Lewis, Chris. *Too Fast to Think: How to Reclaim Your Creativity in a Hyper-connected Work Culture*, Kogan Page, 2016

Lewis, Michael. *Moneyball: The Art of Winning an Unfair Game*, W. W. Norton, 2004

Lyttleton, Ben. *Twelve Yards: The Art and Psychology of the Perfect Penalty*, Transworld, 2014

Palacios-Huerta, Ignacio. *Beautiful Game Theory: How Soccer Can Help Economics*, Princeton University Press, 2014

Perarnu, Marti. *Pep Confidential: Inside Guardiola's First Season at Bayern Munich*, Arena Sport, 2014

Schmid, Fritz. *Vom Sager zum Frager: A Systemic Approach to Self-Organising Processes and Chaos in Football*, Reinhardt, 2010

Sinek, Simon. *Start with Why: How Great Leaders Inspire Everyone to Take Action*, Penguin, 2011

Smith, Rory. *Mister: The Men Who Gave the World the Game*, Simon & Schuster, 2016

Strudwick, Tony. *Soccer Science*, Human Kinetics, 2016

Turkle, Sherry. *Alone Together: Why We Expect More from Technology and Less from Each Other*, Basic Books, 2012

Valdano, Jorge. *Los 11 Poderes del Líder: El fútbol como Escuela de Vida*, CONECTA, 2013

Wilson, Jonathan. *Inverting the Pyramid: The History of Football Tactics*, Orion, 2013

Winner, David. *Brilliant Orange: The Neurotic Genius of Dutch Football*, Bloomsbury, 2000

Newspapers and magazines

11 Freunde
Abendzeitung München
Advertising Age
Aftonbladet
The Age
Algemeen Dagblad
AS
The Atlantic
Augsburger Allgemeine
Berliner Kurier
Bild
The Blizzard
Bloomberg Businessweek
Clarin
El Correo
De Correspondent
Creative Review
Daily Mail
Focus
FIFA Weekly
Financial Times
France Football
Frankfurter Allgemeine Zeitung
Frankfurter Rundschau
Guardian
Harvard Business Review
Independent
Leipziger Volkszeitung
L'Equipe
Liverpool Echo
Marca
The Mirror
La Montagne

El Mundo Deportivo
The National
New York Times
NU
Olé
OP
El País
Ruhr Nachrichten
Sloan Management Review
So Foot
Spiegel
Sport
Stuttgarter Zeitung
Tagesspiegel
De Telegraaf
The Times
Times of India
Wall Street Journal
Westdeutsche Allgemeine Zeitung
Wired
Die Zeit

Academic papers

Albrecht, S., Janssen, D., Quarz, E., Newell, K.M. & Schöllhorn, W.I. (2014), 'Individuality of movements in music – finger and body movements during playing the flute', *Human Movement Science*, 35, 131–44

Barnsley, R.H., Thompson, A.H. & Barnsley, P.E. (1985), 'Hockey success and birthdate: The relative age effect', *Canadian Association of Health, Physical Education, and Recreation Journal*, 51, 23–8

Baumeister, R.F., Bratslavsky, E., Finkenauer, C. & Vohs, K.D. (2001), 'Bad is stronger than good', *Review of General Psychology*, 5, 323–70

Berman, S.L., Down, J. & Hill, C.W.L. (2002), 'Tacit knowledge as a source of competitive advantage in the National Basketball Association', *Academy of Management Journal*, 45(1), 13–31

Bernardi, L., Porta, C. & Sleight, P. (2006), 'Cardiovascular, cerebrovascular, and respiratory changes induced by different types of music in musicians and non-musicians: the importance of silence', *Heart*, 92(4), 445–52

Carney, D.R., Cuddy, A.J.C. & Yap, A.J. (2010), 'Power posing: Brief nonverbal displays affect neuroendocrine levels and risk tolerance', *Psychological Science*, 21, 1363–8

Danziger, S., Levav, J. & Avnaim-Pesso, L. (2011), 'Extraneous factors in judicial decisions', *PNAS*, 108(17), 6889–92

Du, Q., Gao, H. & Levi, M.D. (2009), 'Born leaders: The relative-age effect and managerial success', *AFA 2011 Denver Meetings Paper*

Ericsson, K.A., Krampe, R.M. & Tesch-Römer, C. (1993), 'The role of deliberate practice in the acquisition of expert performance', *Psychological Review*, 100(3), 363–406

Engel, D., Woolley, A.W., Jing, L.X., Chabris, C.F. & Malone, T.W. (2014), 'Reading the mind in the eyes or reading between the lines? Theory of mind predicts collective intelligence equally well online and face-to-face', *PLOS ONE* 9(12)

Folkman, S. & Moskowitz, J.T. (2004), 'Coping: Pitfalls and promise', *Annual Review of Psychology*, 55, 745–74

Fumarco, L. & Rossi, G. (2015), 'Relative age effect on labor market outcomes for high skilled workers: Evidence from soccer', *Birkbeck Department of Management*, 1–51

García-Pérez, J.I., Hidalgo-Hidalgo, M. & Robles-Zurita, J.A. (2015), 'Does grade retention affect students' achievement? Some evidence from Spain', *Applied Economics*, 46, 1373–92

Gerrard, B. & Lockett, A. (2016), 'Team-specific human capital and performance', *British Journal of Management*, ISSN 1045–3172

Grant, A.M. & Gino, F. (2010), 'A little thanks goes a long way: Explaining why gratitude expressions motivate prosocial behavior', *Journal of Personality and Social Psychology*, 98(6), 946–55

Groysberg, B., Sant, L. & Abrahams, R. (2008), 'When "stars" migrate, do they still perform like stars?' *MIT Sloan Management Review*, 50(1), 41–6

Janssen, D., Schöllhorn, W.I., Newell, K.M., Jäger, J.M., Rost, F. & Vehof, K. (2011), 'Diagnosing fatigue in gait patterns by support vector machines and self-organising maps', *Human Movement Science*, 30(5), 966–75

Jordet, G., Bloomfield, J. & Heijmerikx, J. (2015), 'The hidden foundation of field vision in English Premier League soccer players', MIT Sloan Sports Conference

Kahneman, D. & Deaton, A. (2010), 'High income improves evaluation of life but not emotional well-being', *PNAS*, 107(38), 16489–93

Kim, J. & de Dear, R. (2013), 'Workspace satisfaction: The privacy-communication trade-off in open-plan offices', *Journal of Environmental Psychology*, 17(36), 18–26

Kraus, M.W., Huang, C. & Keltner, D. (2010), 'Tactile communication, cooperation, and performance: An ethological study of the NBA', *Emotion*, 10, 745–9

Lieberman, M. & Eisenberger, N. (2008), 'The pain and pleasures of social life: A social cognitive neuroscience approach', *Neuro Leadership Journal*, 1, 38–43

Lipnicki, D.M. & Byrne, D.G. (2005), 'Thinking on your back: Solving anagrams faster when supine than when standing', *Cognitive Brain Research*, 24, 719–22

Marianne, B. & Mullainathan, S. (2004), 'Are Emily and Greg more employable than Lakisha and Jamal? A field experiment on labor market discrimination', *American Economic Review*, 94(4), 991–1013

Martin, R.P., Foels, P., Clanton, G. & Moon, K. (2004), 'Season of birth is related to child retention rates, achievement, and rate of diagnosis of specific LD', *Journal of Learning Disabilities*, 37, 307–17

Mills, A., Butt, J., Maynard, I. & Harwood, C. (2012), 'Identifying factors perceived to influence the development of elite youth football academy players', *Journal of Sports Sciences*, 30(15), 1593–1604

Misra, S., Cheng, L., Genevie, J. & Yuan, M. (2014), 'The iPhone Effect: The quality of in-person social interactions in the presence of mobile devices', *Environment and Behavior*, 10, 1–24

Napieralski, P.E., Altenhoff, B.M., Bertrand, J.W. et al. (2014), 'An evaluation of immersive viewing on spatial knowledge acquisition in spherical panoramic environments', *Virtual Reality*, 18, 189

Oettingen, G. (2000), 'Expectancy effects on behaviour depend on self-regulatory thought', *Social Cognition*, 18(2), 101–29

Oswald, A.J., Proto, E. & Sgroi, D. (2015), 'Happiness and productivity', *Journal of Labour Economics*, 33(4), 789–822

Repšaité, V., Vainoras, A., Berškiené, K. & Sendzikaité, E. (2015), 'The effect of differential training-based occupational therapy on hand and arm function in patients after stroke', *Neurologia i Neurochirurgia Polska*, 49(3), 150–5

Strack, F., Martin, L.L. & Stepper, S. (1998), 'Inhibiting and facilitating conditions of the human smile: A nonobtrusive test of the facial feedback hypothesis', *Journal of Personality and Social Psychology*, 54(5), 768–77

Toering, T. & Jordet, G. (2015), 'Self-control in professional soccer players', *Journal of Applied Sport Psychology*, 27(3), 335–50

Van Yperen, N.W. (2009) 'Why some make it and others do not: Identifying psychological factors that predict career success in professional adult soccer', *The Sport Psychologist*, 23, 317–29

Vercruyssen, M. & Simonton, K. (1994), 'Effects of posture on mental performance: We think faster on our feet than on our seat. Hard facts about soft machines – the ergonomics of seating', in R. Lueder & K. Noro (eds), *Hard Facts about Soft Machines*, London: Taylor and Francis, 119–31

Woolley, A.W., Chabris, C.F., Pentland, A., Hashmi, N. & Malone, T.W. (2010), 'Evidence for a collective intelligence factor in the performance of human groups', *Science*, 330(6004), 686–8

Websites

abcnet.au

arsenal.com

bbc.co.uk

catalyst.org

cbsnews.com

coca-colacompany.com

copa90.com

davidmarquet.com

dfb.de

entrepeneur.com

espn.co.uk

evertonfc.com

fenomenodefenomenos.blogspot.co.uk

fifa.com

football-observatory.com

forbes.com

gainline.biz

goal.com

holacracy.org

johancruyffinstitute.com

lfchistory.net

nextjump.com

ostersundsfk.se

positivesharing.com

raconteur.net

royalsociety.org

rulebreaker-society.com

spox.com

sverigesradio.com

ted.com

trainingground.guru

uefa.com

vicesports.com

virgin.com

winningwithanalytics.com

youtube.com

Television and film

Creating a Level Playing Field

The Happy Film

Inside Quest

Les Blues – Une autre histoire de France 1996–2016

See the Man

Zidane: A 21st Century Portrait

ACKNOWLEDGEMENTS

I learned just how important support networks are in the process of writing this book and I am fortunate that so many people have helped me. In the early stages, I was inspired by the wisdom of Annie Auerbach, the research of Geir Jordet and the support of David Luxton. Each of them helped me develop my own edge.

I have loved working with the team at HarperCollins, and want to thank Oliver Malcolm, Simon Gerratt and Charlie Redmayne for their constant encouragement and insightful feedback. Orlando Mowbray, Polly Osborn and Fionnuala Barrett have been brilliant collaborators. I'm also grateful to Mark Bolland, Emily Arbis, Micaela Alcaino and Dean Russell, and to Steve Leard for his wonderful cover design. Steve Dobell was a marvellous copy-editor who taught me how to get an edge using track changes.

My sincere thanks go out to the following talents who helped me enormously: Duncan Alexander, Chris Anderson, Tord Andersson, Simon Austin, Federico Bassahun, Christoph Biermann, Steve Bond, Adam Chmielowski, Martha Christie, Damien Comolli, Nick Corcoran, Dermot Corrigan, Avi Creditor, Alex Di Mascio, Dave Farrar, Patxi Xavier Fernandez, Will Galgey, Simon Gleave, Simon Gottschalk, Jonathan Harding, Margaret Heffernan, Raphael Honigstein, Michiel de Hoog, Graham Hunter, Benjamin Ipolliti, Jose Miguel Jimenez, Motoko Jitsukawa, Dean Jones, Mitchell Kaye, Anna Kessel, Mark Latham, Ola Laxvik,

Steve Lawrence, Matt McCann, Jules McKeen, Olaf Meinking, Ignacio Palacios-Huerta, Ben Oakley, Sarah Oakley, Jacqui Oatley, Chris Peilow, Bernie Reeves, Archie Rhind-Tutt, Cedric Rouquette, Iker Saez, Daan Schippers, Fritz Schmid, Marcel Schmid, Patrick Sjöö, Henry Stott, Simon Strachan, Stefan Szymanski, Kirmen Uribe, Karin Wahlén, Nick Walters, Lucy Warburton, Janine Weise, Mark Williamson, Jonathan Wilson, Rebecca Winfield, David Winner, Hannes Winzer and Tomasz Zahorski.

I am extra grateful to Dermot Corrigan, Darren Tulett, Alex Bellos, Adrian Paenza and Ronan Boscher for their help in facilitating and interpreting interviews for *Edge*. You are all wonderful friends and brilliant journalists.

Other experts read sections of the book at various stages and helped with invaluable comments along the way. These include Annie Auerbach, Marcus Christenson, Dermot Corrigan, Michiel de Hoog, James Eastham, Ben Oakley and Darren Tulett. Thank you!

My biggest thanks are reserved for my wife Annie and daughters Clemmy and Bibi. Thank you for everything – but most of all, for being yourselves.

INDEX